The Women
of *Orphan Black*

ALSO BY AND EDITED BY VALERIE ESTELLE FRANKEL
AND FROM McFARLAND

Women in Doctor Who:
Damsels, Feminists and Monsters (2018)

Superheroines and the Epic Journey:
Mythic Themes in Comics, Film and Television (2017)

Outlander's *Sassenachs: Essays on Gender, Race,*
Orientation and the Other in the Novels
and Television Series (edited, 2016)

Adoring Outlander: *Essays on Fandom, Genre*
and the Female Audience (edited, 2016)

The Symbolism and Sources of Outlander:
The Scottish Fairies, Folklore, Ballads, Magic
and Meanings That Inspired the Series (2015)

The Comics of Joss Whedon:
Critical Essays (edited, 2015)

Women in Game of Thrones: *Power,*
Conformity and Resistance (2014)

Teaching with Harry Potter: Essays on Classroom Wizardry
from Elementary School to College (edited, 2013)

Buffy and the Heroine's Journey:
Vampire Slayer as Feminine Chosen One (2012)

From Girl to Goddess: The Heroine's Journey
through Myth and Legend (2010)

EDITED BY COLLEEN S. HARRIS AND
VALERIE ESTELLE FRANKEL

Women Versed in Myth: Essays on Modern Poets (2016)

The Women of *Orphan Black*

Faces of the Feminist Spectrum

VALERIE ESTELLE FRANKEL

McFarland & Company, Inc., Publishers
Jefferson, North Carolina

LIBRARY OF CONGRESS CATALOGUING-IN-PUBLICATION DATA

Names: Frankel, Valerie Estelle, 1980– author.
Title: The women of Orphan black : faces of the feminist spectrum / Valerie Estelle Frankel.
Description: Jefferson, North Carolina : McFarland & Company, Inc., Publishers, 2018. | Includes bibliographical references and index.
Identifiers: LCCN 2018011632 | ISBN 9781476674124 (softcover : acid free paper) ∞
Subjects: LCSH: Orphan black (Television program) | Heroines on television.
Classification: LCC PN1992.77.O75 F83 2018 | DDC 791.45/72—dc23
LC record available at https://lccn.loc.gov/2018011632

BRITISH LIBRARY CATALOGUING DATA ARE AVAILABLE

ISBN (print) 978-1-4766-7412-4
ISBN (ebook) 978-1-4766-3255-1

© 2018 Valerie Estelle Frankel. All rights reserved

No part of this book may be reproduced or transmitted in any form or by any means, electronic or mechanical, including photocopying or recording, or by any information storage and retrieval system, without permission in writing from the publisher.

Front cover images of DNA string and woman's eye
© 2018 chrisjohnsson/Wavebreakmedia/iStock

Printed in the United States of America

*McFarland & Company, Inc., Publishers
Box 611, Jefferson, North Carolina 28640
www.mcfarlandpub.com*

Table of Contents

Introduction   1

Season Themes
Season One: Rejection and Self-Hatred   5
Season Two: Autonomy   10
Season Three: We'd Do Anything for Family   17
Season Four: Strange Bedfellows   20
Season Five: Self Definition   24

Literature, Games, Symbols and Allusions
Metafiction, Roleplay and Gender-Flipping   30
Games as Metaphors   40
Inside the Credits   46
Thoughts on Genre   48
Literature Behind the Season Titles   52
Allusions and Inspirations   61

The Science, Real and Emblematic
Inside Neolution   70
Cloning Ethics   82
Science versus Religion   89

Characters as Feminist Embodiments
Sarah the Punk   93
Sarah's Matrifocal Family   98
Felix and Art: Cultural Feminists   101
Vic the Bully   107
Helena: From Cultist to Pagan Guide   108
Amelia and Kendra: Black Feminism   122
Alison: Back to the Gothic Home   124

Table of Contents

Donnie: New Man or Family Joke?	135
Cosima: Classic Second Wave	139
Beth Goes Third Wave	147
Siobhan the Rebel	150
Castors: Military Hierarchy	156
Paul the Macho Man	162
Cal Goes Off the Grid	164
Rachel the Gender Traitor	165
Tony's Trans Struggle	174
Gracie the Victim	177
Kendall the Matriarch	179
Krystal Goderitch: Girl Power	181
Scott and Hell Wizard: Sidekicks	185
Delphine: Dead Lesbian?	187
False Prince Ferdinand	189
Mika: Cyber-Anarchist	192
Susan and Coady: Ruling Man's World	195
Ira the Emasculated Assistant	199
Leekie and Westmorland: The Patriarchy	200
The Next Generation: Kira and the Girls	205
Katja to Camilla: Global Feminism	208

Looking to the Future   211

Episodes   213

Works Cited   215

Index   223

Introduction

Orphan Black premiered on March 30, 2013, and its first showing had a decent turnout for the BBC with 927,000 million viewers. The breakout quality came from those early watchers, who discussed the show constantly. Social media swelled with offerings from #CloneClub, memes, art, and endless discussions as the heroines broke all of television's boundaries. "As a result, *Black*'s season finale had more tweets than bigger shows such as *Homeland, Nashville,* and *The Good Wife* had in any week in 2013" (Ross, "Attack of the Clones" 27).

Orphan Black was hailed as groundbreaking, especially because the main characters are all played by the same actress. Visual Effects Supervisor Geoff Scott and his team at Intelligent Creatures bring Clone Club to life with a motion control camera rig called a technodolly (nicknamed the time vampire), which can be programmed to repeat the same complex camera movements identically over and over. First, Tatiana Maslany and her acting double Kathryn Alexandre film the scenes completely in one set of roles, then switch, and a third time with the scene filmed with just the camera motion for a background plate. Maslany has glowingly described her fellow actress's work, all of which goes unseen: "She's so amazing. She memorizes all of the lines, all of my blocking, all of her blocking, my mannerisms, my impulses; she, somehow, memorizes all of that and gives it back to me with a performance I can play off of" (Wieselman, "Meet the Woman").

This suffices for the most common two-person scene, though for three or four they must keep going. There's season two's four-clone dance party, season three's family dinner, two baby showers (real and imagined) and several climactic fights. Phone and screen conversations, along with photos of unseen clones, help supplement it all. Working this way, the pair play Sarah, Beth, Katja, Cosima, Alison, Helena, Rachel, Tony, Krystal, and M.K. (along with quick single-appearance clones Jennifer, Miriam, and Camilla, as well as Helena's unnamed first victim).

"I guess the most difficult part is that I'm always playing Tatiana playing one of her characters," says Alexandre ("Clone Club Insiders"). Indeed, the layering goes further as Maslany is often playing a clone playing another clone, as Sarah masquerades as Beth, or Cosima as Alison. Of playing multiple roles, Maslany notes, "I start as Sarah, and then pretend to be Alison as Sarah would see her, right like all the judgement she would have" (Wheaton). There are also fun breaks in the fourth wall as the clones interact with mirrors, windows, cameras, and certainly one another, all the while searching for self-definition.

Makeup artist Stephen Lynch, hair stylist Sandy Sokolowski, and wardrobe department head Debra Hanson helped Maslany define each clone with strikingly different looks. Sarah has dark smudged makeup over the shadows of previous applications. Cosima has a nose ring and dreadlocks, Alison, bangs and a tight ponytail. "Alison probably orders her makeup from the shopping channel or has a friend who sells makeup in a pyramid scheme," Lynch adds. "She found her makeup look in high school and never changed it. Rachel would find her makeup laughable … the idea of purple eyeliner alone would put Rachel into a coma" (Miller). Helena has red eyes and badly dyed blonde hair that's explosively frizzy, like her unkempt personality. Katja's is short and red, Beth's strikingly straight. Rachel has her hair, makeup, and nails done by high-end salons, showing off her wealth with the light-dyed bob. While costumes and voices play a big part, the actress also describes differentiating the characters by setting them to music on the advice of her acting coach. "If you change the song that's inside you, that changes maybe how you walk or how you express yourself" (Wheaton).

While all this pushes the boundaries of filmmaking, the show is also striking for its gender roles. Sarah and her clone sisters are the heroines, saving each other but almost never rescued singly by a man. In fact, the men are bumblers (Donnie), objectified eye candy (Paul), gentle supporters (Felix), laughably impotent bullies (Vic), oblivious nerds (Scott), terminally glitching constructs (the Castors) or even babysitters to be used or dropped as needed (Cal). Matriarchs and patriarchs alike are villains, which the clone team take down one by one.

With all this going on, the series' gender roles deserve close examination. The clones not only offer a spectrum of female archetypes but also correspond with historic types of feminism. Sarah and her foster mother's clash echoes the tension between second and third wave, down to the women's ages, though both are rebels of their eras. Alison is the quintessential post-feminist and Krystal, a girl power icon, down to her pink tops and perky music. Clever hacker M.K. nods to the emergent fourth-wave as the disabled woman changing the world from inside a trailer. Katja gets in a quick word for global feminism, alerting her oblivious North American sisters to her friends' persecution. Beth has third wave values; Cosima, second. Rachel, the corporate pro-clone, is a traitor to her gender, selling out to the patriarchy for perceived crumbs of respect. Tony adds the transgender struggle, in a clever metaphor for the clones' central conflict. Helena, perhaps the most interesting, grows from a brainwashed tool of organized religion to a rebellious pagan goddess. While the clones all battle the patriarchy, their different approaches salute a spectrum of women's history.

Beyond this, the science fiction or fantasy heroine has a power not seen in real life. The artificial being reflects "social relations, our most important political construction, a world-changing fiction" (Haraway 149). Writing about women in dystopia or fantasy worlds becomes a thought experiment, a way to explore issues. "She is an artificial construction of womanhood that 'does' gender (as well as race, class, sexual orientation, age, ability, nation, and other factors of identification) in ways that reflect back to us what we mean when we talk about gender" (Helford et al.). Throughout the show, the clones are spied on by their lovers, treated as commodities, exploited for their reproductive systems—issues that use the lens of science fiction to explore different characters' relationship to power. Thus, the series also celebrates "the potential for nonrealist writing to provide a new perspective on cultural expressions of gender" (Helford et al.).

Nina Nesseth, coauthor of *The Science of Orphan Black,* says, "When all is said and done, *Orphan Black* remains one of the most true-to-science sci-fi shows out there" (Griffin and Nesseth). Connections with real cloning history appear, mostly supplied by science advisor Cosima Herter, whose life and studies inspired her namesake character. The show touches on the eugenicists' "world's most perfect baby" at Cold River, Dolly the Sheep, gene sequencing, gene therapy, the religious debate, and movements like transhumanism. Just as feminism is transforming, science is as well. Herter adds, "In our era of synthetic biology—of Craig Venter's biological printer and George Church's standardized biological parts, of three-parent babies and of treatment for cancer that involves reengineered viruses—genetics as we have conceived of it is already dead. We don't have the language for what is emerging" (Newton).

While the show offers real science, it's also a metaphor: clones as property, women as property. Donna Jeanne Haraway explains this issue in "The Cyborg Manifesto," a critical work that views cyborg fiction as an allegory for being marginalized and hybridized. This essay was used for the episode titles, along with the classic poem "Protest," Charles Darwin's *On the Origin of Species,* Francis Bacon's *Plan of the Work,* and President Eisenhower's farewell address. All these works contribute deeper allegory, as do nods to *Brave New World, Frankenstein, R.U.R., The Island of Doctor Moreau,* and more modern works like *Lost Girl.* Further, each season offers particular themes, like body autonomy amid the fertilization cult, or tribal loyalty while facing the Castor clones. Through it all, the Leda clones journey from suspicion and self-loathing to loving pride, not just in their sisterhood, but their individuality.

Season Themes

Season One: Rejection and Self-Hatred

Orphan Black was inspired during filming of the 2001 Canadian TV movie *Lucky Girl*, for which director John Fawcett brought in Graeme Manson as script doctor. "He did this wicked three-week rewrite," recalls Fawcett. "And he really impressed me with that. At that point we realized, 'You know what? We work really well together. We should come up with something to do'" (Ross, "Attack of the Clones" 26). At the time, Fawcett had no story in mind—just a single opening scene. As he explains, "I pitched him a concept that there would be this girl that shows up on a subway platform in rush-hour traffic, and in that moment she sees her identical [twin]. And then—boom!—she jumps in front of the train. All that stuff was in the first idea I pitched Graeme. But I didn't know what it was. I didn't know if it was a parallel universe, if it was an alien conspiracy, no idea. I just said, 'This is a good idea for an opening scene'" (Ross, "Attack of the Clones" 26). The pair kept brainstorming, but kept returning to clones.

This first moment is terribly dark—apparent despair and self-contempt so great that a woman kills herself ... while wearing Sarah's face. As the series begins, Sarah hates her life enough to leave all of it except for her foster brother Felix and abandoned daughter Kira. All her fantasies involve escape, and when she sees opportunity, along with Beth's belongings, she takes it. Facing this mirror-image of herself, Sarah must face the suicidal and addictive elements her own biology may offer, even as she differentiates herself from Beth and the other clones who soon appear.

Science advisor Cosima Herter (called the "Real Cosima" on set) says: "Identical (monozygotic) twins do indeed share the same DNA because they develop from the same parental egg-sperm combination. But if you've ever met a pair of identical twins you will notice that they do not at all appear as exact copies of each other! While their genetics are identical, physical (and some behavioral) differences are generally attributed to something called 'epigenetics'" (Herter, "Nature vs. Nurture"). This process changes genetic activity, both in utero and out, adding to the nature versus nurture tension. Separated twins will have striking differences ... but also striking similarities. "Tracking twins has also allowed scientists to discover that even though identical twins may share eighty percent of things in common, biology is not destiny" (Carveth 43). However, the clones all face self-loathing.

As Sarah discovers an apartment she admires, clothes too fancy for her taste, and a sexy boyfriend, she explores how much of her twinship with Beth is genetic. Meanwhile, she also explores the contrasts within herself, as she outwits the traps of love and patriarchy that Beth fell for. Ironically, Beth and Sarah share unhappiness, though their lives are so strikingly different. Tatiana Maslany, who plays all those clones, has attributed her emotional mastery of all the characters to Cosima Herter's insights. "She briefed me on the insane science behind cloning and it just gave me such a key into that world. It's emotional, it's about humans, it's about life" (Newton). Using this key, she sets out to play a spectrum of parts ... many of whom despise themselves and each other.

The episode ends with a third clone, Katja Obinger, who arrives, realizes Sarah isn't really Beth, and is shot moments later, as it turns out, by another clone, Helena. She has been trained to destroy all who look like her, to wipe out all the impure copies. As she obediently, even psychotically, does so, she establishes the others as less than human in her eyes.

Helena is raised as an abomination, though she's told her sisters are worse. The nuns called her a "devil child," and one dunked her head in bleach, dying her hair in the flashback of "One Fettered Slave" (509). In the prequel comic, her mentor Maggie Chen tells her, "You are a blessing born out of great sin. But the others, they are abominations. They must be cleansed" (*The Clone Club #2: Helena*). After her first murder, she begins cutting herself, slicing her back into a pattern of angel wings as she punishes herself. Trying to kill all her clone sisters, Helena tracks Sarah-as-Beth while believing this murderous dogma. Sarah insists she's a new clone, and Helena feels a strange connection. With this, she finds herself rethinking all the Protheans have taught her, including how she is only worthy if she kills.

Sarah understands her sister's struggles: "Well, but if you were a messed up, abused loner whose faith compels you to belong and somebody that you trusted told you that this was the way to redeem yourself in the eyes of God, I mean, yeah, I might become an angry angel too" ("Effects of External Conditions" 104). With these words, she shows how closely she empathizes with the other woman's struggle through self-loathing and isolation.

Meanwhile, Sarah tracks Alison Hendrix, the suburban housewife clone, who meets her with the words, "How dare you show your face in front of my children?" and "Hide your ugly face on the way out of here" ("Instinct" 102).

All this suggests loathing for the intrusion into her peaceful life, but also hatred of the clones who look so much like herself. Alison's always staring into mirrors and fussing over her appearance—something better explained when her mother's first move is criticizing her hair in "Community of Dreadful Fear and Hate" (307).

Through the lens of the women's movement, self-loathing takes many forms. Some women in abusive situations hate themselves for not breaking free or consider themselves worthless as their partners insist. Some women hate parts of their bodies—faces that aren't alluring enough, or legs and waists that are too fat. Feminists encourage women to stop putting themselves down or judging themselves by such painful standards instead of by their accomplishments. As the Clone Club overcome their self-hatred, they guide the audience on a similar path to understanding. Meanwhile, women's groups hating other women's groups is more common yet, using dividers like race, politics, religion, and stance on abortion to exclude. Following this model, the clones turn on each other, even to the extreme of Helena's murders. They slowly become a sisterhood, but he progression takes time.

Alison is especially horrified when her neighbors air her dirty laundry—her descent into drinking and pills. She calls for Felix, who doesn't judge her, only shares her pills and counsels her in confidence. He advises her, "Put your chin up, be a woman. This is Backstabbing 101." With his support, she faces the crowd armed with perfect cattiness, reclaiming her pride instead of letting them shame her: "I thank you. For scrutinizing every detail of my life, since the day I moved into this fish pool. You have pried and snooped and gossiped about me, like I was your own, personal, laboratory subject. How would you like it if I turned your life inside-out? If I told all these people that Chad, your husband, slept with a spin class instructor long before me. Well, maybe he acts that way because you blew the roofer at the cabin!" With this, she takes back her own.

Evolutionary Developmental Biology student Cosima Niehaus appears comfortable with herself, but she leaps at a new romance with fellow scientist Delphine Cormier, suggesting she's lonely and vulnerable. Though she teases geeky Scott Smith, she doesn't have close friends and companions. Further, she's sick, realizing that her body is shutting down and betraying her. She struggles to gather clone samples from all affected, even as she realizes she may not find a cure in time. She also becomes closer to her corporate creator Doctor Leekie and agrees to work for him. This compliance suggests a deep-seated lack in her life.

As Sarah meets her clones, this issue of self-hatred soon expands to the jarring presence of near-duplicates. Maslany says of the show's core theme, "You think you know everything about yourself, and then you see a woman who looks exactly like you. Who is she? And what does that say about me?"

(Schneider). Beginning in episode one, Sarah pretends to be Beth, and as she does, she learns who she could have been, if she'd finished school and chosen a career of public service. Sarah begins playing at being a cop, even having sex with her boyfriend Paul Dierden, to divert suspicion and win Beth's $75,000 dollars. Her goal is simply escape and a chance to reclaim Kira. However, Cosima gives her a new mission, in a conversation that addresses the central mysteries of the series. She reveals, "So, six months ago, Katja contacted Beth with this crazy story about her genetic identicals being hunted in Europe."

> SARAH: But who is the original? Who's created us? Who's killing us?
> COSIMA: We need to know, but, we lost our cop, so, however you manage to get into her shoes, we really need you to stay there.
> SARAH: Stay a cop to help you?
> COSIMA: To help us. Help us find out who's killing us ["Variation Under Nature" 103].

Sarah protests that being Beth is what messed up her life. However, Cosima counters with "You can't run away from her. Look, we are your biological imperative now, okay?" She frames the conflict about being one of abandoning part of one's self and family or standing by them, a geas Sarah hesitantly accepts. With this mission, Sarah gradually begins to take on Beth's responsibility and mission to protect her sisters. Like Beth, Sarah becomes the planner and warrior. Slowly, the untrusting clones Sarah, Alison, and Cosima begin working as a team, even as they track Helena the murderer using Beth's skills and contacts.

At the condo later, Paul wants to go over what Sarah knows. "There's nine of you," he states. "No!" Sarah objects strongly. "There's only one of me, just like there was only one of Beth" ("Parts Developed in an Unusual Manner" 107). However, Paul makes a valid point. Co-creator Graeme Manson explains, "Every time you meet a clone, you create another identity crisis" ("Send in the Clones"). On meeting Tony in season two, Sarah must wonder about the transgender potentiality within herself. M.K. makes her consider her own paranoia and antiauthoritarian tendencies. "There's a large part of me in each of them. And a large part of myself is revealed in each of these characters," the actress says ("Send in the Clones"). The corporate-raised Rachel is arguably the worst, showing what Sarah-the-sellout would resemble.

Helena, meanwhile, begs Sarah to acknowledge their connection. As it turns out, Helena and Sarah are literal twins, who shared a womb as well as DNA. "The only real difference between clones and identical twins is the process that creates them" (Carveth 42). Twins, by sharing a womb, receive the same nutrition and environmental factors in their growth. The pair spent nine months together and absorbed the same biological factors from their surrogate. They are true sisters, not merely copies.

Like actual biological twins, the clones all start from a place where others assume similarity and they must fight to differentiate. The science fiction twist to the story only makes this job more difficult. "The cyborgs populating feminist science fiction make very problematic the statuses of man or woman, human, artefact, member of a race, individual entity, or body," explains Donna Haraway in her "The Cyborg Manifesto," a critical work that sees cyborg fiction as an allegory for being female and became the fourth season's titles (178). The part of the story where each substitutes for the others, with Sarah borrowing Beth's police powers or Alison-as-Sarah making peace with Mrs. S, emphasizes their different skillsets, used to protect each other and help them achieve their goals. Even as they perform these imposter moments, however clumsily (especially in Helena's case), they show how different their personalities really are, despite their shared biology. Jordan Gavaris (Felix) adds. "I'm not interested in you telling me who I am. I will tell you who I am. I am multifaceted and I cannot be reduced. I hope that's the legacy—the idea that individuality is awesome" (Schneider).

As the season heads toward an end, Sarah and Helena each refuse to turn over the other to DYAD and the Proletheans, suggesting acceptance and love for this person so like themselves. As Tomas insists Helena abandon Sarah and take Kira for herself, Sarah retorts, "He locked you in a cage! He lied to you your entire life. He's going to do that to Kira! He's going to hurt Kira like he hurt you" ("Unconscious Selection" 109). At this, Helena throws herself at him, savaging him and reclaiming her life. Love for her new family outweighs her religious conditioning.

Season end introduces polished, corporate Rachel Duncan, whom Sarah regards with loathing. "So is the part where 20 more of you robot bitches walk in for effect?" she snarks. Though Rachel speaks to her politely, even admiringly, she represents all Sarah has rejected in herself—the clone that gave herself over to Neolution. To Sarah's horror, this reflects a hidden part of herself—she has been signed over to the company without knowing. Cosima calls and warns her, "You can't make a deal! Any freedom they offer is bullshit. They're liars. The sequence? The bar code I told you about? It's a patent. We're property." Though Sarah rejects working with her creators, once again emphasizing her rejection of the very process that made her, frightened Alison and curious Cosima accept.

Sarah spends the season trying to win back Kira but also to reclaim her own origins. Her foster mother Siobhan Sadler (known as Mrs. S or S.) helps with this as much as she can, reaching out to contacts to ask about Sarah's past. At last, Sarah's birth mother arrives. Sarah believes this woman will give her all the answers about herself she's always wanted. However, this too is an illusion—Sarah has formed herself without this mysterious birth mother and must continue to do so. Symbolically aware of this and loathing the mother who gave her to the church, Helena shoots her. After, Helena insists that she can't kill Sarah, "like you could not kill me" thanks to their connection. However, Sarah shoots this copy of herself, ending their relationship, as she thinks. This, like Helena's killing their birth mother, is a moment of self-loathing for all the heroine sees in this close relative so like herself.

Only in the next season does she stop Helena from shooting Rachel and tell her, "You saved my life. You're my sister. Helena, I thought I thought I killed you. I couldn't tell anybody what I lost" ("Ipsa Scientia Potestas Est" 205). She introduces her to Felix and her detective partner Art, then Siobhan, and finally Cosima and Alison, bringing her into the family.

Season Two: Autonomy

"Orphan Black" grapples with the violent intersection between technology and female agency. In the eyes of their creators, the clones' humanity is trumped by their value as intellectual property. The question at the show's heart is whether the clones have free will and the right to lead normal lives, or if they are valuable only as experimental subjects to be monitored, impregnated, sterilized and policed. "It's so thematically connected to feminist issues," Graeme Manson, one of the show's creators [explained]. "Who owns you, who owns your body, your biology? Who controls reproduction?" [Loofbourow]

Manson notes that as soon as he began the research, "I started to get excited about the nature, nurture aspect of the story, the deeper themes and questions of body autonomy" (Bernstein 11). Season two zooms in on body rights—it's revealed that the patriarchal creators deliberately removed the clones' ability to reproduce. Of course, cloning itself suggests an alternate path, as "Cyborg replication is uncoupled from organic reproduction" (Haraway 150). Clones can shake off patriarchal control—reproduction with no men at all, only women's DNA and women to carry the babies. Though damaged by their creators, they quest for the genetic codes to free and perfect themselves. While Leekie has perverted the process, they can perfect it.

Control over one's body has always been central to the women's movement. "Questions about female fertility have typically been dealt with in ways that eclipsed the interests of women, individually and as members of various groups. Debates about who should have the power to manage women's reproductive capacities have often been linked to larger issues—social, cultural, and economic—across the spectrum," explains Rickie Solinger in *Reproductive Politics* (18). These included slave owners forcing their slaves to produce economically useful children, concerns about overpopulation, and different eras' desire to maintain demographic superiority over other groups. Each time, different organizations or individuals have "proposed, enacted, and enforced rules governing women's sexuality and their reproductive capacities" (Solinger 18).

The real Cosima explains: "Season two, we explored the long, complicated, historical relationship between science and religion, and the social practice of science. Eugenics. Control over one's own body, and the existential choices that direct one's own life. Sexual abuse and the use of women's bodies for misogynistic socio-economic gain, especially in regard to reproductive rights and the commodification of women's bodies" (Griffin and Nesseth). For a more provocative conversation, the season introduces Tony, who had gender reassignment surgery. In contrast to many characters, including the sisters all engineered by the corporation, he remakes himself to his own desires. As he brags to Felix about his body and takes a bath, he seems fully comfortable with his skin. After, he doesn't join Clone Club but drives away, unmonitored, master of the road and his life. Cosima Herter, the show's scientific advisor, notes of introducing a trans hero in the second season, "Women are often, throughout history reduced to their biology. And marginalized because of that biology. So it's very timely that you have a character like that. That's very interesting. Some of the other characters like Felix, like the homosexual relationships: homosexuals are people who are also (often) reduced to their biology. (Social) Class, reduced to your biology, different ethnicities are reduced to their biology" ("Q&A with Cosima"). The show addresses the complexities here, as Cosima and Felix break out and have plots unconnected with their sexualities.

Herter also emphasizes how modern life is safe because of the protests of others: "We spend many a night trying to reconcile our families' histories with our own current and contingent privilege of having the chance to live somewhere relatively safe, with having the civil rights to love and partner with whom we choose, to have autonomy of body, to vote, to own property, to have access to education, to be independent women, to gather in public demonstrations against tyranny and greed" (Herter, "Why Protest"). In short, women's rights came about from the women's movement.

During the first wave, in the nineteenth century, women demanded an end to beatings and spousal rape, regulated child labor laws, the ability to see doctors without their husbands' consent. They also demanded "voluntary motherhood"—the rights to their own sexual lives and reproductive choices (Solinger 19). Before this, "Women who attempted to control their fertility were in danger of being exposed and possibly punished by law enforcement. Millions took that dangerous step, which variously mixed desperation and resistance" (Solinger 10). First-wavers inspired a powerful generation in the twenties and thirties: Amelia Earhart, Dorothy Parker, Dorothy Thompson, Lillian Hellman, Margaret Bourke-White, Clare Boothe Luce, and Katharine Hepburn. Societal critic Camille Paglia adds, "The adventurous careerism of those singular women was in many cases a calculated reversal of Victorian conventions, which had exalted prudery and propriety and sanctified motherhood" (214–215). Likewise, in the second wave of the sixties, bodies took a central role.

> The right to control one's body was at the heart of the feminist health movement and was interpreted by feminists to mean possessing knowledge about how their bodies functioned, having the power to make informed decisions about their bodies, and being treated with dignity and respect by the medical establishment. Education and self-help were key components of the early phase of the feminist health movement, but soon feminist concerns about the relationship between sexuality and reproduction would require activists to lobby for concrete changes in medical practices and the passage of new public policy initiatives [Solinger 63–64].

"The 1970 publication of *Women and Their Bodies* (soon to be retitled *Our Bodies, Ourselves*) gave the women's health movement its proverbial shot in the arm" (Berkeley 66). The book became a runaway best-seller with over 200,000 copies sold by 1973 and over 2 million by the end of the decade. After this came free classes on women's health issues. "These and other acts of civil disobedience, like the Redstockings' 1969 'speak-out' on abortion (which coincided with a hearing on abortion conducted by the New York state legislature), helped to redefine the terms of the abortion debate" (Berkeley 66). In 1967, California, Colorado, and North Carolina became the first states in the nation to pass abortion reform legislation and by the end of the decade, twelve more states had passed similar measures. Across the pond in Britain, the 1967 Abortion Act became law. In 1973, the U.S. Supreme Court issued its historic ruling on *Roe v. Wade*. In 1969, the Liberal government of Canada, where the show takes place, permitted abortion to save the mother's life or health, but only in 1988 was abortion fully legalized.

The final episode sees Sarah in flashback sitting outside an abortion clinic with S. There they consider their options as S. warns her of the responsibility and adds, "It's a woman's choice. It's the most personal choice a woman can make." The BBC staff add: "We reached out to Planned Parenthood to ask for some promotional materials and for the OK from them to use their signage in the background. We really wanted to honor the work they do for women and families everywhere in the scene. Lucky for us they agreed and sent us pamphlets and posters that were 10 years old, adding to the details of the flashback" ("Episode 10"). Sarah considers and decides to keep the baby.

All these echoes of the debates over who should control a woman's body are echoed in some startlingly backwards groups. Henrik Johanssen is "an M.I.T.-trained scientist who is also a Christian fundamentalist and leader of the Prolethean cult, whose headquarters are an Amish-style farm, and which appears to date to the nineteen-eighties, too, when the Christian Coalition did battle with advocates of reproductive rights" (Lepore). Henrik rules his small compound as a true patriarch—not only the final law but the father of all. The children are all apparently his, and he even impregnates the animals with his equipment.

Of course, Helena and Henrik's daughter Gracie struggle with forced implantation of Helena's embryos by the zealots there. Gracie's father announces, "It's time for Gracie to bear fruit" and impregnates her with his and Helena's child in the appropriately titled "Things Which Have Never Yet Been Done" (209). Helena chooses to get pregnant but rejects this for Gracie. She tells Gracie's love interest, Mark, "You love her like puppy. But you let him make her broodmare" and tells her new friend, "You're a good girl, Grace. If you don't want to have my babies, don't have my babies." Mark, meanwhile, naively tells the pair "To multiply is divine" and adds, "The women here don't see it that way" ("Things Which Have Never Yet Been Done" 209). Emphasizing how wrong he is, Gracie turns her back in misery.

Helena gets them both out of the compound so they can make their own choices. In a scene played for horror but also triumphant feminism, she straps Henrik down and offers to inseminate him with horse, cow, or whatever kind of fetus he chooses ("By Means Which Have Never Yet Been Tried" 210). This is juxtaposed with Alison's eager embracing of sex with her husband, showing two women taking back power in two very different ways.

In the course of the season, Alison is dragged off to rehab, but Felix persuades her to stay, emphasizing that she isn't a prisoner, as "rehab usually requires some form of consent" ("Governed as It Were by Chance" 204). He persuades her, "Look, a week here is not a bad thing. You go away for a week, you come back from the spa, fresh as a daisy." She concedes that she'll stay. She's enraged, however, when Donnie holds the kids' custody hostage, forcing the issue through legal means.

> DONNIE: You have issues. And, until you get those sorted out, I don't think you should be around the children.
> ALISON: That is not your decision to make.
> DONNIE: It is, if you leave rehab before the program's finished. At least, that's what my lawyer says ["Governed as It Were by Chance" 204].

Meanwhile, Alison discovers Donnie has been watching her and reporting to DYAD. In return, Donnie is so horrified that he has been monitoring his wife without *his* consent—or hers—that he snaps and shoots Dr. Leekie. His revulsion at being used to destroy his own family sends him over the edge. It's the breakdown of his marriage that seems to hurt the most. After, their shared burying of the body unites them and completely removes Leekie's autonomy as they hide his disgusting body and then later dig it up again to remove his head for their own experiments.

"It's no coincidence that the first clones are women on *Orphan Black*. On the series, the female body is a battleground, with the women literally reduced to objects. The more easily controlled or useful the clones' bodies are (read: able to be reproduced), the more they're worth to the government-supported scientists and religious fanatics who continuously lay claim to Sarah (Tatiana Maslany) and the rest of Clone Club," critic Sadie Gennis notes in her essay on feminism in the show. The clones' creator made them all infertile by choice. "Normal development was the prime directive. This was the least-invasive solution. Unfortunately, we didn't, uh, foresee the consequences," Ethan Duncan explains ("Things Which Have Never Yet Been Done" 209). These include the women dying as their wombs and lungs turn against them. For story purposes, that means the pathetic, dying Jennifer Fitzsimmons gets experimented on without ever being told why she's ill, and then Delphine uses problematic treatments on Cosima without telling her. "The game is rigged to begin with to ensure that even the strongest women are subject to having their bodies re-purposed without their consent. Which is why even as much of a bitch as Rachel is, I can't help but empathize with her," Gennis adds. Rachel appears the most devastated to receive the news, since it occurred at the hands of her benevolent-seeming father-creator. Several of the clones, like Jennifer, have died as a result, and Cosima is dying. "That always resonated for me as a woman," the actress told *Vanity Fair* in an interview, "this idea of our bodies not being our own. That they're owned by someone else. That the image of them is owned by someone else" (Loofbourow).

> Though the majority of the villains are men, *Orphan Black* is not the story of women vs. men. (Even Helena, who represents the most radical form of feminism, sweetly dubs Felix "brother sestra.") Instead, *Orphan Black* is about women vs. the system. While the men are nothing more than empty suits, the misogynist system they're a part of gives them power. Leekie's idea to reduce women to man-made synthetic wombs, Duncan's project of creating an endless supply of "little girls," Henrik's religious rape—these ideas, not the men, are the real threats. And since the men who run these projects have wealth and institution on their side, they are able to provide real road blacks to the clones, even though the women are far more intelligent and proficient [Gennis].

Of course, the show provides a safe space where people can discuss these issues—not just for women but for everyone. "Questions surrounding Cos' autonomy have been building all season as she struggles to maintain control over even her own body. As Cos becomes progressively dependent on finding a cure, the DYAD Institute is more than happy to exploit her illness, increasingly reducing her to a medical marvel on which to experiment" (Gennis).

When the DYAD Institute in the person of Cosima's trusted lover Delphine implants Cosima with Kira's stolen stem cells. Cosima is horrified. However, she reluctantly asks Sarah for another baby tooth, only to have Kira willingly pull one out to aid her aunt. In the next episode, Cosima faces the fact that real bone marrow will help her much more and asks Sarah. She and Mrs. S are reluctant, but Mrs. S reminds her it isn't really their choice. "End of the day, it's not your decision. It's not any of ours" ("Things Which Have Never Yet Been Done" 209). They ask Kira, letting her choose whether to give up her cells to save her aunt, and Kira generously volunteers. However, Rachel kidnaps her during the procedure and finally smashes the tube of stem cells out of cruelty. This destroys Kira's sacrifice, taking the potential cure away from all of them. Rachel also sends Delphine to Europe with the words "None of this is personal."

Delphine, horrified to be sent from Cosima without even a goodbye, retorts, "I love her and, if you let her die without me, it is personal" ("By Means Which Have Never Yet Been Tried" 210). While this interference is external, it still takes her autonomy.

In the final episode, with Kira kidnapped to be raised by the soulless corporation, Sarah surrenders to DYAD. The scene opens on Sarah being prodded and interrogated. Mixed in is a flashback of Sarah and Mrs. S fighting about Kira, giving Sarah her motivation here. The doctors fire questions at her, mostly about her reproduction and sexuality—the most intrusive and personal topics. She endures it all, along with handcuffs, only to be told her eggs will be harvested.

When asked to sign a consent form, she's reluctant: There's a difference between being a prisoner and deliberately signing away her body rights, however coerced. After, however, the medical staff strap her to a gurney and haul her away over her protests. She's told that the doctors will instead remove an entire ovary. She struggles and screams. Though she's horrifically tied down and denied all consent, she defends herself—getting a finger free enough to blast the fire extinguisher at Rachel and shoot a pencil into her eye. While Rachel has tried to remove a precious small round organ from her, she reverses this and does so to her foe. "Unlike a lot of what passes for TV feminism, the show's not just about women being confident or comfortable in their own skin. It's about reaffirming that their skin, their body, and their decisions are theirs to control. This is the battle all women in America are living with right now, whether they realize it or not," Gennis concludes.

Season two is set up as the war between Sarah and Rachel (Bernstein 15). Though Sarah and her family seek independence, Rachel seeks control. In the season of body autonomy, Rachel demands the genetic sequence from Duncan so she can create more clones. He tells her it only exists in his head. Possibly anticipating torture or truth drugs, and certainly exercising his own sovereignty, Duncan commits suicide, calmly telling his daughter she doesn't deserve him anymore. As he dies, and she sobs and begs, their happy family memories play in the background, emphasizing how dysfunctional their relationship has become.

Of course, bodily autonomy issues continue through the series. Season three has the Castors seducing and raping women to destroy their reproductive systems, depriving them of body choice. Suddenly, the option of motherhood is taken from them, as it was from the clones. Mrs. S, defender of young women, wants them shut down: "Castor is sterilizing women. We cannot let that happen," she emphatically tells Sarah ("Insolvent Phantom of Tomorrow" 309). In season four, Brightborn has implanted many, including Sarah herself, with deadly technology, close enough to the brain to kill. As it spies, it alters her DNA, increasing the intrusion and horror of the corporations' deadly monitoring.

One issue throughout the show is that women are expected to bear children, and many, like Alison, Rachel, and Gracie, struggle when they discover this choice has been taken from them. The show emphasizes choice and control over one's body, through science fiction like Sarah's jaw maggot and Rachel's spy eye. The women impregnated by Brightborn choose to flee and safeguard their babies. Certainly, women's quest for autonomy stretches beyond pregnancy, or at least it should. Claudette Kulkarni in *Lesbians and Lesbianisms: A Post-Jungian Perspective* explains:

> I am not talking here about "body as destiny"—nor about resorting to restrictive body metaphors, e.g. birthing metaphors which attempt to describe female bodies or "the feminine" only in relation to reproductive functions as if a woman's body is capable of no other metaphors of activity. No matter how important and symbolic such functions might be for many women, they are not so for all women nor at all times in any woman's life. In other words, these are not the only possible metaphors by which we might come to understand a female body which is capable of those functions *and* more. To privilege this aspect of the female body is limiting, distorting, and counter-productive.

Roe vs. Wade upheld a woman's constitutional right to privacy in matters pertaining to reproduction. Before it, in the fifties, "The chief accusation against a woman who ended her pregnancy was that she failed to fulfil her destiny as a woman" (Solinger 66). The show, however, gives its women other choices—Rachel has a clone child in Charlotte. Cosima and Delphine find a triumphant mission in saving clones around the world. Alison adopts. S. takes in older foster children. In fact, all the Ledas are raised by non-genetic parents who sought in vitro treatments to help them with reproductive problems. Even Felix helps raise his foster sister's daughter, in a family he's closer to than his biological one. All the emphasis on chosen families reflects that there are nonbiological, nontraditional alternatives to classic motherhood.

Season Three: We'd Do Anything for Family

A vision of Beth tells Sarah in "Certain Agony of the Battlefield" (306), "We do terrible things for the people we love." This message works well as the season's theme. It begins with Mrs. S giving Helena to the Castors to protect Sarah and Kira, and Paul accepting to help his brothers. Paul insists, "If you thought about it for one second, you'd realize all I am doing for these men is what you do for your sisters ... protecting them" ("Scarred by Many Past Frustrations" 305). They're his family, so he goes down the winding road into illegalities and collateral damage to protect them. He adds, "The military ... is just another family, Sarah. Your genetic siblings are dying. Everything we do is for them."

Sarah, meanwhile, sends Kira away after the Castors threaten her. She gives up the daughter she's fought for for so long, to keep her safe far away. It soon becomes a season of the clones struggling to reunite, understanding that they must protect each other. Editor Jay Prychidny explains, "I mean, these scenes, in this season are just much more about the group of sisters. I mean this is what the sisters are fighting for. They're fighting for this family unit, to keep it together" ("Dissecting the Scenes").

Meanwhile, the Castors were created not only to be superior, but arguably to be mass-produced and expendable, like the clones of *Star Wars* or most other science fiction. This takes a more disturbing twist on doing "anything" for family—even sending super soldiers in their place. Further, these biological brothers are the enemy. While Helena and Sarah show them compassion, they never become friends with these other halves. The real Cosima explains, "Season three, we encounter the Castor clones, the literal, genetic brothers of the Leda sestras—but this relationship of blood (i.e., "natural") siblinghood is confounded by the fact that it has no emotional, or so-called spiritual, meaning between the Ledas and the Castors. The notions of chosen family relations were really important to you for this season" (Griffin and Nesseth).

Even Donnie tells Alison's ex that they won't have a problem "Not unless you come between me and my family" ("Certain Agony of the Battlefield" 306). At season end, he confesses to Helena:

> DONNIE: I should never have gotten involved with Kellerman. But I lost my job, and Ali really wanted to run for trustee.
> HELENA: You do this for your family.
> DONNIE: Now I gotta get us out of it. I've gotta return the pills and get all our money back. And they took this tank thingy from under the counter.
> HELENA: My babies? ("Insolvent Phantom of Tomorrow" 309).

Upon discovering her own fertilized eggs are in danger, Helena follows Donnie to the drug den, bursts in and gets her eggs back. However, when they threaten Alison's children, she attacks them all in a terrible bloodbath. She is the savage mama bear, who will destroy anyone threatening her babies, or her sister's.

Felix meets Rachel while she's painting, linking the pair. However, he humiliates her, drawing an eye on the bandage over her lost one and messing with her wheelchair. Scott is appalled. However, Felix insists, "They've taken Sarah, so I need you to tell me where they took my sister" ("Certain Agony of the Battlefield" 306). When Felix graffitis her eyepatch, it could've been silly, but isn't. Jordan Gavaris (Felix) says, "When we went to shoot it, I was just overwhelmed by the amount of rage and aggression and violence that I felt towards this woman, and you just go with it" (Bernstein 71). He too will do anything to reclaim his sister, even harass someone who's handicapped and recovering.

Rachel has valuable information—they can only decipher Leekie's code with her knowledge, and to share it, she painfully compromises herself—by playing the farm game *Agricola* as cover, no matter how she loathes it. In trade, she insists she'll only work with Sarah's presence. Rachel then sends them on a quest to steal the identity of a new sister, Krystal, whom she uses as a channel to escape, switching bodies with her. Desperate to save Cosima from death, the Ledas agree to all of it, however morally dubious. As critic Sarah Hughes notes, "This is not a drama that deals in moral certainties." She adds, "While we feel Cosima's pain, we also understand why Delphine, who loves her, hides the truth. Our nominal heroine, Sarah, is as capable of doing bad as she is good, and even her foster mother, the supposedly saintly Mrs. S, is more than she seems" (Hughes).

S. of course has traded Helena to the Castors in return for leaving her daughter unharmed. Helena is certain Sarah was the one to betray her. In a story where others commit desperate acts to save her family, Helena has already done such things, from torturing Olivier to offering to murder Rachel—both times to protect Sarah. In "Scarred by Many Past Frustrations" (305), she goes the other way: after helping Sarah with an escape plan, she leaves her in a jail cell with "Now we are even, sestra."

Sarah tells Helena: "Look, Mrs. S, she made that decision to protect her granddaughter. Think of what you would do to protect that baby in your belly. Keep it far away from you. You know, I had to send Kira away again because these Castor assholes came after us, but I knew I had to come find you because we can't fight them alone." Sarah adds, "You leave me here, you've got nobody," but Helena ditches her nonetheless. Only later does Helena finally relent and return to save her. After, S. and Helena meet in a saloon prepped for a gunfight. Both even wear cowboy hats. S. doesn't avoid the meeting, realizing that as Sarah's family they're stuck with each other. However, when S. arrives, she confesses her sins to Helena, and adds, "We have to talk this out, Helena. It's the only way." Helena insists she'll kill the other woman. However, at their big confrontation, S takes the blows and then finally hugs Helena fiercely, helping her work through her pain. She promises, "You're with family now." Helena finally forgives her ("Community of Dreadful Fear and Hate" 307). Fawcett says:

> It was kind of a fun way to do something emotional. We really wanted Helena to deal with her feelings of betrayal. We just knew we had to do something to kind of still the waters to some degree, but also let Helena be real about the fact that she's dealing with these feelings of betrayal.... We wanted Helena and Mrs. S to just fight it out. It was gonna turn into a fist fight in a bar. And we kind of liked that idea! The bigger, goofier version of it was we were going to have people in a big circle, betting money ... it was gonna be more like *Fight Club*, right? But then we were talking to Maria about it and she was like "I can't punch the girl! She's pregnant! I can't actually hit her!" But we loved the idea that it actually would come to blows and we kind of went with this idea, which is a smaller idea, a little less silly but really kind of ends in some strong emotions. And hopefully people believe us that we can move from here [Towers].

Gracie betrays her new family, sharing their secrets with the Castors so she can be reunited with her dying husband. While her choice dismays the others, they understand it. Manson comments, "I do think it's true that we do terrible things for the people we love, which is one of the themes of our season, really. And I think that's true for *Orphan Black* as a whole, especially with the journey they go on" (Dalton, "Creator").

Cosima and Alison's shared political speech also considers family importance: Cosima says, "I've been hearing a lot of people talk today about, um, family values, and in my opinion, the most important family value is, um, accepting your family for who they are. Uh, but that doesn't mean coloring inside the lines, because kids do that. That's their gift." Alison, who's running for school board to keep her kids in their school (another selfless act for her family), finishes up:

> Sometimes family is more than just the people under your roof. Um, they're people who jump in headfirst who aren't afraid to make fools of themselves to help you, who don't hide their faces in shame if you fall down.... If your family is suddenly bigger than you expected and your house gets too crowded, do you tell your family that they need to find a different place to live? ... You make room, you adapt, you find creative solutions to keep people together. Our schools are our family. And as school trustee, I will not divide us. Bailey Downs stays in the Glendale school district. I stand for inclusion, not exclusion. I will be your mother hen, and I will keep our chicks together ["Community of Dreadful Fear and Hate" 307].

This is intercut with S. and Sarah discussing how S. has adopted Gracie and now Helena, while Alison gazes at Felix, Cosima, and her mother. Maria Doyle Kennedy (Siobhan) notes, "The ideas of identity and family are very big ones for all of us. Find your tribe. Kick negative ideas and a-holes to the curb. Live with honor and as little judgment of others as you can manage" ("Maria Doyle Kennedy Q&A"). This becomes difficult for S. when she faces her own mother, who killed her husband. "John Sadler was a drunk and a pikey who plucked you from the cradle," Kendall retorts, unrepentant at what she did for her daughter, though she went to jail for it ("Insolvent Phantom of Tomorrow" 309). S. threatens to kill her, but on realizing her cells could cure Sarah's sisters, reluctantly drags her back to Canada with them.

The season expands from Helena's dream of an idealized family party to all the women's dream of togetherness. The dinner party at season end (in real life, not Helena's mind) emphasizes how they've achieved their goal. Even as Alison waits to see if she's won her campaign, she cooks a fancy dinner for everyone, including all her sisters, Siobhan, Felix, and even Art, who helped get them their happy ending. After, Sarah, Siobhan, and Kendall snowmobile out to Iceland to see Kira. Sarah embraces her in the snow and they have a happy ending, family reunited at last. Fawcett explains: "This is the way we wanted the season to go out, which is with a very different tone. This is kind of almost like an emotional epilogue in a way. I just wanted it to feel like it really had some resolve to it, and yes, there are some cliffhangers and we've left some things up in the air, but what this allows us to do in season 4 is it allows us to breathe and reset ourselves a little bit" (Ross, "Finale").

Season Four: Strange Bedfellows

It's chilling to realize that each clone has one person she trusts completely and that each betrays her as monitor—telling intimate details to DYAD for a cash payout. This is naïve Donnie, Beth's lover Paul, Cosima's girlfriend (with another seen before Delphine in the comics), Tony's best buddy Sammy. Serving a similar function are Rachel's lover Daniel and Helena's adoptive father Tomas. Only Sarah is exempt, leaving Art and Felix free of this taint and truly trustworthy. If the previous seasons were spent discovering this, season four accepts it so much that they work with their enemies.

Fawcett recalls liking returning Sarah to the series beginning "where things are coming at her and she doesn't know who the bad guys are. Those elements of having to lie in the moment … are kind of what made Season One great. We tried to bring that feeling back in Season Four" (Bernstein 41).

"The Collapse of Nature" (401) introduces truly surprising cast, as the flashback episode lets the show bring back the dead characters: Beth, Paul, Leekie, Maggie, Olivier. It's also revealed that Art and Beth were betrayed by a spy—Detective Martin Duko, Beth's treacherous union steward. As the present-day season goes on, he taunts Art with the Hendrixes' drug dealing, trying to convince Art to abandon the Clone Club. Soon enough, Art must protect Alison and Donnie by covering up their crimes, crossing lines he had never expected to protect the criminals. He even lets the Clone Club murder his coworker. When Duko, facing illegal torture at S.'s hands, pleads, "Come on, I know I crossed the line. It's dark stuff, but … you can't let her do this to another cop," Art rejects him. "I crossed the line too, Marty. For Beth" ("The Redesign of Natural Objects" 408). With this, he leaves.

Rachel awakens not only to a mother but to a foster brother, as her mother has adopted the Castor clone Ira Blair. Tatiana Maslany says of the Rachel-Ira dynamic of season four. "We've always been antagonistic towards each other. None of the Leda clones have ever been, like buddies with a Castor clone. So that relationship is familiar and that turn but there's something different about Rachel in the way she speaks to a Castor clone and Ira has been raised singularly as opposed to part of a group of guys raised in the military" ("Closer Looks 403"). This is one of many jarring new team-ups.

Ari Millen, who plays all the Castors, considers the new Rachel-Ira dynamic of season four. "Every time I've worked with a brand-new clone of Tat's, it's always a brand-new energy that she brings, and that we both can contribute to the scene" ("Closer Looks 403"). He also describes Ira's "Mommy issues" ("Closer Looks 403"). As he climbs into the swimming pool with Susan and kisses her passionately, their relationship may be the most jarring.

Meanwhile, Cosima is playing surrogate for Donnie and Felix's baby so she can snoop around the mysterious fertility clinic Brightborn. However, when Krystal shows up, Donnie has to decoy her, pretending to be a masseuse, and listening to her surprising story … all until he reveals too much and she kicks him and flees.

As everyone teams up with the wrong people, Felix tracks down his half-sister Adele and brings her to a painful family dinner in "Human Raw Material" (405), during which Sarah keeps asking how Adele found Felix. At last, Sarah gets the results of a secret DNA test she has had Scott run, and announces to her chagrin that Felix and Adele really are related. Even for the dysfunctional family, this is a new level of drama.

Through the season, Sarah is tortured by the knowledge of a mysterious robot maggot in her cheek—the most intimate and lethal of partnerships. It could kill her at any moment. However, the one best informed is a new Leda clone—one who only communicates at a distance and refuses to get involved. Sarah is desperate to recruit M.K. and repeats over and over that she will work with anyone to be free. M.K., however, trusted only Beth and a strange loner called Dizzy.

In episode four, Alison and Donnie send over Doctor Leekie's rotting head with its own maggot, incongruously in a designer bag. Scott and Cosima start joking with it, showing their triumph over being controlled: Scott smirks, "That's the *head* of DYAD. He never gave me a raise. Not once" and Cosima retorts, "Who's the science now, bitch?" She concludes, "Alison and Donnie are total psychos, but this is a goldmine." The head makes this another terribly jarring alliance, though the Hendrixes are doing things they'd never expected as well.

In her desperation, Sarah-as-Beth allies with a mystery dental clinician who says she can remove the device. However, when Sarah is strapped in with a brace around her head, body horror appears ("The Stigmata of Progress" 403). The doctor tells her:

> I've penetrated the device, which now means that the slightest movement on your part will cause it to erupt. Do you understand? Don't nod, just blink once if you understand. Okay. If you do move, a burst of tendrils will release a fatal dose of tetrodotoxin. So, again, just need you to … blink once so that you understand. Great. Beth, I'm so sorry, but you really don't know what you're getting into here. I had to call my superiors, so…. Well, they'll probably be here any minute. But until then, honestly? No movement. It is … it is super critical. God. You know, when you first came sniffing around here, I had instructions: Misdirect you, send you on your way. But nobody told me you'd be coming back. Or that you're one of the test subjects. God! You don't know how lucky you are to be chosen for this.

Appearing from behind her, the loathsome DYAD "cleaner" Ferdinand suddenly cuts the doctor's throat, compounding the horror. Having saved Sarah, he offers to get Sarah's maggot device removed, but he wants her to find Rachel, his beloved. Their twisted S&M relationship is just one more awkward alliance. Sarah enlists M.K. to find Rachel, but when M.K. discovers she's working with Ferdinand, who murdered her sisters, she tries to murder him as well and then rejects them all.

At last Susan Duncan, Rachel's mother and the clones' creator, offers Cosima an alliance. In "The Scandal of Altruism" (406), Sarah and Cosima decide to work with Susan and give her their progenitor Kendall Malone's DNA and Cosima's research so she can save the Ledas. There's a complex series of exchanges—Cosima will stay as hostage, Sarah will get her maggot removed, while Susan is a hostage she can watch Kendall's DNA taken, she will only get the Leda sample, not Castor. They don't consult with Mrs. S or the Ledas, emphasizing how their alliance pushes them close to the dark side. The complex deal is shattered, however, when Kendall is kidnapped. Evie and her assistant Duko drive her far away, shoot her, and burn the body. Meanwhile, spyware wipes out Cosima's data. It seems the quest is over.

Despairing in "The Antisocialism of Sex" (407), Sarah goes out drinking and partying, hooking up with strange men and seeing an image of Beth everywhere as Beth chides her to protect her sisters and make better choices. Beth's pointed comments and dry humor finally pull her back from the dark side in this unlikely alliance. In another surprising twist, Beth was obeying Brightborn when she committed suicide at their behest. Cosima, however, tries an even stranger bedfellow as she prepares to put Sarah's maggot in her own face to possibly cure her. Only Felix's revelation that her beloved Delphine is alive stops her.

When Donnie is arrested, Alison works with Adele in her lawyer capacity (suspicious as Alison is about her drinking and flakiness). Meanwhile Duko meets with Alison and insists she must betray Sarah or Donnie will die. In another compromised partnership, Alison appears to submit, though she's revealed at last to have set a trap with help from her sisters. Only working together and sharing information, the story emphasizes, can they triumph.

Cosima allies with Susan, sharing her notes, then finally extracting Sarah's eggs and bringing them to Susan's island. Her plan is to fertilize Sarah's eggs with Ira's sperm—technically a brother-sister insemination that takes strange bedfellows to a new level. Meanwhile Scott is more appalled at the concept of working with treacherous Rachel. "She stabbed us in the back. I'm not working with her. She even cheats at Agricola," he protests ("The Redesign of Natural Objects" 408). They speak with Rachel and Susan over the monitor—the women wear white but the shadows make their clothes grey, like the moral compromises here. Ira's in grey as well. At episode end, Rachel is eager to work with Sarah and take back the empire. Meanwhile, Cosima owns her own trip to the morally grey side:

> SCOTT: Have you thought about how insane you are? Jumping on a chopper to a mad scientist's private island?
> COSIMA: Dude, we are mad scientists. Don't be a hater.
> SCOTT: Now you're really scaring me ["The Redesign of Natural Objects" 408].

Meanwhile, the only one nasty enough to take down Brightborn is Rachel, so Sarah arranges to have her infiltrate the building and catch the evil CEO, Evie Cho, admitting to euthanizing babies on camera. Instantly, the Clone Club have blackmail material. However, Rachel ends the season taking her mother's place on Brightborn's board, insisting she will link Neolution and Brightborn by creating bots in clones—the most frightening merger of all. Though she's a clone, she insists on ruling over the cloning process. Back on the island, her mother pleads with her not to choose this path, and Sarah insists, "Rachel! You're one of us." Rachel, however, refuses to be trapped as a clone when she could be a creator. She stabs each of them, leaving them to die of their wounds.

Instead of season four ending with a reunion, perhaps welcoming M.K. to the fold, the sisters are all split up. Ironically, the Clone Club tell Krystal the truth—only for her to disbelieve them and reject membership. Alison and Donnie are safely hidden away with Helena in the wilds of Canada. M.K. has fled. Ferdinand holds Siobhan and Kira at gunpoint, Sarah lies wounded, Cosima and Charlotte are hiding with the secret village of Revival, though they've found Delphine and safety of a sort. This perfectly fits the theme of things falling apart as the most important alliance, the Clone Club itself, splits.

Season Five: Self Definition

The psychologist Doctor Perkins tells S. a meaningful "Your daughter is struggling on the threshold of what it means to become you. Remember that" ("Let the Children & the Childbearers Toil" 504). In fact, all the characters are becoming their best selves, even as they all individuate. The real Cosima adds, "Your genes alone are neither the fullness of your biology nor the extent of your 'existential self' (as Graeme and I refer to it). Neither can be securely located in a string of DNA molecules" (Griffin and Nesseth). Meanwhile, she explores the impact of conditioning on one's life:

> While there are certainly concrete biological reasons why the sisters may have differences in their appearances, there are some very practical non-science related reasons as well. One, of course, is so that they can be visually distinguishable onscreen. But perhaps more poignantly it's important that they are seen as very distinct people with their own idiosyncratic personalities, and as such we continue to emphasize the richness of each character's personal agency. Insofar as they may make choices to act in the world according the principles and concerns that drive them, they also make choices about how they choose to present themselves stylistically (like, for example, one may simply decide to artificially color her hair). And further, they have each have led very different lives that have affected their physical development (like, for example, Cosima's deteriorating eyesight may very well be due to prolonged close-vision eye strain from reading). Again, we stress that simply because they may be genetically the same, their choices—especially as pertaining to their bodies, aesthetically or otherwise—may be influenced by a whole host of factors unrelated to their DNA! [Herter, "Nature vs. Nurture"]

The women define themselves through the crucible of season five—on the island, the new patriarch Westmorland taunts Cosima as he challenges her to surrender her humanity and shoot the "monster" Yannis. She refuses, insisting he can take her life but never her compassion. Meanwhile, in "Let the Children & the Childbearers Toil" (504), Susan is seen healing from the stabbing, and she and Coady reveal some of their history. Susan tells Ira of Westmorland, "Years ago, he chose another path, another scientist, someone who was willing to do the things I wouldn't." Coady, who was less "squeamish," altered the biology, while Susan insists that she was barely involved as she only isolated the genes in her lab. Thus, through their goals echo, their morals set them apart. Goaded by Cosima and Ira, she finally tries to kill Westmorland, but he kills her instead.

For the first time, Kira demonstrates a firm will of her own as she refuses to go on the run in "Clutch of Greed" (502), instead facing Rachel and outwitting her—with this, all of her family remark on how much she's looking and acting like Sarah. In fact, Kira now has her own quest, as she wants to discover what her biology has made her and she decides only Rachel has the answers. Sarah struggles with her emerging temperament, but finally offers to train Kira to become a grifter like herself and fool Rachel. In return for Kira training her in her deep perception, Sarah adds, "I'll tell you whatever you want to know about all the grown-up stuff we do," offering Kira all she herself would want. Each offers her special skills to the other and both grow stronger through the training.

> Too often in television, female characters are reduced to one-dimensional archetypes, barely distinguishable from one another, while in the real world, women are subjected to sweeping and insulting generalizations. By making its heroes clones, *Orphan Black* forces the viewer to recognize that though women might share a lot in common genetically, every woman is a distinctively complex individual. In fact, by highlighting the differences between the clones, *Orphan Black* demonstrates how crucial environment can be in shaping individuals and—especially in the case of Helena—the importance of shaping an environment that actively supports women, rather than degrades them [Gennis].

Alison faces down the community of Bailey Downs from atop a stage and insists that she won't define her entire life by how they think of her, since they're a group of hypocrites—at least she admits what she's done: "I know exactly what you all think of me. But I'm not just a boozer, I'm a pill popper too! That's right. And half of you bought them from me! Oh, God. Don't pretend you're so innocent. You're hypocrites! All of you, hypocrites! Nona, I see you. You know, I've given my heart to this community, and I can't help but feel a little bit hurt that you're pushing me to decide, but, you know I have atoned for my sins." Further, she discovers she doesn't care how they judge her any more, since she's part of a far more worldly community—the sestras. She concludes, "And I have a life that is so much bigger than Bailey Downs" ("Beneath Her Heart" 503). After a lifetime stuck in her small-town borders, she's branching out.

She returns from a retreat in "Gag or Throttle" (507), having chosen to remake herself inside and out. Now she has a purple bob she calls "creative and free" and the hip tattoo "live deep." She changes her craft room into a music room and makes a new relationship with Donnie, one in which she needn't micromanage. She's found healing through loosening her control over everything and can give up the pills and drinking as well.

Rachel's struggle is central this season, especially in the flashback episode of "Gag or Throttle" (507). Beginning with her life as the child raised by the corporation to recite her own barcode number on command, Rachel lives as a slave to the patriarchy. In modern times, she discovers Westmorland is watching her through a camera in her artificial eye—when he promised her total freedom, he lied. She is then ordered to treat Kira the same way she was, experimenting on her and finally bringing her to the island. Through it all, more flashbacks link her life with the younger girl's. When she prepares Kira to have her eggs harvested and implanted, she sees her own childish self sitting there, asking "Why don't you run?" Shaken, she frees Kira and then gouges out the artificial eye Neolution has given her—she's claiming her freedom. In the following episode, S. asks Rachel to betray Neolution, adding, "You saved my granddaughter. I'm willing to take a gamble on nature over nurture." Rachel considers, then finally makes her choice, choosing freedom and the Clone Club over infinite corporate power.

"Guillotines Decide" (508) has a new clone dance party—this time at Felix's art opening where he's painted all the sestras. His paintings showcase their contrasts and personalities—all the differences they've explored through the series. The portraits emphasize his insight into the sisters and how he values and loves their uniqueness. Though Sarah is not dead, her portrait, with x's over the eyes and the inscription "In Loving Memory" continues hanging on Felix's wall whenever she comes by. Her hair is wreathed in flame, and there's a phallus with a face on it, suggesting hybrid toughness.

Other paintings include soccer-mom Alison with an actual soccer ball in the foreground, a bottle smaller and half concealed in her other hand. This balances the side she wants to display and the side she doesn't. Both are round, feminine symbols, emphasizing her war between personal and family, private and public. Her hair is down, softening her beyond her usual look—how Felix gets to see her vulnerability. Her red-yellow halo suggests Virgin Mary, and a winged minivan blends prosaic suburbia with fanciful flight and escape.

Cosima's painting has her labcoat open to display her bra, sexualizing the usually professional young woman. Her face is open, curious and questioning. Red and green solutions in front of her show the same duality of the other pictures—half one thing, half another. Around her is the blue rain of science and ecology, or perhaps tears because she's dying—some are even edged in bloody red. Her halo is a black outline, making her appear to pop out of the picture, or perhaps suggesting a chalky outline of forthcoming death.

Felix's art features lots of human forms, often outlined suggesting a contrast with the superficial versus what's underneath. Glaring primary colors offer a fanciful lens, a new way of seeing the world. A self-portrait has him standing in a field of pink flowers with lots of sunshine. As he lifts up his tank top, he's displaying himself for viewers and also trying to share himself, to be vulnerable. A blue dog faced portrait on the wall is positioned to silently observe everything, like the eyes of T.J. Eckleburg in *The Great Gatsby*. Graffiti on the walls shows a bohemian freedom to personalize as he wishes. When the series ended, his paintings became souvenirs:

> Felix's original pieces of art went to wonderful homes, and we wanted Clone Club to know. Tatiana, Stephen Lynch (makeup), Graeme, John, Jordan, Maria, Kristian, Mackenzie, Kerry, Kathryn, BBC America, and the real Cosima all received pieces that meant a lot to them. We even took down Felix's wall in a way that huge portions of it were saved and auctioned off. And the door, including the screwdriver, will be on display in our Canadian network's offices as a reminder of this amazingly little weird show that could [BBC Staff, "Episode 10"].

In the final season, the three original paintings shown in Felix's loft through the series, now have grown into a roomful. Tony stands before abstract slashes of color, with lots of red for his abrasive personality. Krystal wears her fur coat over a pink top with an "I love me" bubble and open orchids for optimism and sensuality. M.K. is a disembodied head like her avatar, appearing on a split screen of two canvases. A blue outline traces the sheep mask but allows her wounded face to peep through. Rachel's painting is a thin outline and a huge shock of wig and lipstick—all she allows the world to see. Cosima finds herself dancing on it joyously, just as the clones triumph in bringing down her company. Pictures of Felix with his art, Kira with pink butterflies, and Siobhan also appear—with the last standing proudly behind the lady as Felix introduces her. Sarah in black, appears in front of mottled red and blue, her painting near Kira's and S.'s. Helena, gowned in white, bursts from a crimson background, just as the angelic heroine really does escape her past. Black shadows beside her like a door and surrounding her head suggest it still clings to her.

Beth appears in stark outline covered in shadows—the lost clone Felix never met. Red on one side and blue on the other like Sarah's suggests her public/private split. Beside her, sideways, is another photo that could be a homicide report or perhaps a stolen ID. She stands before the arches of what might be a train tunnel. Art and Sarah, who did know her, pause in front of her picture to feel her presence.

In happier portraits, Cosima stands in a mandala of swirling color with more of those colors spiraling across her body—she's one with the science, now that she's discovered a cure. Delphine bids on this one, emphasizing her love for all Cosima's become. There's a new one of Alison in a garden of flowers—and the new purple-haired woman poses in front of it in a flowered top, emphasizing her new self's growth.

Further, at the party, they don't disguise as each other the way they often do. Instead, Felix introduces Alison, Cosima, and Sarah as different goddesses—Hestia, Metis, and Athena—encouraging the crowd to celebrate their differences. His definition of them suggests their true selves as he encourages them to drop the fake accents and show themselves off with dancing, conversation, or whatever they wish, as long as it's true. Alison party-plans and chatters about her life driving the soccer bus. Cosima dances with several women on a platform, ending with Delphine, her love. Sarah makes rude hand gestures at the crowd—her real feelings but also a moment perfectly in keeping with her personality. It's significant that this is a scene of separation—no four-clone dance party, but three clones being celebrated individually for what makes them distinct.

After this overarching celebration of differences, the Ledas end the show on different paths. Cosima and Delphine travel the world, loving and healing all of Cosima's sisters. Meanwhile, Krystal and Tony are free to live outside the club, healed but unburdened by its knowledge. Alison finds music and joy as she returns to domesticity, while Helena's raising of her babies "Purple" and "Orange" is unconventional but delightful. Maslany says, "What I like about that ending is that it is back to just human beings. The conspiracy, and all of that, and all of these kinds of systems—the strongest part in that is the family that these people have created. Whether it's a chosen family, or genetic, or whatever—they've embraced this family and this community" (Ross, "Tatiana Maslany")

> Even when a clone's decision has negative effects on the rest, their support of each other never wavers. Rather than tearing each other down, the Clone Club draws strength from one another. What makes this so important is the fact that they don't *need* one another to succeed. Yes, it's hard to imagine where they'd be now without Cosima's smarts, Sarah's fearlessness or Alison's…. Alison-ness, but the show still gives the impression that, united or divided, the clones are survivors above all else [Gennis].

Rachel, meanwhile, has lost her privileged status at DYAD—the wealth, the magical eye, the knowledge of her own superiority. However, she too revels in her uniqueness by not joining the others. "Ever since I was six years old, I've compared myself to each and every LEDA. Believe me, the last thing I want to do is see another face like mine," she decides. She may not have found happiness, but she has found peace.

Sarah, however, is less settled. In a downward spiral, she considers running away and tells her sisters, "I don't know what I'm doing. I … I carry around all of these mistakes. I don't know how to be happy. There's no one left to fight, and I'm still a shit mum" ("To Right the Wrongs of Many" 510). With her battle won, she doesn't know what to become. The real Cosima explains, "Season five is a long-view discussion of not only what we wove throughout the narratives in the past seasons, but also a launching point into the future that is unwritten—not simply unwritten by the OB writers, but unwritten in the sense that it is impossible to know" (Griffin and Nesseth). This is what most troubles Sarah—that without her five-year enemy, she's back to drifting.

Her sisters comfort her with their different stories of bad mothering, coming together by sharing their individual uniqueness. Manson concludes: "Tatiana did a marvelous job of portraying that real subtle quiet pain, that inability to move forward that Sarah has there. And, of course, it's only her sisters that can help her move forward like she helped them all the way along. This reluctant hero has grown up and she's filled her mother's shoes" (Ross, "Series Finale"). With this, Sarah resolves to do better and create an unconventional, loving family for her daughter.

The final scene at Mrs. S's has Sarah, Felix, and Kira going fishing, leaving their new home awaiting them. Fawcett adds "That place is Sarah, and it is Mrs. S, and it is Kira, and I like the idea that when they left for the beach, they ate breakfast really quick and left breakfast out on the table, and just left. I wanted that feeling that everything is right in the world, and that things are going to be okay" (Ross, "Series Finale"). They've claimed the house instead of running from it. In fact, Sarah has hung up three portraits and a few other pieces of Felix's art. The staff add, "It was a gesture we wanted fans to see to know that Sarah's building her own version of home inside S's" (BBC Staff, "Episode 10").

The real Cosima concludes that the sestras "embody some of the voices representing multi-generational, multi-classed, multi-gendered, multi-sexualities which demand not a perfect world … but inclusion, diversity, heterogeneity, and liberation from violence" (Herter, "Why Protest"). Working together, they celebrate the differences even as they achieve freedom for themselves and their sisters.

The post-show comic *Orphan Black: Deviations* gives the clones' individuality and teamwork even more emphasis. In this alt-world reimagining, Beth and Katja survive. They work with their sisters and bring in M.K. sooner. Thus, the shenanigans of season one like Alison's party are complicated by Beth the coke fiend passing out, but also progress more quickly, with more Ledas teaming up to provide more pieces of the mystery. This time, Sarah explores the differences between herself and Beth, trying to heal the other woman instead of mimicking her. Though ill, Katja shows her heroism too. Even as Helena continues to target the clones, Rachel kidnaps Kira and Cosima in an echo of the season two epic finale. Increasing the teamwork, Beth and Sarah go in together to save them with S., Felix, and Katja as backup, though conscience-struck Delphine beats them to the rescue. M.K. helps but also entraps Ferdinand and triumphantly blows him and Rachel up together, in a more empowered ending for the character. Though Helena is yet to be redeemed in this arc, the other women emphasize how much stronger the Clone Club becomes with each new sister.

Literature, Games, Symbols and Allusions

Metafiction, Roleplay and Gender-Flipping

In their 1987 article "Doing Gender," sociologists Candace West and Don H. Zimmerman introduced their notion of gender not as a trait or role in society, but rather as an accomplishment, created by daily social practices and behaviors. They specify sex as biological criteria, while doing gender, as they put it, "involves a complex of socially guided perceptual, interactional, and micropolitical activities that cast particular pursuits as expressions of masculine and feminine 'natures'" (127). Only Tony is seen literally choosing a different sex than the one he was born with. After this, he not only identifies as male but uses exaggerated male behavior, describing his genitals to Felix in order to provoke him. Like some transgender people, he over-performs gender, reclaiming it. His clone sisters all identify as female, but some of their actions are more nuanced.

West and Zimmerman point out that those performing gender feel accountable to society—which, for instance, dictates that men open doors for women, rather than the reverse. "To 'do' gender is not always to live up to normative conceptions of femininity or masculinity; it is to engage in behavior *at the risk of gender assessment*" (136). Each clone has a difference response to society's expectations. Alison is the most frantic about them, hiding all her inappropriate behaviors, from drugs, to torturing Donnie, to any sort of sloppiness or imperfection. However, in season five, at the Church Fall Fun Fair, she finally stands before her community and owns all this, confessing the drugs and nearly confessing the strength of her sisterhood as well. Hilarious Helena goes the other way, caring nothing for society's judgment and acting the same in public or private. Sarah acts tough publicly, but it's privately, around her family, that she's softer and admits her many failures. Cosima is usually seen privately, hanging out with Delphine or Scott in her lab or at home. This emphasizes her free spirit role, as she rarely even goes into judgmental society. Rachel, raised by a corporation and in a room filled with spy cameras, has always had to be perfect and arguably has never has privacy at all. In "One Fettered Slave" (509) Westmorland smirks, "Secrets. I know yours, Rachel. I know how you cup your hands just so, so you can hide that digging at your fingernails that you can't stop. I know how you constantly write letters to your biological mother—who you never met.... I know how you touch yourself in the shower, where you think it's clean."

Sorting through gender roles, S. and her mother Kendall both prefer tough trousers, parkas, and flannel shirts to dresses. Both are skilled with guns as well. While S. has long hair, her mother's short hair, name, and status as the Castors' progenitor all code her as male before she reveals her biological secret. This, that a woman can have male DNA, helps call into question the shadings of gender. S., who is called this more than the feminine Siobhan, defends her home Mama Bear style and puts Kira above all ... but she is also a freedom fighter who keeps secrets close.

Of course, Sarah has been neglecting her duties as mother, something S., Felix, and society in general drive home. Her punk look is technically feminine but not at all soft. Meanwhile, her interest in casual sex (as she dumps Vic and Cal, who beg her to come back) codes her as a rather masculine loner. However, she achieves a desire for community through the story, centered on her daughter, mother, and sisters. With Cal, she tries domesticity, and appears open to it.

Beth is a cop whose boyfriend complains about her lack of intimacy. She too performs the masculine standoffishness, though in a different way than Sarah. She insults Art in a friendly camaraderie, calling him "dipshit" at the police station. Her big hobby is running—a loner sport but not a feminine one like Alison's figure skating. However, season four sees Beth embracing M.K. in a gentle sisterhood and rushing to Art's place late at night, seeking comfort. While hidden, she can be vulnerable.

Rachel is the classic businesswoman who wears expensive suits as armor. Her relationships are ones of control—in fact, she uses them to keep her monitors and ally Ferdinand obeying her orders. She never declares love for any of them, only that she's using them. However, beneath this is a desperate desire for motherhood.

Helena is a serial killer sniper—as the detectives remark in season one, this is unheard-of in a woman. Many of her props, like gun and motorcycle, are masculine-coded. She also leaves childlike crafts and drawings, but decapitating Barbies suggests a hatred for femininity as well as for her clones. She wears parkas and has a clumsy dye job, though her hair is wild and curly—suggesting nonconformity. With this, she's more bag lady than tomboy. The Proletheans dress her in a wedding dress and nightgown, emphasizing how foreign these are to her. In the fantasy of her baby shower, she wears a pink dress—basically the only time she does such a thing, and imagines her friends in gender-conformist attire—a British schoolboy look for Felix and Ukrainian folk dress for Cosima. On her travels she meets Jesse, whom she admires for his blend of rugged toughness (he's a truck driver) and chivalrous gentility (he's polite and defends her in the bar instead of hitting on her). Like Donnie, he's polite and lets her take charge, suggesting he's happy taking the submissive role in their relationship.

Cosima the nonconformist is rather balanced in her gender approach. She's a scientist who can play RPGs with the guys, but also plays caregiver, aiding her friends as much as possible through their emotional upheavals. Her relationships are with women, but with Delphine and Shay, she's seen deciding and giving way, comforting and being comforted, rather than ruling the relationship as Alison does.

Alison determinedly performs gender, from propping up her husband to being a perfect "soccer mom." In fact, when she's biologically unable to have children, she adopts them to mimic the biological role she wishes. She rules the family more than Donnie … something that's not necessarily a gender-flip, considering how long the domestic sphere has been in the women's control. As "Community of Dreadful Fear and Hate" (307) reveals, Alison's mother is the same, expanding beyond the home to a feminine pursuit that's also a full-time job with her fuchsia soap store. Nonetheless, Donnie is well aware that his wife "wears the pants" and he's emasculated in many ways society would consider the weaker role—he takes Alison's last name, and with this, her mother loses all respect for him. When he faces the Portuguese gangsters, he needs the stronger Alison and then Helena to save him.

Critic Joan Riviére describes the masquerade of femininity as a kind of reaction-formation against the woman's trans-sex identification. Womanliness is "assumed and worn as a mask, both to hide the possession of masculinity and to avert the reprisals expected if she was found to possess it" (38). For instance, Riviére describes a housewife hiding her knowledge of building when anyone comes to work on the house and giving suggestions "in an innocent and artless manner, as if they were lucky guesses" in order to appear nonthreatening to the male ego (39). Another woman, a university lecturer, wears feminine clothes and jokes about her topic, as she also seeks to subvert her power in the male arena. As Riviére concludes, "The reader may now ask how I define womanliness or where I draw the line between genuine womanliness and the masquerade. My suggestion is not, however, that there is any such difference; whether radical or superficial, they are the same thing" (38). Women, forced into feminine roles by society, use them manipulatively as they conform.

The Ledas, switching roles, often play different kinds of feminism in this way. Helena-as-Alison acts meek before the drug dealers. In "The Stigmata of Progress" (403), Helena-as-Alison coos, "My biggest supporter was my husband. He's my rock" and expertly describes Alison's campaign details for the police. Likewise, Cosima tries to tone down her pro–LGBTQ stance while giving Alison's campaign speech. Sarah-as-Rachel charms Ferdinand while channeling her real rage into Rachel's accustomed S&M sex play. Confronting the evil patriarch Westmorland, Sarah-as-Rachel pretends to sob, all while demanding why Westmorland never loved her enough. Several times, Sarah plays Krystal, the ditsy self-appointed investigator who waylays suspicion through prattle about cosmetics and conspiracies. Cosima similarly allays suspicion as a naïve surrogate at Brightborn—their victim not the scientist investigating them. When Susan dismisses her questions with "it's all rather technical, actually" ("Human Raw Material" 405). Cosima must straddle roles of ignorance and knowledge as she admits to being just a biology major. Breaking into a mental institution to find Dr. Coady, S. plays a psychologist and Sarah, her clumsy assistant, as both dress more harmlessly feminine. All of these roles are taken to reassure and fool men (and occasionally women in the patriarchal system) that they are harmless.

Other role-switching lets the Ledas borrow their counterparts' strength—Sarah emulates and soon becomes Beth the capable cop, and Alison borrows the power of rebellious Sarah. Sarah plays Rachel several times, stealing her power and discovering her secrets. There's also Helena's imaginary friend Pupok.

> Pupok has given Helena a pep talk while she was imprisoned in her crate ("Nobody said it would be easy, kiddo.") and drooled over the possibility of mangoes. And if the voice of Pupok sounds familiar, there's a reason: Maslany added the scorpion to the many roles she plays on the show. "Tatiana is doing the voice of the scorpion as well," Fawcett says. "We talked to her very early on ... to create a sound that you could hear the scorpion before you saw it, so you knew it was around. I had this idea that the scorpion would kind of purr, partly like a cat and a velociraptor. The clicking and the purring and all of these different sounds that normally would be sound design and sound effects guys.... Tat has created all of those sounds herself" [Nguyen, "Here's the Story"].

Of course, the actress is playing many roles and playing characters who occasionally play *each other's* roles. While many note how Tatiana gets to show off her acting chops, fewer notice how much her characters show about acting itself. Maslany compares her parts with the acting experience and the publicity machine that impacts so many music stars. "This is about volition and autonomy," she said of the show, "and that was resonating with me, being an actor who was suddenly being interviewed or being dressed" (Loofbourow). In fact, the Ledas offer a myriad of personalities: housewife, punk rebel, professional, lesbian free spirit, villainess, madwoman, vamp. These are in fact "encompassing almost every trope women get to play in Hollywood and on TV" (Loofbourow). Thus, as the characters break stereotypes, they challenge Hollywood's view of women—Alison is a housewife, but she fights off thugs with pepper spray. Helena and Rachel are sometimes villainesses, but they have surprising vulnerabilities for family. The Ledas are nonconformists, determined to break out of their roles.

Alison, the biggest conformist, plays roles as she performs before her community—with the Family Day at rehab, the speech as she runs for office, and the Harvest Fair talent show, as well as two literal musicals. These all emphasize the roles she must assume and her life in the community spotlight, with everyone watching and judging her—her part in the musical is just as artificial as the smiling face she dons each day.

Further, the beautiful modellike uniformity of the clones gets deconstructed, not just because of the women's differences, but also through Helena's learning that their cookie-cutter consistency is a lie.

> By structuring the story around the clones' differences, *Orphan Black* seems to suggest that the dull sameness enforced by existing female archetypes needs to die. Early in the first season, there is a serial killer hunting down the clones—it turns out to be Helena, the Ukrainian—who ritualistically dismembers Barbie dolls after dyeing their hair to match that of her next victim. It's a creepy touch, but one that can also be read as a metacriticism of how women are used on TV: the punishing beauty standards to which they're held, the imposed uniformity. (Need a new sitcom wife? Grab the prototype and change the hairstyle.) Our low tolerance for difference among female characters means that they will almost always be less interesting, less memorable and less beloved than their male counterparts. In this context, Helena becomes a kind of hero, slaughtering televisual conformity and constituting, in both her savagery and her warmth, a radical expansion of what women on television can be [Loofbourow].

The show also straddles genre, as Sarah-as-Beth and Beth's stories are police procedural, complicated by their secret knowledge. Alison's stories are suburban gothic as she conquers her hidden drug problem as well as the community's judgement. Cosima solves scientific puzzles, and Sarah sells coke and parties at clubs as she fights to reclaim the daughter she abandoned, in a gritty drama. Wherever there's Helena, there's masochistic violence and savagery, from survival and escape dramas to revenge fantasies. Of course, the women unite, thus bringing their skills earned in their respective genres so they can fight together.

> In its subject matter, *Orphan Black* broods on the nature-nurture debate in human biology, but in its execution, the show cleverly extends the same question to matters of genre. What does the exact same woman look like if you grow her in the petri dish of "Desperate Housewives" or on a horror-film set in Eastern Europe? What about a police procedural? The result is a revelation: Instead of each archetype existing as the lone female character in her respective universe,

these normally isolated tropes find one another, band together and seek to liberate themselves from the evil system that created them [Loofbourow].

Gender-flipping and gaze also subvert the conventions. In most shows, someone like Paul, the ex-military good guy who loves the persecuted heroine, would be the hero. However, Sarah and Rachel each use and take advantage of him. "Couldn't just be pretty and dense, could he?" Sarah thinks in the spinoff comic, in a delightful gender-flip (*The Clone Club #1: Sarah*). By thinking of him in these terms, she firmly establishes *herself* as central hero, with all the agency and decision-making power. Marginalized Paul is only the love interest. At last, he gives his life to stop a great evil but also to defend Sarah and aid her own quest. Much more often in fiction, it's the woman who is sacrificed to give the hero pain to struggle through, as he bravely completes his quest nonetheless. This task, once again, falls to Sarah. The actress notes of the show, "It sort of normalizes having a lead female" (Wheaton).

This time, women don't die to affect the male characters, but to affect each other and the audience, as everyone reels from Kendall, Siobhan, and M.K.'s deaths. All are mentors, perishing to make the heroines succeed on their own. Meanwhile, the big corporation DYAD is taken over by young women, Rachel then Delphine as Evie rules their competitor Brightborn ... and then Rachel takes it from her. Finally, as Cosima destroys Westmorland's power on his mad scientist island, Rachel is the one to dismantle DYAD itself. Each time, this becomes the women's world, not the men's.

Much more than Paul, Donnie is emasculated, leaving Alison and Helena to fight for the family and save him repeatedly as well. Even tough woodsman Cal has a place in the story as much as Sarah dictates, as she leaves him waiting and arranges for him to babysit Kira during her heroic quest. Kindly Jesse will wait for Helena as long as she needs. Actor Wil Wheaton describes "how strongly the show has resonated with women." As he adds, "We have the potential for so many things and not defined because how we look—because it's just me" (Wheaton).

Strong men like Tomas and Henrik are beaten nearly to death in the former case and strapped down to be "impregnated" with his own equipment in the latter. Both times the warrior is Helena, once the madwoman, who takes the central fighting role. The patriarch Leekie is killed by a man, but it's fumbling, goofy Donnie who accidentally pulls the trigger. To emasculate them both further, a grossed-out Donnie, retching all the while, must obey Alison's orders to dig him up and pass his putrefied head to Cosima for study.

Felix, the other lead man in the series, offers a nonconformist perspective, teaching Alison how to beat the catty wives of suburbia, or playing peacemaker between Sarah and S. Nonetheless, this role of his emphasizes how he's only support in the women's story, much like the other men here. Everyone's raised by mothers, not fathers, or the relationships like Sarah's and Alison's focus on dealing with their maternal figures.

The men are treated as love interests in a more subtle yet significant way. Laura Mulvey pioneered the study of gender-bias in cinematic gaze, explaining: "There are three different looks associated with cinema: that of the camera as it records the pro-filmic event, that of the audience as it watches the final product, and that of the characters at each other within the screen illusion." She describes "the woman as icon, displayed for the gaze and enjoyment of men, the active controllers of the look." Mulvey emphasizes the difference between the delight of admiring a figure onscreen (especially one in a skimpy outfit) and identifying with the character (especially one fully dressed and powerfully posed): "In a world ordered by sexual imbalance, pleasure in looking has been split between active/male and passive/female. The determining male gaze projects its fantasy onto the female figure, which is styled accordingly. In their traditional exhibitionist role women are simultaneously looked at and displayed, with their appearance coded for strong visual and erotic impact so that they can be said to connote to-be-looked-at-ness."

Orphan Black contains quite a few shots of naked bodies, but no obvious gratuitous shots of breasts and bottoms. In the first episode, Sarah's butt is visible as she strips and seduces Paul, inviting him to look at her. However, along with this female sexualized nudity is also male sexualized nudity, with shots of just Paul's naked body next. Unusually for television, the camera lingers on Paul, as Sarah's gaze lingers on his body, suggesting she is the active participant and he the passive object. The next morning, he walks around the flat naked, and she can't stop sneaking glances. In episode two, he's naked again, coming out of the shower to ask about her feelings and try to reconnect with her, to her disconcertment. Through season one, she continues to objectify Paul, who's often seen underdressed in their encounters.

Rachel objectifies him even worse: "Even when she uses sex as a distraction—jumping Paul when he begins to suspect her identity last season—Sarah isn't a femme fatale or vixen. The focus is her desire, not his. When Paul has sex with Rachel this season, he's like a stallion at a livestock auction. She commands him to undress, inspects his body, appraises his teeth, pours him a glass of wine and won't let him drink it" (Breger).

"In sex scenes, the camera glances past Maslany's body to linger on beefcake abs. Sarah's two love interests, Paul and Cal, take on the role of Bond girls—objectified eye candy who spend their time helping our heroine or betraying her. Paul is a Ken Doll, and Cal is Your L.L. Bean Boyfriend come to life" (Breger). Mrs. S, who sizes up Paul for his looks when they meet, introduces the two men while smirking to herself and holding back the information that Paul and Sarah are lovers. The two clueless men greet each other.

Meanwhile, she objectifies and admires them, commenting, "Just look at the two of you. I don't know how she does it" ("By Means Which Have Never Yet Been Tried" 210). Alison and Cosima also weigh in on how hot they find Cal. When Rachel and Sarah play S&M games with Ferdinand, he's the one stripped and tied to the bed—in both cases, an intruder (Delphine then Ira) enters and sizes him up.

Alison has her own moment as she eyes her best friend Aynsley's husband as they sit in her van smoking pot. "You ain't so bad yourself. Tight glutes, nice pecs. I bet you could bench press me. Easy. I bet you could bounce me like a ball." When he protests, she retorts, "I'm objectifying you, sexually, to get back at Donnie," and seduces him on the spot ("Entangled Bank" 108).

Despite all these romantic moments, likely the most objectified character is Felix, who paints wearing only an apron, naked rear end hanging out. Generally, whoever comes in comments on it and can't stop staring. Sarah also catches him in the shower when she returns at the beginning of season four. Like the audience, she gets to stare at his body, and even jokes, before she lets him get dressed. Felix in turn gets a chance to leer at a male dancer, commenting over and over on his appearance:

> FELIX: Now, wait, what about your eye? Is that a permanent augmentation?
> ATTENDEE: It will be, one day. I've got other enhancements.
> FELIX: Right. Well, a philosophy so physical makes for a very handsome tribe. What about Olivier? Is he enhanced?
> ATTENDEE: Darling, you have no idea ["Parts Developed in an Unusual Manner" 107].

He's objectifying the dancer, who's objectifying Olivier, even as Olivier observes and monitors the clones. As season four begins, many male and female investigators stare at a dead Neolutionist's genitals, with the excuse that they're unusual because he had them strangely enhanced. While the audience doesn't get to see, they can picture and wonder as the onscreen characters gawk.

"Precisely because of their destabilizing potential, the popular representations of cyborgs are sentimental, existential, sexualized, and fetishized in alarming ways" (Kakoudaki 166). Thus, it's a mark of special commendation that the show avoids making the clones into sexy eye-candy, as occurs on *Battlestar Galactica, Torchwood,* and other programs. There are many moments—when Felix has clones play dress up, even when Cosima's taking a bath, when the clones might be fetishized but aren't. Cosima, vulnerable in the tub, manages to look wounded but not exploited. She tells her new lover about her deathly illness, only to start bleeding at that moment, turning it tragic rather than sexy ("Community of Dreadful Fear and Hate" 307). Ironically, the other clone seen in a bathtub is the male Leda, Tony. As he lounges, describing his genitals in a way that gets Felix picturing them, he objectifies himself—but only because he's now male.

The dehumanizing interrogation when in season two Sarah is prodded and questioned by medical examiners about her sexual history is cruel but not exploited with nudity. Helena and Sarah, tortured by Castor, likewise remain fully dressed. "Women are tied up, tied down, held captive, inseminated, their mouths sewn silent. On another show, these images might be filmed as torture porn. One of *Orphan Black*'s singular virtues is the way it avoids this voyeuristic lens" (Breger). A nun masturbates onscreen in "One Fettered Slave" (509) but not much can be seen. Further, Coady tells Art of Helena, "put your fingers in and tell me how open her cervix is!" in "To Right the Wrongs of Many" (510) and still the show manages not to show anything exploitative.

The male clones, the Castors, are more exploited. Sarah meets Rudy, the Castor in the basement, when he's shirtless in "By Means Which Have Never Yet Been Tried" (210). In "The Weight of This Combination" (301), he does pullups pantless as well, enjoying his body but also presenting it for viewers. In "The Weight of This Combination" (301), Delphine shows Sarah the hall camera, through which she sees a new clone, Krystal Goderitch, seducing Rudy. "I don't wanna see this shit," Sarah says, repelled by this sexualized self-image.

The Alison and Donnie twerking scene objectifies them both, but hilariously. They dance wildly in their underwear, hurling money, in a scene that's silly because ordinarily they're both so straight-laced and reserved. Further, as shown when their daughter tries to come in, the pair definitely don't want anyone gazing at them. In another humiliating moment, this one just for him, Donnie trips and his kilt flies up as he falls, giving an entire church audience a show. Finally, Donnie actually stripteases for Alison in "To Right the Wrongs of Many" (510) stripping down to his boxers and dancing for the gaze of the audience as well as his appreciative wife.

While all this watching goes on, cameras are central as characters spy on each other constantly, though often watching through others' cameras or spying on their own past actions. All this suggests fluidity to the spying and watching—many conspiracies and secrets rather than one all-encompassing Big Brother. Speaking to Cosima onscreen in season one is just a variation. Art discovers the Sarah-Beth switch from watching the playback. Neolution's symbol is an eye, suggesting the corporate Big Brother keeping watch over the clones. Soon enough, they create a new bionic eye for Rachel, communicating with her from within even as she spies on her sisters. Murals of eyes around the police station emphasize the constant watching theme. Even Alison lives on a Neighborhood Watch block where the neighbors are all spying on each other. Sarah watches her own memorial service through binoculars, and many other characters spy on each other through S.'s binoculars or Helena's gunsight, watching other characters just as the audience does and nodding to the fictionality of it all.

Paul watches his videos of Beth while Sarah plants bugs in his office, emphasizing how each spies on the other. When Sarah as Beth brings Paul lunch at work in "Conditions of Existence" (105), Felix watches from the car, spying as the audience is. He confronts her about her missing scar and everything changes. Paul asks to see it again, but Sarah/Beth giggles, "You will really try anything," and holds him off. "I will," Paul agrees in the same light tone, but his eyes are cold and the skin around them pulls tight. As each dismisses it and bids the other a pleasant goodbye, each knows the other is lying. They're playing parts for each other and the spy camera on top of the real roles the actors play.

Further, there are many mirrors, which reflect one's self—or at least the self others see, much like the many faces of the clones. In episode one, Sarah looks into three mirrors: in the restroom after she steals Beth's purse, during her transformation into Beth, and in the precinct bathroom when she realizes what a tough deception she's committed to. All three are moments at which she considers her transformation. Spy cameras suggest gaze, but mirrors, introspection and how one presents a gender-performed self to the world.

There are other significant moments where the heroine negotiates with herself in a mirror even while sparring with the enemy, casting them in parallel. As Sarah gazes at Kira in the DYAD pink room, Rachel gazes into the two-way mirror and addresses Sarah, pointedly saying that sometimes even mothers have to do what they're told. Plotting his death in "From Instinct to Rational Control" (404), M.K. watches herself in Ferdinand's glasses while Sarah reads through the newspaper clips on a projected screen. Side by side both reveal the history of Helsinki. In season five, Rachel confines Sarah at DYAD and Ferdinand shows her video feed of her loved ones, then an image of Rachel she needs to speak with. Once more, Sarah gazes at mirror-Sarah, watching herself even as the audience watches her.

Somewhere between the two, windows are frequent, with characters staring through them. Shattering Beth's windshield when Katja is killed suggests shattering Sarah's illusion that she's safe and plunging her into a vast conspiracy. Rachel is often shown in front of windows, emphasizing her role as observer of the world. Windows also suggest transparency and truth: Rachel is the only clone that was raised self-aware and knew about her origins from the start. The clone who knows she's being watched often watches herself—not in mirrors, but in the home video of her idyllic childhood, before she learned the truth.

When season four returns to the Paul and Beth story through the unusual medium of flashback, it calls attention to itself as fictional. More, it returns to the spy camera motif. In "The Collapse of Nature" (401), Beth implants a round spy camera to watch Paul then looks through a round hole to see the neolutionists extract a maggot from someone's cheek. In "Transgressive Border Crossing" (402), Art gazes at the painting and tells Sarah, "Come see this." They're looking at the camera as it scrutinizes them in turn. These moments add to the show's paranoia and oppression when Neolution watches, or to subversion and power when the Ledas plant their own. Moreover, as they constantly communicate through video chatting, the take back the patriarchy's power and reclaim it for their own.

Games as Metaphors

Cosima establishes her geek cred when she instructs Scott in *Runewars*, and his friends quickly invite her to play. Symbolically, the game has deeper implications. *Runewars* is an epic board game of conquest, battles, and area control, for two to four players. Players must gather resources, raise armies, and lay siege to heavily fortified cities while they compete to take control of six Dragon Runes.

Like the show, *Runewars* is fast—events keep coming with little downtime. Both take place over a series of seasons and have a set ending, and each player controls a different faction with specific strengths and weaknesses seeking to dominate the others. The factions cannot work together—one wins, and the others all lose. The Ledas, Castors, Neolution, and Proletheans seem drawn into just this sort of competition. Since many factions fight for control and only one can win, the game resembles the *Orphan Black* storyline from the first.

Julian Meynell, the board game consultant for "Variable and Full of Perturbation" (208), describes his experiences with it:

> Because it is his hobby, [John Fawcett] thought it might be interesting to put a board game in the show and have a scene where the character Cosima plays board games with Scott, so we started discussing which game we would use. John wanted a game which would be visually striking and also have a geeky theme. It also had to have incomprehensible board game lingo. We also wanted the game to be a good one. Naturally a lot of the games we discussed were Fantasy Flight games. We discussed *Runewars*, *Descent* and *Twilight Imperium* the most because they do not have other intellectual property that *Orphan Black* would need permission to use. We also discussed games that were not Fantasy Flight games primarily *Eclipse* and *Mage Wars*. In the end, *Runewars* was John's first choice because it met all the criteria, but most importantly because it is John's favorite game [Meynell].

Fantasy Flight gave their permission and Meynell found himself an extra in the scene, while also helping the others with the language and setting up the game between takes. "I wanted a game that took up table space, had a big wow factor, and looked really complicated," Fawcett says. "I like the fantasy element to *Runewars*—from an initial look, it repped geek board-game culture. We contacted FFG to see if we could use it—they'd already put out the second edition, which doesn't have the mountains—so I brought my copy of the first edition because I like the 3-D plastic mountains on the board" (Law).

Fawcett added that none of the actors knew any of the games beforehand. "You have to teach them enough to make them look proficient, give them enough that they look good on camera and it looks authentic when they're doing it," he explained (Law). Meynell amusedly describes Tatiana Maslany having more trouble with the game terminology than the science of other episodes.

A further joke is how good Cosima is at the traditionally male geeky activity that Scott calls a "bit of a sausage-fest" ("Ruthless in Purpose, and Insidious in Method" 308). Battling the boys at strategy and smarts, she quickly rules the board. "I also liked it from a story point of view," Fawcett continued. "There's no possible way that Cosima would know this game, but she blows us away. We realize in that moment, not only does she know that game, but she's incredibly versed at the game—as the guys at the table get their socks knocked off by this science girl. It added some depth to the character" (Law). Cosima's girlfriend Shay actually notes that she's good at it too: "I play this game with my brothers all the time" ("Ruthless in Purpose, and Insidious in Method" 308). Both women can play in the male sphere, emphasizing their power and transgression. In real life, many women are playing the board games, finding a variety beyond the traditionally boys' world of D&D. Further, even the cool girls like Cosima can play. Julian Meynell adds:

> Board games starting to show up on TV is part of the process of them moving into the main stream. It's really a symptom of their growing popularity. Over the last few years, geeky activities are moving out of a marginalized ghetto where they are seen as strange and incomprehensible into just other activities that people can be into. I suspect that board games will continue to show up in the background of scenes from time to time, because they can be used as ways of building character quickly. In the past, indicating the geeky side of Cosima's character might have been done through *Star Trek* references, or comic books or whatever. In *Orphan Black* it was done through board games.

Scott's game playing works as a metaphor for the chesslike maneuverings required to outwit the patriarchy. The actual games, however, are closer to worldbuilding, echoing the clones and their struggles to build a safe community even as DYAD has literally built their biology. Further echoes appear in M.K., who uses the internet as her personal playground and dominates the virtual world, though she's small and shy in the real one. Gaming let those who are shy and socially awkward, or even disabled or ill rule civilizations and topple empires—an excellent parallel for the clones themselves. Being powerless in the real world can thus be transcended, all in virtual space.

Meynell comments that games create social communities both online and in person—something seen in the increasingly close bond of the clone club. Each challenge they defeat together makes them more of a team. Games also show one's personality—aggressive, friendly, skilled, or conciliatory. "While Scott is very smart, he's very linear, and he's blown away by Cosima because she can improvise," adds his actor, Josh Vokey. "The game drives home the point that she's the smartest person in the room, and that she's very good at thinking outside the box" (Law).

Meanwhile, Scott protests of the scheming Rachel, "She stabbed us in the back. I'm not working with her. She even cheats at *Agricola*" ("The Mitigation of Competition" 409). Scott first plays Lookout Games' *Agricola* onscreen in "Community of Dreadful Fear and Hate" (307): Rachel sees it and asks to learn as a cover for deciphering her father's code book. Immediately, she finds the multi-hour board game foolish but Scott, mustering his determination now that she's playing in his world, tells her that she must learn for appearance's sake. "A medieval farming game where you have children and raise cattle seemed very weird" for the show, Fawcett says. "I picked it because it seemed one of the least appropriate things you could play with Rachel Duncan. She would completely abhor it. It's more like torturing Rachel rather than having fun with her" (Law).

The goal to *Agricola* is not conquest but survival—keeping one's people fed each winter and creating a prosperous community. "It's the model for many games since then that force players to confront limited resources while placing workers on a central board" (Law). This is precisely the Ledas' goal—staying alive when there are so few of them and so many life-threatening disasters keep coming. Rachel, trapped in her DYAD wheelchair, has a similar struggle. "It becomes like a game of chess between Scott and Rachel," says Vokey. "They end up trying to eliminate each other, and it ends up in a big double cross. Plus it's a funny idea, a cutthroat businesswoman doing this agricultural farming game, who's forced to play it to get what she wants" (Law).

Agricola has more parallels with the theme as Scott explains to Rachel, "Each turn, you get two choices to build your farm … one for you and one for your spouse. You can build fences, plant crops, have children." In fact, each family member gives the player another turn so having a spouse (whom one starts with) and producing children is an enormous advantage. However, barrenness proves a handicap: Scott even says, "If you don't have any children, you can only take two actions." Game play includes his comments like "Instead of mending this fence, I'm going to take this clay oven. Look at this guy. He's going to starve our kids." With Neolution actually preying on children like Kira, Charlotte, and young Rachel, there's extra significance.

Gaming soon transforms to reality as Scott's gamer buddies help break Rachel out of the lab with planning and coordination. "Dude. You rule. It's like your game life has overtaken your real life," his gamer-nicknamed buddy Hell Wizard tells him. Scott replies that it seems the other way around. Meanwhile, Hell Wizard shuts down the cameras, and they're off ("Ruthless in Purpose, and Insidious in Method" 308).

Gaming takes an even bigger role in the fourth season with their new secret base: Rabbit Hole Comics and Games Emporium works well with the rabbit hole they've all fallen into. Cosima jokes, "Secret lab under a comicbook shop, what more could a girl want, right?" ("Transgressive Border Crossing" 402). Adding the game store base was Fawcett's idea. Moreover, the staff at the BBC reveal:

> "The Rabbit Hole Comic Book and Gaming Emporium," name came from a game our production plays every year. We always give our different seasons a nickname (to protect the show from getting spoiled), and our whole office crew votes at the beginning of prep on what the name will be. This year, we called ourselves Rabbit Hole Productions, and when we needed a name for the comic book store, assistant to the showrunners, Evan Moore, suggested The Rabbit Hole, and everyone loved it! [BBC Staff, "Episode 2"].

While a convenience store forms the store's exterior, the products are real. Funko Pop! and IDW, along with other supporters of the show, contributed inventory to fill up the shop. Further, the creators supported local Canadian and Torontonian illustrators by using their posters on the walls.

"*Orphan Black* kind of gathers its audience and has this feeling of collecting ragtag groups of outsiders," says Fawcett. "Board-gamers are like those people that live in the cracks and crevices. And I've been playing and collecting for a lot of years—it's my other hobby—so I wanted to push for that, to highlight certain games I really loved" (Law). Hell Wizard, assistant in Scotty's new store, greets Sarah's family when they return to Canada, and emphasizes that he'll be a regular part of their team. *Agricola* sits on the top of his game pile, once again emphasizing building a community and keeping their people safe.

In "The Stigmata of Progress" (403), he teaches Kira a D&D style quest game called *Descent: Journeys in the Dark* and calls her "Fair Cinderel." *In Descent*, one player plays the great villain and the others are adventurers, exploring dungeons and caves to try to defeat him. With the introduction of Brightborn and the shadowy board it shares with DYAD, the Clone Club indeed are struggling against one monstrous villain, not the multiple players of the previous seasons. Further, this foreshadows the appearance of Westmorland at season end. Kira, however, gets frustrated and scatters the pieces. "Here's one of Hell Wizard's favorite games, but you can see in that scene, it's going right over Kira's head, she doesn't want to play, she's bored," says Fawcett.

"They never tell me when things are bad," Kira says to Hell Wizard. "But I always know." In fact, Sarah has just discovered her cheek maggot, which could kill her at any moment—thus, Kira resists being distracted with a frivolous game because she realizes how truly serious things are. With delightful synchronic symbolism, the show's solution is not an epic quest to save Sarah but actually to turn over the board—to play a different game than the one Brightborn has chosen.

In "The Antisocialism of Sex" (407), Kira plays *Minecraft,* a computer game that's likely a product of the game store. The creative and building aspects of *Minecraft* enable players to construct out of textured cubes, echoing Kira's interest in art. Rather like real life, the game has no specific goals for the player to accomplish, allowing players a great amount of freedom in choosing how to play. They can be spectators, builders, adventurers, warriors, just like the clones. *Minecraft* offers quests and campaigns across fantastical lands, much like Kira's trips to DYAD, the woods, and Iceland. Further, as she sits under her castle mural and her first-person view crosses a moat and climbs a mountain, they parallel. She isn't just playing but really questing, much like the visions intruding on her real life.

Suddenly, M.K. in her sheep mask bursts into the screen to greet her. Fantasy has turned real. In season five, Felix tracks down M.K. in the game to get her help. He manages this by creating players called Sarah Manning, artificial avatars that encourage M.K. to reach out. Since the game allows players to create worlds and share them with each other, they've reached a state of cooperative play in which working together will help them win.

The nasty Detective Duko confronts Hell Wizard in "The Redesign of Natural Objects" (408), and the metaphor gets overt. When Duko asks who's in Hell Wizard's D&D party, he responds, "Uh, a tenth level paladin, a twelfth level thief and a half-elf cleric named Albus Dimpledots." Indeed, the real Clone Club is nearly this amateurish.

Duko retorts, "You could run a hell of a campaign with a party like that. Unless someone were to roll up a dragon ... not some wyvern or some pansy-assed wandering reptile, but a real-life adamantite. White-hot fire breath. You'd have to be a real smart player to survive." Of course, Brightborn is just such a surprising dragon with a new power and ferociousness. Duko considers himself a representative of just such a powerful threat. However, the Clone Club "party" arrives and rescues Hell Wizard on the spot. In fact, they *are* running a "hell of a campaign" and promptly defeat Duko.

In "From Dancing Mice to Psychopaths" (410), Hell Wizard and Scott get Krystal to play with them, keeping her busy while Sarah's out. This time it's *Dead of Winter,* a zombie-apocalypse cooperative board game—as the end of the world comes, all the players win or lose together. Since Krystal resists joining the Clone Club and wants to go on spy missions all on her own, there's a clear message that all the clones must play together if they want to win.

It's a massive game, with a listed playing time of 45 to 210 minutes and a 20-page rulebook. Thanks to this, Fawcett thought it would be the last thing Krystal would want to play. "I tried to pick a game that seemed like it would be a favorite of Scott and Hell Wizard, and it's the wrong game for Krystal," he says. "She's peeved to have to be sitting there with these guys to play this 'stupid' board game" in a scene where she's supposed to be getting some answers about the mysterious things that keep happening to her" (Law). Like Rachel, she's uninterested in gaming, and like Kira, she's too perturbed by real life to be distracted. "Ugh! This is so boring. I don't care about the zombie apocalypse. I'm dressed like this to go on a real mission," she complains.

Season five introduces other games, more of Fawcett's favorites. *Gloomhaven* is a "legacy" game, meaning the board and components can change permanently whenever people play. Since quests and careful choices on how to use one's cards are central, the game reflects the Clone Club's journey through blackmail and investigation as Cosima and Felix cross the world to unravel different pieces of the Neolution puzzle. Fawcett, who adores the game, describes the difficulty of getting it at all:

> "You couldn't buy [*Gloomhaven*] anywhere," he recalled. "The Kickstarter was over, so we contacted [designer] Isaac Childres, and it all went down very fast. The game showed up the morning we were shooting. I'd never played it or seen it played before. I downloaded all these snapshots of people playing it, but didn't have time to read the rules. We just had to look at how the board was set up from all these shots on the internet. There are some inaccuracies, but I think it's pretty close. It was so important to me to get it on the table" [Law].

In "One Fettered Slave" (409), Cosima and Scott stare at it as they plan. By kidnapping Helena, Westmorland has indeed changed the game. The Clone Club will need to use all their pieces to rescue her. In turn, Hell Wizard reveals that he can help save Helena from imprisonment in the old DYAD building, since he once worked security there—he's back to the real-life gaming scenario. Sarah-as-Rachel uses her sister's knowledge to get admitted. At the same time, Scott disguises as a doctor transporting a human organ, and they break in, leaving Hell Wizard to disarm the codes while Art provides the fighting power. With their contrasting skills, they resemble a D&D party in truth. Their quest has once again turned external, allowing the geeks to save the world.

Scythe cameos in the finale, as Scott helps Cosima find the world's Ledas and plan their salvation. "*Scythe*'s artwork is incredible—I love that game," smiles Fawcett. "Unfortunately, in the final edit of that scene, it's not as featured as I would have liked, but the scene isn't really about a board game. It's probably an Easter egg for the serious board gamers watching" (Law). This

2016 version of *Gloomhaven* is more of a traditional Eurogame, set in an alternate universe after World War I has left five European powers rushing to fill the vacuum left after "the Factory" has closed. Of course, Westmorland's defeat encourages just such a powerplay, with Coady, Rachel, and the board all considering claiming power in their unsettled world. "Each player represents one power with specific abilities, begins with different resources, and has a unique goal that s/he keeps hidden from other players," quite like the factions on the show (Law). All of these intense, multi-hour strategy games emphasize the skills and strategy all the show's characters must hone for their own faction to win the day at last. Of course, it's the Clone Club who triumph, eliminating the enemies one by one, and then saving hundreds of clones to forge a truly unbeatable team.

Inside the Credits

> In Technicolor's opening titles for *Orphan Black,* what begins as an apparent journey through the cosmos—complete with an alien encounter—soon becomes a twisting, abstract journey through inner space. Manipulated genetic material grows, divides, morphs and mutates, revealing the biological makeup of Sarah and her clones. Guided by a chorus of airy female voices and glitch hop courtesy of Two Fingers (aka Amon Tobin), this is a symbolic trip from not-so-immaculate conception to birth.—Chandoo

The credits are filled with deep symbolism. Viewers rush through the galaxy to end up in the inner world as these two reflect infinitely. A single drop of water splashes and bursts, offering a rich microcosm—an entire ecosystem confined in such a tiny space. The series, of course, focuses on the interdependence of a single genome—a few women and their struggle with their corporate creators, all taking place blow the public's notice.

The credits' kaleidoscope-like feel suggests a hidden inner world of symbols. An actual kaleidoscope constantly generates changing symmetrical patterns from small pieces of colored glass, and therefore represents constant change, like the surprising new clones and allies with shifting allegiances. The colors and shapes mean escape in time of difficulty and self-doubt. The kaleidoscope, a symbol of constant change and beauty, encourages new perspectives. It releases blocked creativity, allowing people to see themselves in the bigger scope and connect to its meaning. This the clones do as they break out of their sheltered lives and confront their creators as well as cloning's impact on the world.

The blooming orchids symbolize careful breeding, prized as they are today for their rarity. Their uniqueness suggests the clones themselves. Orchids are connected with reproduction: Greek women believed that if the father of their unborn child ate large orchid tubers, the baby would be a boy. If the mother ate small ones, she would give birth to a girl. Darwin, whose book supplied the first season episode titles, admiringly describes an orchid's complexity as it lives in symbiosis with honeybees: "How, it may be asked, in the foregoing and innumerable other instances, can we understand the graduated scale of complexity and the multifarious means for gaining the same end" (143). Like the clones, it can fertilize itself and independently reproduce, with aid from an outside force—in this case, bees. The sea green tint means growth but also more uncommonness when applied to an orchid.

DNA strands, in two ladderlike chains, symbolize the cosmic serpent binding the world together, enfolding all it touches. Meanwhile, the snake is a feminine symbol, endlessly shedding and regenerating as it binds the world together. Snakes "are also known for their transmutational power, which is exemplified in their ability to shed their skin. This life-death-rebirth cycle is the energy of wholeness and the ability to experience anything willingly and without resistance. It is the knowledge that those things which might be poisonous, hurtful or uncomfortable may be ingested, experienced, integrated and transmuted if one is in the proper state of mind ... thereby producing divine, cohesive energy" (Spencer).

> Depicted coiled in several successive rings, the serpent mimics cyclical evolution and reincarnation. It coils sinuously as the seasons and the fluidity of female cycles, devoid of straight lines. "The serpent represents immortal energy and consciousness engaged in the field of time, constantly throwing off death and being born again." The snake that sheds its old skin, or eats its own tail, is a Goddess symbol of constant decomposition, constant renewal. Thus the Aegypto-Greek Ouroboros or Norse Jörmungandr (Midgard serpent) surrounds the cosmos, biting its own tail in a symbol of perpetuity and infinity, never ending, always regenerating [Frankel 70].

Like ladders, the DNA strands climb toward enlightenment and understanding: "In a world in which man was learning to walk upright, and reaching toward heaven as the source of divinity, towers and ladders were signs of strength, of civilization, of contact with god-force. Thus upright man is separated from animal, sky parted from earth" (Frankel 50). With DNA's paired structure, it also offers symbolism of twins. Casting the DNA in deep pink links it specifically to the women's realm.

Splitting cells is the biological process, creating life itself through the magic of cloning but also through Helena and Sarah's superpower—giving birth. Cells, like eggs, represent the woman's realm of creation. Throughout antiquity, "the circle was one of the primary female signs, representing a protective or consecrated space, a room where all were equal" (Frankel 50). Once again, these infinite circles are pink, ushering viewers into the women's realm.

The color changes again, returning to the sea green orchid with a wavy pattern suggesting fluidity and flexibility. Once again, this is life, fertility, and the birth process, doubled when a pair of reflecting Sarahs burst from the orchid's center as the questing heroine and her clones all give birth to themselves. The camera moves past her, through a suggestively pointed oval to reveal the show's title. Diving into an orchid often reveals the shape of a woman's genitals, as Georgia O'Keefe famously symbolized in all the flower centers she painted. Passing through this long dark tunnel of abstraction, the viewers have finally been born.

Creative Director Kevin Chandoo of Technicolor Toronto explains some of the original concepts he was given by the showrunners: "Abstract, Twinning, Orphans, Dark, Poetic, Soulful, Biological Mystery, Human Evolution, Patent Human Genetics, Synthetic, Random Selection, Black Humour." Together they viewed slime mold videos, as well as mushrooms growing and clips of "Crazy" by Gnarls Barkley with its symmetrical inkblots and the surreal bluish titles of *Fight Club*. Chandoo adds: "It was a bit overwhelming at first, trying to create a concept that would complement the show in a cool way. I tried to keep certain guiding principles in mind during development. How to create a pretty blossoming flower based on fungus, was the first thing that jumped out at me. I felt this image was important to convey, for it was symbolic of Tatiana." He distilled the concepts down to a few: "Abstract, Human, Biological, Synthetic, Tatiana, DNA, Dark, and Poetic."

Thoughts on Genre

The show finds its echoes in story patterns from bygone centuries as it wrestles with the autonomy of created people.

> *Conte philosophique* translates as "philosophical story" or "fable of reason." The *contes philosophiques* were used for centuries in the West by the likes of Voltaire, Johannes Kepler, and Francis Bacon as one legitimate way for scientists or philosophers to present their findings. The *conte philosophique* employs the fictional frame of an imaginary or dream journey to impart scientific or philosophical content. In a sense, the fantastical or science-fictional adventure became a mental laboratory in which to discuss findings or make an argument [VanderMeer].

Of course, one of Bacon's works supplies the second season titles. These early philosophers contributed to a historical weakness of the speculative fiction genre. Early fantasy and science fiction, modeled after the early works of Wells, Verne, Burroughs, Tolkien, and others, tended to be very straight, white, and traditional, with male warrior-heroes saving the day—even when women and minorities created it. Though many of the short stories created in science fiction's Golden Age (the thirties and forties) arrived through pulp magazine delivery systems and cheap paperbacks seen as "low art," the genre slowly gained recognition for its discussion of philosophical themes. The New Wave writers of the sixties and seventies shook stories up with new voices from feminists and minorities. Ursula K. Le Guin wrote, "The women's movement has made most of us conscious of the fact that SF has either totally ignored women, or presented them as squeaking dolls subject to instant rape by monsters—or old-maid scientists desexed by hypertrophy of the intellectual organs—or, at best, loyal little wives or mistresses of accomplished heroes" (qtd. in VanderMeer). However, an inevitable eighties backslide returned temporarily to the male protagonists.

Writers of science fiction (and also those outside throughout the modern era) "grapple with the changing nature of reality and technological innovation" (VanderMeer). Many define science fiction simply: "It depicts the future, whether in a stylized or realistic manner," as science fiction editors Ann and Jeff VanderMeer explain. Thus, *Orphan Black* technically does not qualify, though the currently-impossible technology gives it science-fiction elements. There are fantasy tropes too—though Westmorland's longevity fairytale is disproven, and Kira's regenerative power is a product of science, her empathy and telepathic connection with the clones are notably fantastical. As the clones battle the big corporations, the story is a modern thriller, to be sure. It's closest to dystopia, a world gone wrong, with the heroines battling for freedom in a world that restricts them.

"In her essay on the history of subgenres, A. J. Dalton asks, "Is it, then, the task of the modern fantasy author to subvert the dominant gender-, identity- and sexuality-formulations of the fantasy literature that precedes them, if they are to express their own voice and assert their own 'self' and values?" Since the modern genre author does not start with a blank page, he or she must consciously analyze what's being produced. Obviously, *Orphan Black* subverts classic stories as *all* of the central protagonists are female, with the men aiding them in fulfilling their quest. The show is strikingly non-exploitative, highlighting the female characters' strength, not their cleavage. Meanwhile, as part of this subversion, modern sub-genres as "dark fantasy," "metaphysical fantasy," "dystopian YA," and "grimdark fantasy" sprang from the traditional patterns. Dalton adds:

> The proliferation and competition of "steampunk," "flintlock fantasy," "comedic fantasy," and "urban fantasy," with the arrival of the new millennium, marked the end of the numerous decades in which a single sub-genre dominated, represented or defined the genre, its social moment and its wider society. The fractures, class divides and competing groups and voices within society were becoming more obvious. Social certainties were replaced by social anxieties, and competing values now informed social and individual identity. The early 2000s thereby foreshadowed

and predicted the greater crisis of 2008/ 09 onwards, the time of the credit crunch and the time during which UK politicians were found guilty en masse of the Expenses Scandal, the tabloid press were culpable in the Phone Hacking Scandal, and the police were found guilty of the Selling Information Scandal. It was clear to all that we were not ruled and safeguarded by those of superior moral standing, of a noble conscience and with a sense of social responsibility.

Science fiction also fragmented into subgenres. The two movements most associated with the eighties and nineties, cyberpunk and humanism, both redefined the world of science fiction. Cyberpunk (popularized as a term by editor Gardner Dozois) reflected the technological hybrids possible to imagine in the new computer age. "Cyberpunk usually fused noir tropes or interior design with dark tales of near-future technology in a context of weak governments and sinister corporations, achieving a new granularity in conveying elements of the Information Age. Trace elements of the recent punk movement in music were brought to the mix" (VanderMeer). Sarah is a punk, and Brightborn, Rachel, and M.K. use season four to stretch into internet hacking and futuristic cybertechnology to accomplish their goals. Using this technology helps the show explore complex moral issues. The real Cosima explains:

> Season four was predominantly situated around the difference between science and technology/engineering. Where, for example, science aspires to speak to and uncover something called truth, and engineering aspires to a construct that is simply a sum of its parts, we look at a body as a kind of machine that can be "fixed," improved on, rebuilt according to particular specifications for order; the commercialization and profit-driven machinations of industrialized reproductive capacities; the aesthetics of designer babies; the limitations (and the public's hopes and expectations) of gene therapy, and germline manipulations; socially constructed values of desire and how that affects consumer-driven choices; the tangled mess between definitions of scientific success and failure; the unreliability of technology and technological interventions into living systems that are barely understood; and, of course, issues of consent [Griffin and Nesseth].

"Humanist SciFi" brought in more three-dimensional characters, as *Star Trek: The Next Generation* focused on the interpersonal much more than its sixties' inspiration. "whereas New Wave and cyberpunk fiction arose out of a starker, darker impulse…. Humanist SF grew out of another strand in which human beings are front and center, with technology subservient, optimistically, to a human element" (VanderMeer). *Orphan Black* fits neatly into this genre, among others, as the personal is central here, not the technology or philosophy.

At the same time, the evolution of fantasy connects with *Orphan Black* through its stages. The gleaming epic fantasy of the eighties "with its second-world whimsy, noble kings, beautiful queens and heroic males," gave way to the grittier, more realistic urban fantasy of the early 2000s, "with its first-world grit, street life and battling females empowered by several male lovers"

(Dalton). *Orphan Black* takes place in disguised Toronto, with the police turning a blind eye and corporations murdering people in the streets, all unnoticed by the general populace. The women rule here—brave and strong, with several of them proficient with weapons or personal combat.

Later that decade came dark fantasy. From here, genre fiction, especially in the *Game of Thrones/True Blood* vein, grew darker and more violent, with body horror equivalent to the cheekbots and Rachel's eye. The works, including *Twilight* and its many imitators, were also known for "diversity of lifestyle, sexuality, personal definition and representation. The groups that were previously hidden, demonized, marginalized or condemned by society (be they Goth, Emo, LGBTQ, androgyne, dysmorphs, multi-racial, non-identifying or other) were at last given open and explicit representation" (Dalton). Likewise, the VanderMeers note, "The more radicalized third-wave feminism science fiction of the current era fits more comfortably with New Wave and 1970s feminism despite not always being quite as experimental." Of course, the series emphasizes marginalized characters, from Sarah and Felix to M.K. and Tony, as all struggle for freedom. Felix gets to introduce his unconventional lifestyle even into dull Bailey Downs, and Alison, sporting purple hair and tattoo, finally establishes that she can express herself, and even help Helena raise her babies, in its confines.

Alongside dark fantasy came the rise of teen dystopias (*The Hunger Games, Divergent, Wither, Matched*). With these, *Orphan Black* shares the plotline of the evil corporation preying on young women. "Very much, we are presented with admirable but lonely protagonists. Their sense of self, gender-formation and sexuality are oppressed to the extent that they are elided or prevented from developing. The true 'self' can only be realized by breaking free of the society that forces them to conform. There is a sense of constant monitoring and scrutiny, a need to hide the 'self' so that it might be protected from exploitation and a creeping paranoia" (Dalton). Megan, 13, says she appreciates dystopia, "Because it shows everyday life in stories that aren't every day. From the way teenagers hang out in cliques, to the frustration with adults." Isaac, 15, says, "It can present a moral observation about society, even offering solutions to current problems." Ellen, 16, thinks, "It's the way the characters are oppressed and have to fight to get their voices heard—that's how you can feel as a teenager, silenced and unable to really express yourself" (Campbell). All these themes resonate through the show.

Notably, these series have the young women turn on the patriarchs that played God with their genetics and choices, rebelling and creating a new society of freedom. While the *Orphan Black* protagonists are in their twenties, not teens, the genre is otherwise strikingly close. While the book series in question mostly take place in the far future, some dystopias are set in the modern day, filled with secret government or corporate conspiracies and unjust experiments. *Dark Angel*, following an augmented young woman with a barcode on her neck, whose military creators seek to reclaim her, takes place in the ruins of post-apocalyptic Seattle. This genre flourished post–September 11th, as audiences appeared comforted by thought experiments of the worst possible scenario, followed by a fight for freedom. Young adult dystopia can reflect the "older generation getting it wrong, younger generation feeling trapped and powerless ... signposts to resolving some of the big issues" (Campbell). Teen writer Alex Campbell adds, "If one of the biggest factors differentiating the present from the past is the internet, could technology be the answer? It's true that social media can certainly feel like another world, futuristic at that. And one that can control you to an extent, with non-stop exposure to the world's problems coupled with a personal pressure to be seen fitting in."

"Both near-future, first-world 'dystopian YA' and second-world 'grim-dark fantasy' describe an immoral or lawless society in which those at the top are the most corrupt, immoral or bullying. There are themes of abuse, betrayal and abandonment present throughout both sub-genres" (Dalton). Of course, this nebulous enemy began extending into real life. *Orphan Black* concluded in the Trump-Brexit era, as many science fiction shows dropped in cynical comments about "alternative facts" and government power. Many wonder where the science fiction is going now. Dalton comments, "There is more intolerance of difference and more insistence upon traditional values ... but also more resistance and more protest than before. We are seeing subversion, assertion and reversion. Societies are more polarized and fraught than ever before." In this multitude of possibilities, the series ends as many of the dystopias do, with the heroines defeating the evil corporation. Their new world is imperfect, with the greatest threat the chance that society will fail to learn from its mistakes. However, the heroines, for the moment, have triumphed. The ending of the series also carries a trace of dark fantasy:

> The plot progression of "dark fantasy" and "metaphysical fantasy" therefore involves the protagonist's fraught quest to discover a sense of identity and self, to find a place in the world, and to find safety and contentment. Invariably, however, these two sub-genres ultimately describe terrible sacrifice, loss, anti-climax and resignation. The self-realization, place, safety and contentment that are achieved are illusory or temporary at best. There is no true "happy ending," as the existential quest of life continues on through the next generation(s), some progress made but the results of past mistakes born into the future, the problems of society and the past inherited by those that follow on after us [Dalton].

Literature Behind the Season Titles

Each season, famously, takes its ten episode titles from a work of literature. In fact, the real-life Cosima, science advisor Cosima Herter, chooses the inspiration for them (Nguyen, "Here's Everything"). Season one is Charles Darwin's *On the Origin of Species* (which Cosima reads in the bar in season one). Historically, this work founded evolutionary biology, explaining how species evolved into others through natural selection. Of course, cloning represents a different kind of evolution, guided by the hand of man, not by chance. "Darwin's book changed the course of science with the creation of his theory of natural selection and his ideas on evolution. Natural selection refers to the differential survival and ability to reproduce among individuals of a given species due to phenotype—that is, the presence or absence of specific traits playing a role in an individual's ability to survive and pass on their genes," Griffin and Nesseth explain in their book *The Science of Orphan Black*. The real Cosima adds: "For the first season, we had many conversations about some of the basic principles of (Darwinian) evolutionary theory; contesting visions of contingency, chance, and determinism; individuality; identity; (autonomous) selfhood; what it means to have (or not have) ownership of one's own body; and bodies, tissues, cells, genetic lineages as forms of property and profit" (Griffin and Nesseth).

The Neolutionists appear to appreciate Darwin, even while pushing his theories to a new level—not survival of the fittest but "self-directed evolution." Doctor Leekie's name salutes Dr. Louis Leakey (1903–1972), the Kenyan paleoanthropologist and archaeologist who helped prove humans evolved in Africa. Further, Darwin arrived at his theory by observing finches on the Galápagos Islands: the show nods to this with a display of Galápagos finches on the island ("History Yet to Be Written," 310).

Darwin also addresses and refutes the theory at the time that animals and other life were all created to delight man—a human-centric belief system that insists on man at the center of the universe. Traces of this issue can be seen in Neolution's belief that the clones are their property to treat as they will. Manson comments, "I think there's a fundamental human hubris in trying to play God. That's a trope of a lot of great sci-fi" (Bernstein 101). Darwin continues, "When two forms vary, which already differ from each other in some slight degree, the variability will not be of the same exact nature, and consequently the results obtained through natural selection for the same general purpose will not be the same" (143). The Neolutionists' variations have injured Leda and Castor in different ways—one set of small modifications destroys lungs and wombs; the other, brains and motor skills. As he discusses how interdependent species are, he emphasizes a major theme—that the Ledas can only survive together and can only cure themselves with aid from Castor.

The book also describes how animals, including humans, reproduce biologically, while descriptions of the parasites and power of self-healing share ties into the injuries and artificial parasites of the series. Darwin even adds that compared with animals, a human's "wounds are repaired by the same process of healing, and the stumps left after the amputation of his limbs, especially during an early embryonic period, occasionally possess some power of regeneration, as in the lowest animals" (397). This describes Kira and Helena's fetus's near-magical power of healing even as it paves the way for stem cell research.

The real Cosima explains: "The first time I read Darwin and *The Origin of Species*, it changed my life." She'd been reading books recommended by a philosopher who "was trying to understand Darwin in a feminist sense," how Darwin's ideas have played through philosophies and modern politics. Then she started reading Darwin himself, as she said, "and I loved it. I hadn't realized that it wasn't just science theory. This guy was writing philosophy, writing the history of life, and I am really moved by it. That's actually what I really want to do" (Newton).

Feminist Darwin certainly becomes a major theme, since Helena and Sarah's fertility appears to be nature's way of fighting back. Manson adds, "Their fertility is a true product of chance. It's anomalous, it's a natural selection amidst all this science" (Ross, "Tony the Transclone"). His description of the struggle for existence is reflected in the clones' lives. As Sarah explores during the first season, she discovers other moments of natural selection as Beth, weaker than herself, apparently succumbs to addiction and commits suicide, while Helena preys on her own more vulnerable sisters. Sarah must step up and become a warrior while battling these Darwinian threats within and without. Near season end, she discovers Kira's biology has adapted to help her heal speedily, a miracle that comes from Neolution's meddling but only in the second generation—something they never expected. Blessed with these gifts of transcendent biology, Sarah and Kira must contend with Neolution, the movement devoted to directed evolution, rewriting the human genome and defying nature.

Season two's text was Francis Bacon's *Plan of the Work*. It's the steps to create his *Great Instauration*, the restoration of a state of paradise through the illumination of mankind. This would be a second Eden, but one filled with pure enlightenment rather than innocence. Of course, the clones are struggling towards understanding, even as the false gods Leekie and Westmorland guide them down flawed paths. Bacon comes from a religious background, stressing man's gift of differentiation between good and evil after Eden, an issue Rachel, Helena, and Cosima must face as they choose sides. Alison and Donnie take it a step further, as each deals with the impact of murdering another person. Bacon's titles for the six stages of work are given in the "Distributio Operis" ("Plan of Work") of his Instauratio Magna ("Great Instauration") published in 1620.

The plan begins with a general inventory of the existing state of human knowledge, which echoes the Clone Club's research into the existing science of Neolution and their quest to Cold River to discover Neolution's history. Then there's the discovery of a true scientific methodology, echoed by Cosima's working with DYAD to find a cure. Next comes the collection and then application of a natural history of factual evidence: natural phenomena together with human behavior and divine operations in Nature. Once again, Cosima researches the science angle, performing an autopsy on Jennifer and comparing her sisters' biologies, even adding Kira's stem cells. Like Bacon, she commits to first discovering what the clones are, then to bringing them health and enlightenment. Meanwhile, Henrik takes a different angle, implanting Helena and Gracie with Helena's fertilized eggs. Tying in with Henrik's cult, "Bacon urges us to regain our God-given right over nature, as defined in the Bible" (Dawkins). This is Genesis 1:26: "And God said, Let us make man in our image, after our likeness: and let them have dominion over the fish of the sea, and over the fowl of the air, and over the cattle, and over all the earth, and over every creeping thing that creepeth upon the earth." Like Henrik, Bacon links knowledge and the search for God. However, Henrik's direct arrogance in controlling the biology of lesser beings (on the show including the clones) makes him their enemy.

Last comes "the storehouse of final axioms or truths concerning the laws of the universe, divine, human and natural, as proven by the New Method, by the test of time and by the maxim 'truth prints goodness'" (Dawkins). This is more problematic, as Rachel seeks to claim everything—Kira, Sarah's ovary, Cosima's research. Only by rebelling can all the clones find freedom instead. They end the show not with a storehouse of scientific information, but with a single cure Cosima can use to save her sisters.

> Sometimes referred to as the "Father of Experimental Philosophy," Francis Bacon was an English scholar in the late 16th and early 17th centuries who focused most of his work on philosophical and scientific ideas, most notably the development of the scientific method. The scientific method is a process of inquiry that involves developing a hypothesis based on observations and testing this hypothesis through experimentation. This, of course, ties into Orphan Black in that the clones came about as a result of experimentation based on laboratory observations and the hypothesis that human cloning was possible. Bacon's emphasis on inquiry and induction is mirrored by Ethan's work, making it a good match for the second season. Bacon also wrote many works focused on philosophy and religion, and particularly on morality. Once again, this dovetails perfectly with a season in which we meet the Proletheans and examine their questionable practices in the name of a higher power [Griffin and Nesseth].

Meanwhile, the overarching second season plot has everyone questing for a "plan of the work" indeed—Professor Duncan's book with his knowledge of the original. He shares the clones' true reason for existence with them: "Proof of concept. How everything starts" ("To Hound Nature in Her

Wanderings," 206). Further, his book contains the original science of creation—the location of the original DNA source. On finding it, the clones have a potential solution to save themselves through the power of science. "Bacon's work, specifically his focus on discussing ways to improve mankind, also mirrors themes brought up in season four. He touched on topics such as prolonging life, reforming law, and scientific innovation" (Griffin and Nesseth). Bacon also created a system of logic he considered superior to the syllogism.

Season three is "Eisenhower's Farewell Address to the Nation" from 1961, as the Cold War spawned the Korean War and then the Vietnam War, threatening a never-ending reign of violence. Fawcett explains, "The Eisenhower farewell address really hit a number of thematic elements that really were important to us in Season 3 ... technology and science and warfare. It's about the military-industrial complex, and since the Castor clones are a military product, it spoke volumes to us" (Nguyen, "Here's Everything"). Eisenhower cautions: "We face a hostile ideology global in scope, atheistic in character, ruthless in purpose, and insidious in method. Unhappily the danger it poses promises to be of indefinite duration." On the show, this is the Castors, a small military unit waging a war on women's fertility in general and the Ledas in specific. Beyond them, however, lies the larger military branch of government.

"Eisenhower discussed the role of the country's military-industrial complex in the context of the political state of the world, believing that military power was necessary. When considering the military branch of the clone project, it becomes a bit terrifying to think of them as a necessary power, especially with the Castor arm of the clone disease doubling as a sterilization method" (Griffin and Nesseth). In fact, Eisenhower describes how different the modern world is thanks to new military production. The clones' world has been forever transformed by their own new science, and season three focuses on its military applications. Eisenhower warns, "In the councils of government, we must guard against the acquisition of unwarranted influence, whether sought or unsought, by the military-industrial complex. The potential for the disastrous rise of misplaced power exists and will persist." Of course, the "unwarranted influence" on the Castor project results in Paul's military contact helping the Castors retake the base from Paul, so they can continue their experiments. Wielding their "misplaced power," they prize Castor's destructive capability more than they care about vulnerable civilians. The real Cosima explains: "Season three was guided by questions of authority, homogenization of a population according to the violent rubrics of white-Euro superiority, masculinity and aggression, how those ideologies have colonized concepts of self and body and expectations of identity" (Griffin and Nesseth).

Eisenhower adds, "Down the long lane of the history yet to be written America knows that this world of ours, ever growing smaller, must avoid becoming a community of dreadful fear and hate, and be, instead, a proud confederation of mutual trust and respect." Certainly, as the Castors poison mankind and Neolution builds alliances to exploit the clones for corporate greed, cloning offers just such a threat. Eisenhower insists, "Such a confederation must be one of equals. The weakest must come to the conference table with the same confidence as do we, protected as we are by our moral, economic, and military strength." The Ledas try to negotiate as just these equals, not pawns and subjects to be exploited.

The real Cosima describes season three's themes including "the insertion of different arms of industrial funding of scientific research (like, of course, the military) and how that affects the general praxis, thus the outcomes, of scientific research; contemporary aspirations of patriotism, nationalism, and mass eugenically genocides; bioterrorism and bio-power; siblinghood and family" (Griffin and Nesseth). Eisenhower discussed the upswing of scientific research and warned against letting policy help create the scientific elite. Of course, Coady the scientist is maiming innocents and torturing soldiers in the name of progress. Paul is the first to caution his superiors that they have too much power.

Taking more of Eisenhower's advice as the president advocates "disarmament, with mutual honor and confidence," the Ledas struggle to disarm the glitching clones as Coady unleashes them upon the population, with their very DNA a terrible weapon. The president warns, "America's leadership and prestige depend ... on how we use our power in the interests of world peace and human betterment" and describes a government meant "to foster progress in human achievement, and to enhance liberty, dignity and integrity." This is Neolution's problem: they too have lost sight of this path, preferring wealth and military power instead of improving freedom and self-worth—exactly what the Leda clones fight for.

The first female author of the lineup appears for season four's titles: It's Donna Haraway, a feminist intellectual whose work fits perfectly with *Orphan Black*'s aesthetic and themes. Her "A Cyborg Manifesto" considers how a cyborg—an enhanced person with added mechanical capabilities—symbolizes being female. She focuses on woman's hybrid nature, as well as her agency and relationship with their own existence.

The real Cosima describes the show by quoting Haraway: "The cyborg is a matter of fiction and lived experience that changes what counts as women's experience in the late twentieth century.... Contemporary science fiction is full of cyborgs—creatures simultaneously animal and machine, who populate worlds ambiguously natural and crafted. Modern medicine is also full of cyborgs, of couplings between organism and machine, each conceived as coded devices, in an intimacy and with a power that was not generated in the history of sexuality" (Herter, "Eat Me/Drink Me"). As she concludes, "So we've fantasized Haraway's cyborg in our own strange and disturbing ways" (Herter, "Eat Me/Drink Me"). This essay was one of her inspirations for a feminist approach to science and cloning.

Boundaries blur onscreen between people and objects as women are created with barcodes and men as weapons. The delving into genetic code emphasizes how everyone is numbers and chemicals. "The phallogocentric origin stories most crucial for feminist cyborgs are built into the literal technologies—technologies that write the world, biotechnology and microelectronics—that have recently textualized out bodies as code problems" (Haraway 175). Of course, the created Leda clones function as marginalized cyborgs. As "trickster figures that might turn a stacked deck into a potent set of wild cards for refiguring possible worlds," the cyborg shatters boundaries (Haraway 66). With this, the Ledas not only shapeshift into each other, but break boundaries with surprising mental powers. Each is a nonconformist in some way, from violent Helena and frightened M.K., to Alison who plays by the rules but indulges in affairs and pills underneath. Meanwhile, the women save each other through the series, focusing on sisterhood and independence from men. "Unlike the hopes of Frankenstein's monster, the cyborg does not expect its father to save it through a restoration of the garden; that is, through the fabrication of a heterosexual mate, through its completion in a finished whole, a city and cosmos" (Haraway 151).

> Although there are few women writing cyberpunk fictions, cyborgs have nonetheless been adopted by feminist theorists as a tool for imagining hybrid identities and categorical disruptions. While cyberpunk fictions do not openly address feminist concerns, the cyborg itself disrupts restrictive categories of identity in a way that can be friendly to feminist politics. If the cyborg blurs the boundaries between "human" and "machine" and calls into question the purity of such categories, cyborgs (both in fiction and in reality) are conceptual tools that challenge the stability of many other conceptual categories (human/machine, human/animal, man/woman, heterosexual/homosexual, etc.). Donna Harraway's famous essay "A Cyborg Manifesto: Science, Technology and Socialist-Feminism in the Late Twentieth Century" (originally published in 1985 and also collected in Harraway's 1991 book *Simians, Cyborgs, and Women*) challenges readers to use the concept of the cyborg to move beyond isolating categories such as "man" and "woman" and to begin imagining these categories as fields of affinity offering different possibilities for expression and play beyond typical social limits [Higgins 79–80].

It's no substitute for true racial diversity, but in science fiction, cyborgs, androids, and aliens often stand in for minorities. As the clones' personhood is called into question, a slavery metaphor emerges, as well as a disability model for characters who can be fixed with technology or opt to remain as they are.

Moreover, the fourth season offers true cyborgs—Brightborn's genetically modified babies and cheek maggots, technology that rewrites people's original biology. Another story point is Rachel's mechanical eye. It gives her a hybrid nature of her own, as she receives mystic visions from her creator, Westmorland. According to Haraway, the cyborg's split condition offers extra insight and perception (4). With this, cyborg characters can begin to disobey the system, drifting into grey areas that defy categorization.

> Many of the episode titles in season four have roots in Haraway's essay "The Biological Enterprise: Sex, Mind, and Profit from Human Engineering to Sociobiology," which looks specifically at human engineering and capitalism—themes explored through Evie Cho, who acts independently of Neolution to commodify genetically modified humans and to secretly launch her own eugenic projects through Brightborn's offerings. Part of Haraway's essay focuses on American psychologist, primatologist, and eugenicist Robert Yerkes, who envisioned human engineering to benefit culture, society, and industry, and who described it in a way that almost sounds like an overview of Project Leda [Griffin and Nesseth].

The real Cosima concludes with a final Haraway quote: "Taking responsibility for the social relations of science and technology means refusing an anti-science metaphysics, a demonology of technology, and so means embracing the skillful task of reconstructing the boundaries of daily life, in partial connection with others, in communication with all of our parts" (Herter, "Eat Me/Drink Me"). Of course, even the insidious Brightborn technology can potentially save lives as CEO Evie Cho recovers from her "bubble girl" condition and Leekie uses a maggot bot to stave off Alzheimer's. The goal of the series is balancing the technology with love and family, not rejecting one or the other.

For the final season, Herter explains on her blog why she chose the 1914 poem "Protest," which she considers a hail to women's suffrage: "*Orphan Black*—in so many ways that I cannot even begin to do justice with my words here—is, has always been, to me an allegory of evolution, resistance, and protest. It is a testament to what we can achieve, what we hope to achieve, and what we have to yet to imagine that might be achieved through collective and collaborative efforts" (Herter, "Why Protest"). As she adds:

> I felt, for this concluding season of *Orphan Black*, that the titles should be less science or theory specific, and more about the overall sense of not only women's suffrage, but inclusive of some of the most important (at least to me) themes that underpin the entire show: body autonomy, political and personal agency, continual resistance to oppression and ideological authority, courage, hope, and change. The idea of protest is deeply embedded in and woven into the OB narrative on so many levels. I felt that "Protest," being short and poignant, was pertinent because it reflected the strength and perseverance not only of these characters that I've come to love, but of something more deeply philosophically and politically meaningful

to me as person. The question then, is less, "Why 'Protest'?" the poem, and more, "Why protest as an action in the world?" [Herter, "Why Protest"]

Herter describes her mother, an immigrant, being sterilized without her consent during Cosima's own Caesarian birth in 1970. "Once aware of what had happened—the reason given to her was that she'd already had 'too many children that could barely be supported as it was' (I was her fourth child)—despite it being illegal, she'd felt she had no recourse, nowhere to complain, no one to appeal to for help. She could not protest" (Herter, "Why Protest"). She salutes silenced women around the world—reflected by women on the show kept in compounds and convents with their lips sewn shut and tongues cut out, women locked away, women forced under duress or poverty or lies to sign contracts giving away their very bodies and children. As Herter insists, all women deserve the power to speak out:

Ella Wheeler Wilcox
"Protest" (1914)

> To sin by silence, when we should protest,
> Makes cowards out of men. The human race
> Has climbed on protest. Had no voice been raised
> Against injustice, ignorance, and lust,
> The inquisition yet would serve the law,
> And guillotines decide our least disputes.
> The few who dare, must speak and speak again
> To right the wrongs of many. Speech, thank God,
> No vested power in this great day and land
> Can gag or throttle. Press and voice may cry
> Loud disapproval of existing ills;
> May criticise oppression and condemn
> The lawlessness of wealth-protecting laws
> That let the children and childbearers toil
> To purchase ease for idle millionaires.
> Therefore I do protest against the boast
> Of independence in this mighty land.
> Call no chain strong, which holds one rusted link.
> Call no land free, that holds one fettered slave.
> Until the manacled slim wrists of babes
> Are loosed to toss in childish sport and glee,
> Until the mother bears no burden, save
> The precious one beneath her heart, until
> God's soil is rescued from the clutch of greed
> And given back to labor, let no man
> Call this the land of freedom.

The poem condemns sinning by silence, and demands people come forward, even by acknowledging all the victories previous generations have won.

The Clone Club win against Neolution by publicizing its crimes, financial and biological. While Ferdinand wants to hush up their secrets, using them instead for blackmail and personal power, even Rachel finally accepts that, as S. puts it, exposing them is "a chance to be truly free" ("Guillotines Decide," 508). According to the poem, there is "No vested power in this great day and land" that can gag speech—through careful, determined research, the clones piece the puzzle together and bring Neolution down.

Another patriarch, Westmorland himself, is destroyed when Cosima publicizes her own knowledge of him, exposing him publicly before his loyal disciples. "The lawlessness of wealth-protecting laws/That let the children and childbearers toil/To purchase ease for idle millionaires" is what she battles, as Westmorland drains the blood of children to try to prolong his life and dines in Victorian splendor while his followers live in rickety huts and eat seaweed.

When the poem concludes, it describes the chained wrists of slaves (Rachel), babies (Helena's sought-after twins) and mothers (Sarah), who must all be freed before the struggle is won. "God's soil," the earth and the natural process of biology, must be redeemed from the "clutch of greed"—Neolution and its corporate deals. Only thus can the clones dwell in a "land of freedom." The real Cosima concludes, "Protest is not only an attempt to fracture the existing structures of inequalities, but a perseverance towards a different future. It is the embodiment of hope for change, a hope that courage and fortitude do and can produce change. Hope that one day, even if it isn't *this* day, our bodies that have been legislated and governed by violence and inequality may one day gain autonomy, equality, safety, and political and personal agency to determine our own futures."

Allusions and Inspirations

Manson mentions influences of first-person sources like *Run Lola Run* and *Memento*. "You're in the shoes of the protagonist, and the protagonist doesn't know what's coming next." He includes existential science fiction like *Frankenstein* and *The Island of Doctor Moreau* for the moral questions and *Breaking Bad, Six Feet Under,* and *The Sopranos* for the pacing (Bernstein 10).

Throughout the series, more specific moments appear when mentioned fictional works reflect the plot. As Felix remakes Alison as Sarah in "Effects of External Conditions" (104), they actually discuss both *Pygmalion*, the play about men shaping women into their desired protégés, and *Steel Magnolias*, the female-centric film about women's love and sisterhood. These highlight two contrasting views of fictional women, which the Ledas must struggle between. Alison, meanwhile, has grown up in the world of *Pygmalion*, making herself society's perfect lady, though she's unaware Doctor Leekie has created and is reshaping her through DYAD's endless monitoring. *Steel Magnolias* is her goal—loving her sisters instead of rejecting them to exist separately, confined by her tiny suburb.

Aldous Huxley, author of *Brave New World,* gives Aldous Leekie his first name. *Brave New World* introduces an artificial society, with everyone grown in bottles and raised in family-free schools. The population are engineered to fulfill social functions—some as Alphas, the smartest, tallest, and strongest, and some engineered down through Epsilons. More, everyone is emotionally conditioned to love their society. The Castors are similarly designed to be soldiers while Rachel and Helena are disturbingly brainwashed to love their controllers' agendas. Since Rachel is raised by a corporation, not a family, her utter inhumanity criticizes this choice.

Just as the clones' dynamic has existed for decades before wild Helena shakes them up and brings them to self-awareness, *Brave New World* is rocked by the introduction of John, a "savage." He desperately tries to inform and awaken the complacent citizens, only to find they aren't interested. Sarah of course tries to enlighten her own people, though some, like Krystal and Tony, reject exchanging their happy lives for one of knowledge and persecution. Likewise, Alison is happy to stay in Bailey Downs, pretending Neolution doesn't exist, so she signs their contract. However, as John protests, "I don't want comfort. I want God, I want poetry, I want real danger, I want freedom, I want goodness. I want sin," he echoes Sarah with her demands for truth, not ignorance (215). Now that the clones have realized they're created and monitored, they're desperate to break free.

The Controller, Mustapha Mond, finally reveals the secrets of their society to John, explaining that some people are deliberately crippled to make them more compliant, similar to the backstory of the Leda and Castor damage. As he adds, "A society of Alphas couldn't fail to be unstable and miserable. Imagine a factory staffed by Alphas—that is to say, by separate and unrelated individuals of good heredity and conditioned so as to be capable (within limits) of making a free choice and assuming responsibilities ... it's an absurdity!" (200). Another interesting reference is that the citizens "too self-consciously individual to fit into community-life" are sent to a mysterious island, there to live in a society of misfit intellectuals practicing pure science that the mainstream forbids (204). Westmorland's island echoes this concept. On it, he and his strange cult create clones and genetically engineered monsters, enacting science unimaginable in the outside world. The novel shows a world not only of artificial beings, but of a patriarch who squashes free thought and brainwashes his people into compliance. *Orphan Black* responds to this scenario, with the Ledas beginning in this world, yet shattering it.

Allusions and Inspirations

Susan and Westmorland, on the island, recite a poem together.

"Lines Written in Early Spring"
William Wordsworth, 1798

I heard a thousand blended notes,
While in a grove I sate reclined,
In that sweet mood when pleasant thoughts
Bring sad thoughts to the mind.

To her fair works did nature link
The human soul that through me ran;
And much it grieved my heart to think
What man has made of man.

Through primrose tufts, in that sweet bower,
The periwinkle trailed its wreaths;
And 'tis my faith that every flower
Enjoys the air it breathes.

The birds around me hopped and played:
Their thoughts I cannot measure,
But the least motion which they made,
It seemed a thrill of pleasure.

The budding twigs spread out their fan,
To catch the breezy air;
And I must think, do all I can,
That there was pleasure there.

If this belief from heaven be sent,
If such be Nature's holy plan,
Have I not reason to lament
What man has made of man?

The poem admiringly describes nature, typical of the Romantics. "What man has made of man," however, decries the evils of human behavior: massacres, war, injustice, poverty, industrialization. If nature is innocence, man has corrupted it with experience. As Susan recites the key line, villagers set the buildings afire, descending into savagery. Wordsworth likely speaks of war as well—though he chooses not to specify which of man's evils he's responding to, leaving the poem to apply to many. At the time, the French Revolutionary Wars offered twenty-three years of almost unbroken violence: he had once supported the Revolution, but it descended into savage slaughter without end. Revolutions were replaced by counterrevolutions, even as on the show, one enemy rises to take the place of the last. The line gains extra significance because Westmorland, a man, has literally "made" his fellow man into horrors. Only a return to nature can guide his people past the savagery.

When Cosima meets Westmorland, he offers to help her continue her research and she asks why. He smiles.

Conan Doyle penned a poem on the very subject. You know, we delighted in theological satire back then. Cheeky Arthur. He imagined a debate between microscopic cheese mites trying to determine the origin of their chunk of cheese, whether it came down from above or rose from the platter below. "They argued it long and they argued it strong, and I hear they are arguing it now. But of all the choice spirits that lived in the cheese, not one of them thought of a cow."

This quote is condescending—the cheese mites are so circumscribed by their tiny world that they cannot even conceive of the scientific truth so far outside their sphere of reference. When Cosima asks what Westmorland intends, he similarly responds that she is such a tiny mind that she cannot even imagine his larger plans. Of course, this is traditional Victorian white male arrogance. Jeremy Boxen, the writer of "Clutch of Greed" (502), comments:

> Some backstory for one of my favorite small moments: the Arthur Conan Doyle poem P.T. Westmorland quotes is called "A Parable," and it came to my attention by chance through my spouse, who was reading a graphic novel called *The Thrilling Adventures of Lovelace and Babbage* for her book club. Its author and artist, Sydney Padua, compiled tons of research for her story of Ada, Countess of Lovelace, and Charles Babbage, as they partnered to create a steam-powered computer in Victorian England. Padua featured Conan Doyle's poem in footnotes as an example of Victorian theological satire, and I thought it fit perfectly in the mouth of our Victorian-era scoundrel, Westmorland. As our science advisor Cosima Herter would say, chance and contingency drive evolution—in this case, the evolution of a script! ["Jeremy Boxen"]

Critic Jill Lepore notes, "It could be said that *Orphan Black* is a feminist *Frankenstein*, if it weren't true that *Frankenstein* was a feminist *Frankenstein*. (Mary Shelley, after all, was the daughter of Mary Wollstonecraft, who, in 1792, wrote 'A Vindication of the Rights of Woman,' and died five years later, in agony, of an infection contracted while giving birth.)" *Frankenstein*, like "A Cyborg Manifesto," arguably pleads for the rights of those man considers lesser—like Frankenstein's monster, rejected and condemned for his pleas for equality. Henrik Johanssen, a Doctor Frankenstein himself who builds clone babies, reads to the children at his farm: "So, the doctor sailed north to the arctic, amongst the icebergs, but his creation pursued him with a terrible vengeance because the doctor had never shown his creation any love. And so, when they finally came face-to-face, they sat down and they had a great, big bowl of iceberg cream" ("Things Which Have Never Yet Been Done," 209). His remaking the story suggests his control over all aspects of life, even fiction. The original novel is one of the creator abandoning the artificial child who sought only love, and the created being pursuing his creator through all eternity. Henrik sees himself as human, made in God's image to do God's work, while Helena is a monster, a construct he's free to use. Neolution has of course created its Ledas and Castors. The more monstrous love appears between the Castors and female creators Coady and Susan, both of whom have an incestuous love for their children, whose very sperm can kill. While Rachel echoes the novel's monster, pitiably seeking only love and acknowledgment of her humanity, the other Ledas reject this dynamic.

Rabbit Hole Comics beckons Sarah and her friends down the rabbit hole—somewhere they've arguably been since they learned of secret clone projects and corporations. Certainly, like Alice, they're discovering new ways of consciousness, befriending monsters and working with roaring patriarchs and matriarchs. The trailers for season four actually used lines from *Alice in Wonderland.* The comic book shop, appearing in season four, offers the team a haven of protection, even as the fantasy aspects of the show take on new life, with cheek maggots sprouting inside Sarah and other characters. Continuing the fantasy connection, Kira and Sarah paint a mural of a fantasy castle, suggesting the idealized world they wish to escape to, even as they play games that serve a similar function. The castle, guarded by a fire-breathing dragon, has no princess, emphasizing how the heroines are more like the story's dragons. It also foreshadows the fantastical island where Cosima and Sarah will soon find themselves.

The Island of Doctor Moreau appears through season two as Ethan Duncan references through metaphor how he played God to create the Ledas. Ethan reads to Kira, "You cannot imagine the strange, colorless delight of these intellectual desires! The thing standing before you is no longer an animal, a fellow-creature, but a problem!" ("Variable and Full of Perturbation," 208). Sarah worries that this is inappropriate, while Ethan voices a central issue of the series—the Ledas' quest to be acknowledged as people, not property. Of course, he gives Kira his copy of the book, filled with a code that can get them the original Leda DNA and save them all.

Ethan watches a childhood tape of himself reading to Rachel: "Suddenly I heard a thud and a hissing behind me and, looking round, sprang to my feet with a cry of horror. Against the warm dawn great tumultuous masses of black smoke were boiling up out of the enclosure.... Shot flickering threads of blood-red flame" ("By Means Which Have Never Yet Been Tried," 210). In the 1896 H. G. Wells novel, a mad scientist on a remote island vivisects animals in horrific experiments that mirror Neolution's massive death toll and Brightborn's brutal surgeries. Duncan is especially struck by the scientist's lack of moral responsibility. He asks Rachel, explaining her infertility, "Do you remember I used to read you *The Island of Dr. Moreau*? How does it go? Um the bit about how he'd be forgiven for hate, but not for irresponsibility" ("Variable and Full of Perturbation," 208). Unlike Moreau, he insists on containing his creations, though both cause anguish and suffering in their hybrids.

The story is told by Edward Prendick, the horrified castaway escaping the mad scientist's island, a role Sarah, Rachel, and Cosima all play (especially Cosima, who leaves in a rickety boat). All visit a similar island in season five, where the architect of all, P.T. Westmorland, has remade a boy into a monster that prowls the forest at night. The protagonist of the book, fleeing into the jungle, meets a similar group of half-human/half-animal creatures. Their leader, the monstrous Sayer of the Law, loves Moreau as his savior, much like Westmorland's true believers. Eventually, the brutal doctor is killed in an accidental fire, like the one seen in the revolution when Cosima reveals Westmorland is no more than human.

A few other shows have dealt with the nature of body ownership, especially for clones and cyborgs. Joss Whedon's *Dollhouse* (2009–2010) allows the "dolls" (predominantly shown as women) to rent their bodies out for five years with other minds downloaded into them. This results in the main actress, Eliza Dushku, playing a new personality each week, which sometimes interacts with another copy. As the show goes on, however, it's revealed the "doll" architecture is permanent and the evil corporation running the place tries to claim bodies forever. Like M.K. and Sarah, the heroes end up running away and living off the grid. Meanwhile, protagonist Echo (Eliza Dushku) has an innate superpower like Kira's—glitches that let her remember pieces of her various engagements and finally harness them to use their personalities as she wishes. Gradually she becomes self-aware as she quests for her original identity, Caroline Farrell, and takes down the evil corporation. Dollhouse ruler Adelle DeWitt mirrors Susan as the mother figure and corporate sellout, willing to abuse the dolls to please her patriarchal masters. However, she finally joins the escaping dolls in their rebellion, creating a "safe haven" far from the world of evil technology.

Caprica (2010), the prequel to *Battlestar Galactica*, has the teen heroine, Zoe Graystone, die in the first episode's suicide bombing. Left behind is her brilliant AI, which copied many of her brain patterns, so much so she could be deemed a life form. Her grieving father, meanwhile, takes this AI and downloads it into a robot body so she can live again. The Vancouver-shot series explores the ethical implications of artificially creating life, even as the young heroine struggles for autonomy, while her best friend Lacy Rand is enticed by a religious cult. As the corporations entangle Zoe's father, he creates monstrous cyborgs that will replace humanity and destroy his world as irrevocably as Brightborn tech. AI-Zoe rebels, seeking freedom despite her artificial origin, in this notably feminist show.

The *X-Files* episode "Eve" from 1993 also has a plot that echoes *Orphan Black*. Mulder and Scully meet a pair of identical twins, Teena and Cindy, conceived via in vitro fertilization and raised separately with no knowledge of each other. Both families were treated by Dr. Sally Kendrick, who was fired for conducting eugenics experiments. She has been creating genetically-modified supersoldiers called "Adam" and "Eve," who have superhuman intelligence and strength, as well as homicidal psychoses. Even as Mulder and Scully try to protect Teena and Cindy, they soon discover the girls are homicidally violent like their older sisters. They lock them up in a psychiatric ward, though at episode end, one of their sisters comes and releases them. The episode confronts people's fears of genetic tampering and, like *Orphan Black*, the unexpected side effects of modifying babies to become "better." This show also features an eerie sisterhood and connection among the Eves.

Orphan Black's first season aired just after *Doctor Who* in the U.S. on BBC America. While both are science fiction shows, one celebrating its 50th year in 2013 and one its first, some found the juxtaposition quite startling as in trailers, they appeared to have the same plot. That year, *Doctor Who* was running the "Impossible Girl" arc. The Doctor, an alien traveling through time and space, routinely travels with young women from earth. However, on meeting Clara Oswald from modern times, he was quite surprised, as he had bumped into several copies (played by the same actress). One was a Victorian governess and one an entertainment officer on a futuristic spaceship. None of them knew about any of the others. Season end finally revealed that modern Clara had heroically split herself into infinite copies, to leap into every moment of the Doctor's life and protect him. In contrast with *Orphan Black*, Clara lacks agency until the end, as she's unenlightened like Krystal—it's the Doctor seeking to solve her mystery. Thus, her plot arc is arguably less feminist.

Lost Girl (2010–2016), a Canadian supernatural drama, parallels *Orphan Black* in several ways. Vic's actor was on *Lost Girl* and many other actors from the show stop by. In episode one, as Art hustles Sarah-as-Beth inside police headquarters, a woman wishes her good luck—it's Inga Cadranel who played Aoife. When Sarah visits Paul's workplace in "Conditions of Existence" (105), "Beth" is called back by a leggy blonde (Miriam McDonald) who played Anita. At the Neolution club, Felix is greeted by *Lost Girl*'s warden. All these wink at fans while binding the two programs together. As far as plot, *Lost Girl* follows the life of a bisexual succubus named Bo (Anna Silk), who learns to control her superhuman abilities as she seeks the truth of her origins. It's fantasy where this one is science fiction, but both offer agency and empowerment for the questing heroines. Like Sarah, Bo grows up unaware of her biological heritage until it's thrust upon her. When her succubus powers kill her boyfriend, she is horrified and goes on the run. Though the Fae push her to choose a side, Bo maintains neutrality and independence, instead opening a detective agency to protect women in danger. Like Sarah, she values autonomy and protection of innocents above all.

Groundbreaking feminist work *The Female Man* by Joanna Russ (1975) foreshadows the clones of this story as they all discover what could have been. In the novel, four genetically identical women from parallel worlds meet and compare their lives. Joanna (obviously named for the author) is an emerging feminist in a world that's similar to seventies Earth. Jeannine lives in a world where the Great Depression never ended, as a librarian settling into a traditional marriage. A powerful police officer and mother, Janet lives on Whileaway, a utopia in which all the men died. With a new independence from emerging technology, the women can combine two eggs to produce children, so they live in male-free lesbian relationships, mostly farming for food. The assassin Jael (named for the Biblical woman who killed a great general) lives in a dystopia where men and women literally fight in a "battle of the sexes" and women must trade children for resources. "Haraway's reading of *The Female Man* highlights the ways in which these four protagonists subvert each other's certainties" (Thweatt-Bates 91). Even without comparing the four heroines to educated Cosima (with a touch of Beth the cop), traditional Alison, rebellious Sarah, and murderous Helena, the plot of identical women discovering types of feminism by meeting the selves they might have become seems a strong influence. Through both series, the women teach each other about different kinds of autonomy and strength, modeling these for the readers.

Czech writer Karel Čapek's play *R.U.R. (Rossum's Universal Robots)* introduced the term "robot" in 1920. The play begins with the heroine Helena, daughter of the president (so, in fact, a parallel to Rachel) visiting a factory that makes artificial people, called *roboti* (robots). Since they've living flesh, they're actually more like clones. Old Rossum, their inventor, sought to prove that not only was God not necessary but that there was no God at all, mirroring the Duncans and Leekie, true believers. Meanwhile, his nephew saw the commercial potential. Young Rossum locked his uncle in a laboratory to play with his monsters and mutants, while he built factories and created thousands of artificial, disposable people. This of course is one of DYAD's goals. Čapek's engineers tell Helena that the world of robots will be a good world, with living machines doing the labor. Helena hesitates, but her efforts to treat the robots as people with rights soon fail. Giving in to the patriarchy, she eventually marries the director of Rossum.

A decade later, Robot Helena is created, hinting at a theme that the real Helena is not so different from an artificial copy. In secret, Helena burns the formula required to create robots, an act paralleled by Duncan and Evie's similar destructions. However, by the final act of Čapek's play, all of humankind has been killed off, except the last engineer, Alquist, who slaves night and day to recreate the formula and save robotkind. The entire series, Cosima and Susan similarly labor to recreate cloning, though Cosima only wants to make a cure for her own near-extinction. At last, the robots give

Alquist permission to destroy some of them to complete the formula, as Susan horrifically proposes doing with little Charlotte or Coady does with her creations. When Robot Helena self-sacrificingly offers to be vivisected in place of her beloved, she reveals she has learned to love. With this, Alquist finally gives the robots what the Ledas seek—he acknowledges them as "people" and humanity's heirs. The artificial people have evolved to have the same rights and abilities as humanity, and in fact take their place as earth's new heroes.

The Science, Real and Emblematic

Inside Neolution

"Neolution" specialist Dr. Aldous Leekie, part of the mysterious DYAD Institute (owned by the Topside Corporation), has scattered roughly 300 clones around the world, with "monitors" of lovers and family to report on them. Under his direction, doctors perform illegal experiments and medical testing on them in their sleep. The word DYAD (two) refers to duplicated chromosomes produced during mitosis, an early stage of fetal development, as well as any pair or set of twins. The name thus references the Ledas and foreshadows their other half—Castor—as well as their biological creator Kendall, who carries the DNA of twins.

Aldous Leekie's first name suggests the author of *Brave New World*, a dystopian novel in which designer babies are grown in bottles. The last suggests Dr. Louis Leakey (1903–1972), a Kenyan paleoanthropologist and archaeologist who helped prove that humans evolved in Africa. Leekie is moving beyond the latter and trying to bring evolution toward the former. Manson says, "I think there's a fundamental human hubris in trying to play God. That's a trope of a lot of great sci-fi." He adds that in the case of DYAD, the story has "got the banality of evil, because once you've done that, you have to administer the whole thing" (Bernstein 101). Traditional gothic "centers of the transgressions of a male over-reacher who defies social taboos, and includes graphically detailed violence, often sexual and directed against objectified women" (Hughes et al. 234). Though Leekie is not the protagonist, this *Frankenstein* plot certainly mirrors his actions. His followers mutilate and remake themselves in *Island of Doctor Moreau* fashion, hurling themselves into the lifestyle. However, the clones emphasize many times that this is not his story but theirs.

Cosima and Delphine attend the lecture at their school, where Leekie explains his philosophy:

LEEKIE: Neolution, a philosophy of today for tomorrow. Rooted in our past, in the evolution of the human organism. But before we go to the future, let me take you back to the great, Greek philosopher, Plato, and his twilight years. Poor old Plato was going blind.
 Going lame and losing his hearing. Now, imagine if he knew we could correct his sight, restore his hearing and replace his ailing body parts with titanium ones. Plato would have thought we were gods. But we're not. We're just fundamentally flawed human beings. Your glasses, for example, make you somewhat, um Platonic. But within the very near future, I'll be able to offer you the ability to see into a spectrum never before seen by the naked eye. Infrared, X-rays, ultraviolet. You interested?
COSIMA: Maybe I'll just start with basic LASIK.
LEEKIE: And so you should. That's making an evolutionary choice. Neolution gives us the opportunity at a self-directed evolution. And I believe that's not only a choice but a human right.

In "Parts Developed in an Unusual Manner" (107), Sarah tells Cosima that Olivier, her monitor's handler, owns a club called Neolution. "Felix says it's a bunch of bio-hack, body-mod freaks. Uh, Olivier's supposed to have a tail." This sort of power over the self is Neolution's great goal: "The freedom to enhance the body is thus articulated as the freedom to dispose of the body as one wills, in an argument clearly continuous with liberal humanist arguments for bodily autonomy, integrity, and freedom" (Thweatt-Bates 79).

Self-directed evolution is ironically the opposite of what's happened to the clones, who are someone else's experiment, created and monitored by others. The power of the male-run company to prey on young women throws them into a historically familiar gender dynamic. They are not (yet) self-creators, but pawns, living and dying under DYAD's direction, as the incident in Helsinki reveals. "Their exaggerated gender is what makes cyborgs matter, and is the reason contemporary feminist discourses have appropriated and proliferated cyborg femininities" (Kakoudaki 166). These created women, always fashioned by the patriarchy in works from *Pygmalion* to *The Bionic Woman*, become a metaphor for the men in power reconstructing women to fit their own models.

While *Buffy the Vampire Slayer* had a "watcher" and many secret agents have "handlers," monitors spy without making their subjects aware (except in Rachel's case). Since the DYAD Institute recruits loved ones (Donnie) or sets people up then manipulates the clones into falling for them (Paul, Delphine), this creates a sinister gothic story, in which the heroines cannot trust their closest family. Alison's paranoia pushes her to let her friend die, while Beth's suspicion of Paul is a source of endless pain to her. This becomes torture, not just a loss of autonomy.

Dr. Leekie finally speaks directly with Paul, telling him, "I've searched for the lost clone, Helena, for years. She's my white whale, Paul." Though

Neolution monitors 300 young women, Helena and Sarah, the unreported twins, have escaped control and must be contained. When he learns about Sarah from his monitor and spy Delphine, he wants to meet her. "Your interests have aligned. You can get answers," Paul tells Sarah, and blindfolds Leekie to come meet her on her terms. "I oversee data collection and quantify your well-being. I look after you," Leekie tells Sarah blandly. The benevolent-looking white haired figure casts himself as patriarch and caretaker of her world. He asks Sarah to bring him Helena so he can de-program her, and offers tempting bribes: "You do this, and we can move forward with a new understanding. You and your friends will be free to live as you choose. No monitors." As he insists, he doesn't represent an evil force: "You've always had lives. They haven't been directed, just observed" ("Unconscious Selection" 109).

He comes to Alison's door and offers her freedom, and then promises Cosima an amazing lab and a lucrative job pursuing the research on the clones she's already doing. Afterwards, the three sisters sit together considering the offer. In a truly feminist moment, they agree to support each other even if they each make different choices. When Alison protests, "If there won't be any more spies in my life, if my kids are safe, I'm sorry, but I have to tell you I'm inclined to take the offer," the others tell her "That's totally your choice" and "no judgment" ("Endless Forms Most Beautiful" 110).

However, Cosima discovers a synthetic sequence in their DNA, like a barcode, and finally translates it through binary and ASCII. They have all been patented as property. She warns Sarah that the corporation will want Kira: "You are the first one of us to ever even have a child. I mean, there's not even taxonomy in the offspring of a clone" ("Unconscious Selection" 109). This places the emphasis on their fertility and what they as women can produce. In Canada, patents have been allowed on genes and individual cells since the 1980s, but not on entire organisms and certainly not on cloned humans. It's unlikely this would hold up in court, but just the concept that the clones have been tagged as property puts them in disturbing ethical waters.

> In the season two episode "Nature Under Constraint and Vexed," Rachel Duncan has a phone conversation (in German) with a stakeholder about how "most of the patents were submitted immediately after the decision of the Supreme Court." Later in the same episode, she tells a group of Korean stakeholders that "the recent Supreme Court decision characterizing the legal status of natural versus synthetic DNA was the successful result of our lobbying strategies. We are proceeding with the next tranche of patent claims." She's referring to the June 2013 U.S. Supreme Court case of Association for Molecular Pathology v. Myriad Genetics, Inc., in which the court ruled that human genes could not be patented in the United States because DNA is a product of nature and not an invention. (As a fun timeline-related aside, this episode aired in April 2014, and so Rachel was commenting on relatively current real-world events.) [Griffin and Nesseth].

"Science is political. Science has always been political," the real Cosima says, citing Richard Lewontin, a Marxist evolutionary biologist who's "very interesting in terms of what we can actually use genetics for" (Newton). Season one ends with the corporation revealing what it wants—the women to serve them willingly, fully. The episode also introduces the powerful insider clone Rachel. Later she explains, "I've known Leekie my entire life. When my adoptive parents died, he became something of a guardian to me. But, now, my position in the corporation essentially outranks his DYAD directorship. He can become too attached to his subjects, myself included. Sometimes he can't make the hard choices" ("Ipsa Scientia Potestas Est" 205). Since she sees herself and her fellow clones as "subjects" rather than people, she's a chilling part of the problem.

Graeme says of the cloning concept, "it was logical that you would create females. And that immediately made it a feminist drama, because it immediately put questions of body ownership at the fore. Who owns your body is one of the central questions of the show, and a central issue of feminism" (Griffin and Nesseth). From here, the women become more involved with DYAD, as Cosima agrees to work for them. The design of DYAD, even with its open spaces and whiteness suggests boundaries, control, and clinical sterility. While the open, light-filled head office sparkles with spaciousness and luxury, it's a place of lies and secrets. The old building was once an asylum, and the screens everywhere emphasize surveillance. Underneath, in creepy gothic fashion, are windowed cells, shackles, laboratories where the women undergo nonconsensual surgery.

At the end of season one, Amelia, Sarah's birth mother, finds Sarah and tells her she and Helena are twins. She gives Sarah a photo with the Duncans in lab coats, and the code name Project LEDA. In "Governed as It Were by Chance" (204), Cosima sees the photo and tries to explain: "Okay, so Zeus, the big guy of the gods, he comes down from Mount Olympus in the guise of a swan and he gets it on with this human queen called Leda. They have twins and the kids are half-human, half-God. Weird, right?" The symbolism emphasizes two children, Leda and Castor, that are more than human. She adds, with foreshadowing: "Project LEDA I mean, it's total military-speak, isn't it? And what's with that soldier in the background?" ("Governed as It Were by Chance" 204).

Mid-season two, Sarah and Helena go hunting "Swan Man," as Helena calls him. This is Professor Ethan Duncan, who designed them all and raised Rachel. Helena guides Sarah to the Cold River institute, "A place of screams," where Sarah discovers his hiding place. She sits with her creator and gets her questions answered at last:

> SARAH: Project LEDA. What are we for?
> DUNCAN: Proof of concept. How everything starts.... But an oversight committee declared us an ethical failure. Um, are you sure you won't have some tea?

SARAH: How was DYAD involved?
DUNCAN: Contractor. When the military scuppered our work, DYAD persuaded us to, um, push on to full term.
SARAH: So DYAD hijacked Project LEDA.
DUNCAN: Once you've gone too far, it's hard not to go all the way.
SARAH: Why? What did you want?
DUNCAN: Babies. Little girls ["To Hound Nature in Her Wanderings" 206].

Sarah rejects this summation, protesting, "You know we're not just a concept, right? That we're your consequences?" She pleads for Duncan to take responsibility for his creations—now real, individual people: "Your daughter is lost. There's just me. And Alison, a housewife with two adopted kids. And Cosima, a brilliant scientist,—just like you…. We're real, Ethan. Cosima is unlike anybody I've ever met. And she's sick. We're sick. Your little girls are dying. It could happen to Rachel too. Try to stop it. You can help us now" ("To Hound Nature in Her Wanderings" 206). An auto-immune disorder is attacking their epithelial tissues, resulting in their coughing blood, and then eventually dying, as Cosima discovers through the autopsy of Jennifer Fitzsimmons. To make the clones infertile, Duncan created the flaw that's killing the Ledas, and knows their original DNA source—the best hope of a cure. Analyzing their DNA with nowhere to start is hopeless—"If you imagine a base pair as a single letter in the code that writes your DNA, finding a tiny difference between two genomes is like trying to find a single typo in a 200,000-page book by comparing it to another 200,000-page book" (Griffin and Nesseth). Only Duncan's notes can solve the mystery.

Duncan blames Dr. Leekie and DYAD for taking Rachel and making her a monster. Mrs. S and Sarah decide to reunite them so Ethan can tell Rachel DYAD killed her mother and turn Rachel against Leekie. Rachel accordingly banishes Leekie out and takes over the company. Delphine worriedly tells Sarah, "I believe Aldous was the lesser of two evils. But it's too late, now" ("Variable and Full of Perturbation" 208).

Meanwhile, DYAD's deeper plans begin to emerge. Sarah's love interest Cal tells Mrs. S, "The DYAD group has these key people on dozens of corporate boards, you know. I'm talking superpacs and research groups and lobbyists. All a concerted effort to try and effect biogenetic patent law" ("By Means Which Have Never Yet Been Tried" 210). When Cal tells a mysterious force on the Dark Web (apparently Marion) that he's with Siobhan, the response is that he should ask her about Project Castor. When he does, she replies, "Don't know your mythology, do you, Cal?" ("By Means Which Have Never Yet Been Tried" 210). Castor was the demigod son of Leda, an identical twin and powerful warrior. Project Castor, as it turns out, is the male militarized equivalent of Leda, intended to be super-soldiers. However, the clones are all dying even faster than Leda, with seizures and neurological problems.

Their genetics result in a brain-destroying prion disease, in which a misfolded protein causes other proteins to misfold. With the disease's rapid neurological degeneration, Cosima likens it to mad cow disease.

Doctor Nealon debuts in the season two finale, in which he gets Sarah to sign her consent on medical procedures and prepares to perform her oophorectomy. As she protests that since she's already chained to a table, a contract means little, the evil corporation still focuses on having her submit legally, not just physically. They don't just want her body but her rights. "By Means Which Have Never Yet Been Tried" is a compendium of feminist battles: "Sarah Manning ... is heavily interrogated about her sexual orientation, number of sexual partners, contraception, and abortion. The interrogation is, obviously, conducted by men, the ones who are always placing women under surveillance" (Berns and Aguilar 143). Sarah fights free and escapes with her friends' help, but the evil corporation continues grasping for her rights.

Nealon proves a villain through the next season, agreeing to work with Cosima but plotting behind her back and smuggling Rachel to Taiwan while leaving Krystal in her place as a helpless coma patient. In both cases, of course, he preys on clone women on behalf of DYAD, casting himself as a crueler replacement for Leekie. Meanwhile, after Rachel gets a pencil in the eye, Delphine takes her place as the head of DYAD. While less cruel, her obsession with Cosima, now her ex, leads to an imbalance of power as she spies and dictates Cosima's choices.

In season three, a kidnapped Helena meets the Castors' foster mother, Doctor Coady. She is surprisingly maternal, establishing herself as a powerful woman in the military hierarchy. As she explains, "The irony of it? I never wanted kids. Didn't think it was for me. Next thing I know, I've got more than I can count" ("Transitory Sacrifices of Crisis" 302). While she cuddles and comforts the dying boys, she also experiments on them as needed.

Further, she encourages them to have sex to pass on a disease she wishes to study. The Castors can transmit the misfolded proteins to a sexual partner, who is then rendered infertile. Apparently, there exists a similar ability in nature—though only in the fruit fly. The male, when mating, produces toxins that can make his chosen female infertile after, to encourage her to lay more eggs. The toxins act as a weapon to prevent other males from breeding (Davis). This hyper-masculine form of genetic competition echoes symbolically with the show. There's a gender war here, and the Castors are destroying civilians.

> SARAH: You're infecting innocent women with it.
> COADY: To understand it. I didn't put it in the boys, I just found it.
> SARAH: So it's engineered. Who engineered it? Was it Duncan?
> COADY: It's a weapon.

SARAH: You're field-testing it. You want to isolate it, to develop it in other forms.
COADY: It could end wars in a single generation without spilling a drop of blood ["Certain Agony of the Battlefield" 306].

When she refuses to stop, Paul destroys her. Coady, a woman, uses men to rape and disable women, and Paul the hero ends the carnage … though Coady survives for Helena to finally kill. Mark and Ira survive, but none of their brothers appear again. Fawcett says at the end of season three, "We've kind of put an end to Castor, loosely. We have the original. And there's been a very big victory for the sisters by the end of this season" (Ross, "Finale").

The gang ends season three with two enemies—Castor and Topside (representing the military-industrial complex and late-stage capitalism, respectively). Sarah and Delphine meet with greedy, ambitious Ferdinand the cleaner (i.e., the mass murderer at the Helsinki event), calling Topside the lesser of the two evils. Ferdinand tells Delphine he plans to capture the original DNA supplier for Castor and bring him to Topside so he'll have a "seat at the table." Still, Sarah offers him Kendall's samples in return for his taking down Coady, which they can't manage alone.

In the finale, Delphine and Nealon face off. "We were there from the very beginning," he brags, almost drooling with excitement. "Topside pursues its profits, the military pursues its weapons … and we steer it all from within." This steering force is Neolution: Leekie was its face, while Castor and Leda "were our Adam and Eve" as he puts it ("History Yet to Be Written" 310). Nealon teases, "Wherever you think the science is at, I guarantee you're wrong," foreshadowing Brightborn. He offers her a partnership but when she scoffs, he cracks open something like a cyanide tooth to reveal a frightening cyber maggot. He attacks her, and in a scene coded as rape, tries to spit the worm into her mouth. She shoots him with her pocket gun. As he dies, he gurgles, "You won't live till morning." Fawcett says:

> It's good to have something sick and gross. What's kind of shocking about it, which I thought was fun, is that this goes from Neolution are the bad guys, to the reveal that Nealon is part of Neolution, to suddenly he's on top and he's strangling you and there's something creepy coming out of his mouth—there's blood, there's this wormlike creature and he's trying to force him into Delphine's mouth. I love leaving that mystery hanging in season 3 [Ross, "Finale"].

As with the end of season one, the women realize they can't make any deals with the corporation. Fawcett says at the end of season three: "It was important to us in this finale that there are a lot of answers and there is resolution and there is the feeling of a finale, but we also are at the brink of almost a brand-new rabbit hole. It's interesting to come to the end of our Castor mystery, and how that fits in with Leda and Topside and then to introduce our new foes that we're expecting to see more of in season 4, which is

Neolution, which we set-up in season 1" (Ross, "*Orphan Black* Finale"). Delphine bids Cosima a touching goodbye, but is apparently killed by a mystery assailant, leaving the position of DYAD's head open. With no one officially researching the cure, Susan and Cosima independently try.

Season four introduces Neolution's tech side. While the previous three seasons explored biological alterations, the story begins incorporating machines as robo-maggots are implanted in Sarah and others without their knowledge in an example of body horror ("Body Horror"). Of course, Sarah struggles through the season with having such a device implanted within her, leaving her vulnerable to be killed at any moment. When the Brightborn thug checks for it in "Transgressive Border Crossing" (402) and warns her not to bite him as he sticks a finger in her mouth, he has her on her back in another clear rape metaphor. Clearly, the women are once again at the mercy of the corporate entity.

Further, the biological hacking they thought they were investigating has turned technological. Fawcett adds, "As we dug deeper into Neolution we wanted to discover that it's kind of more than just science. That there is a biotech side to what Neolution is doing. So Rachel's eye was the perfect thing to kind of illustrate that" ("Body Horror"). An eye is the symbol of Neolution, and Leekie actually shows an image of Rachel's prosthetic eye as early as "Variations Under Domestication" (106). Donnie's antagonist in the prison uses such an image to mime "I'm watching you" ("Body Horror"). This creates a *1984*-style paranoia from the giant company with spies and cameras everywhere, always monitoring its subjects.

Cosima says in "From Instinct to Rational Control" (404), "It's like a whole new side to Neolution." Manson explains that the maggot bot "is trying, by a process of elimination, to determine why she is fertile. Whatever it is that has made Sarah immune and fertile, that has made her the anomaly among the clones. It's flipping genomic switches on and off, trying to make her sick. [Brightborn are] trying to flip switches to see if they hit the 'right' button. It's an entirely irresponsible, unethical form of scientific research" (Bernstein 101). Once more, the clones become acceptable collateral damage for the bureaucracy.

Brightborn is a fertility clinic, one that can produce superior babies, especially to infertile mothers. Their promotional video introduces "Evie Cho, CEO and founder of the Brightborn Group," who promises, "We can help provide you and your family with the best chance at a fast conception, a smooth pregnancy, and a healthy and thriving newborn. But why stop there? Mainstream reproductive technology? It's like a whole new side to Neolution. All of our children are born stronger and healthier" ("From Instinct to Rational Control" 404). Cosima notes that "embryo enhancement" can mean anything—but probably nothing good, since they haven't published a thing in scientific journals. She's curious enough to volunteer as Donnie and Felix's surrogate to infiltrate their research facilities ("Human Raw Material" 405). There, Cosima sees a deformed baby born and meets her "creator" Susan, who fervently justifies her actions. Manson says, "Susan Duncan is not just evil. She's very rich in her ethics, in her science. She's thought long and hard about what she's doing, and, yes, she may be a eugenicist, but she truly believes in her heart that she's trying to improve the human race and the human lot on the planet" (Bernstein 167).

George J. Annas, a professor of bioethics and human rights, reveals in an essay the primary arguments for genetic alterations and cloning: "Cloning is a type of human reproduction that can help infertile couples have genetically related children, and cloning is part of human 'progress' (potentially leading to a new type of genetic immortality) so to prevent it is to be antiscientific" (22). Brightborn supports both these concepts—many proud Brightborn parents walk out with healthy babies. However, Annas worries about this kind of designer child. After a conference in 2001, he and his partner proposed a Charter of the United Nations to affirm human rights, establishing that "no individual, nation, or corporation has the moral or legal warrant to engage in species-altering procedures, including cloning and genetic alteration of reproductive cells or embryos for the creation of a child" (20).

In fact, the clinic's work is brutal. While they claim a mission helping women get pregnant, helping them achieve their reproductive desires, the women actually become uniformed subjects for gruesome experiments, as another set of babies are born with serious defects. The callous Evie—a young woman like Rachel who serves the corporation and preys on society's most helpless for profit—then orders them killed. "Although Brightborn does uphold their facade of a fertility clinic by helping infertile couples to have babies, the real purpose of the clinic is to explore and understand genetic diseases and abnormalities. To do this, the scientists manipulate specific genes of an embryo, then hire women to carry the fetuses to term" (Griffin and Nesseth). Cosima, the ethical scientist is appalled by both projects. While the latter is horrific, she has moral problems with the former, too, insisting, "You can't perfect the human genome! You can't know what perfect is!"

Evie, who was born damaged, believes firmly in creating perfect babies. To do this, she insists that the scientific ends justify the means, retorting, "Da Vinci robbed graves to study anatomy. In a hundred years they'll call me a pioneer" ("The Scandal of Altruism" 406). Such technology would have stopped her own childhood suffering, and she's willing to create and murder countless babies to achieve it.

The next stage of their planning appears to include spreading the maggotbots through the world. With them, the wicked baby-killer Evie can deliver transgenes to people without their consent and even unethically edit their genomes. She's advanced from experimenting on babies to the general public. S. notes, "I think we have two factions of Neos with competing technologies. Bots versus clones. And if we're not careful, we are gonna get screwed again" ("From Dancing Mice to Psychopaths" 410). Of course, the bots essentially give Neolution control over every human who purchases one, expanding their reach through society. A brief plotline follows to find Kendra, the last surviving surrogate to escape with a deformed baby and video that proves Brightborn is killing the babies they've created. Cruel, expedient Rachel and Ira intercept both woman and video before Sarah and Art can. Rachel confronts Evie to demand a seat at the table in return for Kendra and her video. However, the conversation is staged—Rachel blasts her own video through Evie's press conference with Evie's confessed killings and destroys her. Clearly the outmatched Clone Club need the cruel, conniving businesswoman to take down her counterpart.

After, Dr. Ian Van Lier takes over as interim CEO. Creepily, he's Evie Cho's personal doctor as well as mentor—he not only displaces her, but when she protests, he kills her with her own maggotbot. As she dies in his arms, he tells her, "Technology is subject to natural selection too, Evie. It changes and adapts.... You built it. Let it take you." With this, he sets himself up as the next patriarchal adversary. Evie, who thought herself so superior to Rachel the clone, is merely another disposable experiment. Throughout the series, the hierarchical corporation and army destroy its own people, emphasizing that within the system only useful corporate drones survive for as long as they have something to offer. The metaphor here is women convinced that the hierarchy respects them, even as they're only welcomed for serving their masters' agenda.

Annas, questioning the ethics of immortality through cloning, points out that the increased power of genetic science "has the power to fundamentally diminish humanity by producing a child through human cloning or through intentionally producing an inheritable genetic change" (20). The show introduces both, as the clones fight to shake off DYAD's control, and Kira suggests the possibility of a new kind of humanity. Annas further worries that the clones or their children will be labeled as other than human and thus become second-class citizens or other types of lesser or nonpeople legally. Creating clones as perfect organ donors is popular in science fiction but disturbingly unethical—sacrificing all or part of a living, thinking individual for another. The series uses this a few times, as in the comics M.K. is given skin grafts from a more-damaged clone as a child, and Sarah's cheekbot tests her DNA to try to cure the other Ledas by killing her. After, Cosima considers sacrificing herself by implanting Sarah's cheekbot to help her sisters.

Rachel pushes this to extremes as season four ends and she decrees the total nonpersonhood of clones, taking the commercial, exploitative side. In "From Dancing Mice to Psychopaths" (410), Rachel tells the sinister board that she will combine and accelerate human trials with bots in clones, keeping the latter as lab rats: "We operate in countries where human cloning is not illegal. Where our corporation supersedes their citizenship, their personhood. So why grant them this illusion of freedom? If we want to know if our lab rats' tails will grow back, we damn well will cut them off and see!" By turning on her sisters, she reclaims her own biology and proclaims herself as better than they are, or so she hopes. Like Evie, she is delusional about her value.

Meanwhile, on the mysterious island where Rachel was convalescing, Cosima actually creates a cure, but is forced to evacuate before she can use it. The cure, notably, requires a viable Leda egg (Sarah's) combined with sperm from a Castor (Ira). This is only possible because Sarah's biology circumvented the infertility disease meant to control her—instead, the biological dice fought back against man's control and pushed toward fertility and gave her the chance to not only procreate but use her body's rebellion to save her sisters. Ira too is not what he was created for—becoming a rather effeminate schemer instead of a soldier. Finally, the cure to the disease is a zygote—creating the life that was forbidden to both Leda and Castor.

At the end of season four, it becomes clear that Rachel and Susan's island is far from deserted. In fact, the village holds P.T. Westmorland, the Victorian industrialist and true architect of Neolution. Susan describes him as "Born to industry, drawn to Darwin and early eugenical thought. He used his resources to essentially create a secret scientific society. Percy sought to bring science to the task of breeding a better human" ("The Antisocialism of Sex" 407). Believers flock to the island to share in his alleged longevity as he promises them cures. "PTW's 'fountain,' or what he believes is the key to live forever, is in the manipulation of the gene Lin28a. This gene (an actual gene!) encodes a protein that regulates developmental timing and stem cell self-renewal. That is, Lin28a is important in determining when certain processes stop or start, as well as controlling the size of the stem cell pool during development" (Griffin and Nesseth). All of Neolution has been his schemes, down to Doctor Leekie's book. In his rural paradise, he protects his chosen people like a feudal lord. There, Delphine reveals to Cosima she's been hiding out, and slips her the cure. Delphine is soon sent away, but Cosima decides to stay and investigate, even as Westmorland treats her as his subject, at the mercy of his whims. Meanwhile, Westmorland reveals himself to Rachel, who's seeking a new master, and she becomes his adoring disciple.

Like his genetics, Westmorland's philosophy has real world parallels: Paul Niehans (1882 –1971), a Swiss doctor, was one of the developers of cellular therapy. The Transhumanism movement, which he began, injected fetal sheep cells into humans, in an attempt to prevent aging and death (Shannon 42). Of course, Cosima is experimenting to prevent her own death, but only after her life has been tragically shortened. Her last name may deliberately reference his. The Transhumanism movement has a goal of defeating death through "supplements, diet, exercise, computers, biotechnology, cryogenics, and possibly cloning" (Shannon 44). Their goals involve replaceable genes, upgrades, and a more positive, enlightened person who can transcend the limits of biology (Shannon 45). The desperation to defeat death is, to many, anti-religious as well as unnatural. Unlike the Ledas' goals of healing, the goal is "to become better than well, by using technologies to redefine or remove the naturally given limits of human embodiment" (Thweatt-Bates 43). While Westmorland seeks this path, he hasn't found it, as he's faked his enormous age. Further, he's dying, and is desperately preying on his subjects, especially the children, for any possible cure.

In "Guillotines Decide" (508), Delphine tells Cosima of disturbing new legislation, as hundreds of millions of people will be required to submit their DNA, thanks to Neolution. S. adds to Rachel, seeking her help, "Westmorland wants unprecedented access to human genetics, and Hashem Al-Khatib was bribing governments worldwide to get it.... Neolution want to sell curated, commercialized evolution to the one percent who can afford it. So they can live forever, grow a bloody tail if they want to. The rest of us are Coady's department, targeted for sterilization." At last, Neolution's agenda is revealed. Felix and Adele have followed the finances, but only Rachel has kept incontrovertible proof. Rejecting the corporation at last, Rachel gives it to S., who releases it worldwide. However, the knowledge of the clones is held back, allowing the Ledas to continue in safe obscurity. Manson comments, "We never wanted that sort of news conference-y [moment or] the plot to turn to, 'Oh, it's all going public.' That took out the mystery and the heat and the clandestine tone of what the girls were going through, so we were never interested in that. It's our secret, and we're off to cure our secret sisters" (Gelman, "*Orphan Black* Boss").

In the next episode, many suicides or murders dispose of the once all-powerful board, including Van Lier. When Art and Felix burst in, only two remain, stressing the shadowy organization's depowering without Westmorland's illusion of power. Mr. Frontenac, about to eliminate Al-Khatib, draws his gun on Art, who shoots him. With Rachel's help, they push Al-Khatib for information and track where Westmorland and Coady have taken Helena, whom they've kidnapped for her twins' stem cells. The fragile Westmorland is quickly dying, and the stem cells are his final chance of survival—once again, preying on his younger creations to sustain himself.

At DYAD, Coady devotedly obeys Westmorland, even to the point of killing Mark, the last Castor. At last, Sarah rescues Helena and then kills

Westmorland, even as he gloats. She retorts, "You never caged us. Not me and Helena. You got nothing to do with who we really are." Westmorland tries smothering her with plastic, in a final attempt to silence her. Nonetheless, she fights free and proclaims, "We survived you. Me and my sisters together. This is evolution." As nature incarnate, they have outcompeted his hidebound philosophy. In the midst of his final comeback, she smashes his head in. Helena, even while giving birth, does the same to Coady. With this, the evil schemers are all defeated, their plans revealed to the world.

With this, Helena, Alison, and Sarah can resume normal lives, together with their children. Meanwhile, Cosima, united with Delphine, sets out to save her sisters. Though they don't know it, it's Rachel, final heir to Neolution, who supplies them with the names of 274 Ledas across the world—with all the patriarchs destroyed, its final offering is one of healing as the information will let Cosima distribute the cure. While the technology is abandoned, the creators and weaponized Castors all dead, the Ledas can live on and raise their miracle children as a family at last.

Cloning Ethics

Fawcett explains that the show's topic came to him easily, since, in science fiction, clones have never been explored deeply; "There's great opportunities for humor, for mystery and conspiracy, for body horror and science" (Bernstein 11). There are also opportunities to study gender roles and biology, as the history of cloning ties in closely.

A great deal of science appears on the show. Real Cosima explains, "I'm a resource for the biology, particularly insofar as evolutionary biology is concerned. I study the history and the philosophy of biology, so I do offer some suggestions and some creative ideas, but also help correct some of the misconceptions about science. I offer different angles and alternatives to look at the way biological science is represented, so (it's) not reduced to your stereotypical tropes" ("Q&A with Cosima"). As she adds, "We mined historical events and now-defunct beliefs, as well as popular trends in contemporary research in biology, biotechnology and bioengineering, ethics, policy, law, and philosophy. Some we chose because they mobilized the narrative; some because we needed a way to solve a narrative problem" (Griffin and Nesseth).

Scientists love studying twins separated at birth (though these are hard to find) because with their identical biology, any differences must be in how they were brought up—their diet, amount of exercise, what they were taught. Many issues like disease and mental illness straddle the nature/nurture question—do people become overweight because of their upbringing and what they were taught and fed? Or was it predestined from their genes? What of depression? Schizophrenia? Alcoholism? Behavioral scientists and psychologists place many issues on the spectrum with nature and nurture contributing.

Of course, the Ledas (less so the Castors who were raised together) can study this in person with examples many scientists would adore: who can the same person become when raised by a religious cult? An abuser? A nurturer? What factors result in homosexuality or becoming transgender? What about the suicide risk Beth represents? "We try not to sacrifice the accuracy, but its science fiction. It's not a documentary," says the real Cosima ("Clone Club Insiders").

While in countries without slavery no one can own another person, "Patents have been granted to fragments of genetic code, methods for identifying DNA or RNA sequences in an individual, nucleic acids, and genetic diagnostic techniques, among other things" (Dvorsky). With the ambiguous state of patent law today, parts of the human genome may indeed be patented. In 2005, MIT researchers Kyle Jensen and Fiona Murray reported that over 4,000 human genes had been claimed by U.S. patents. Isolated DNA was ruled different than natural-occurring DNA by the court system (Dvorsky). The "barcode gene" seen onscreen appeared in 2012, when geneticists from Harvard and Johns Hopkins Universities "developed a novel method of DNA storage, and demonstrated its potential by encoding a 5.27-megabit book containing 53,426 words, 11 jpg images and one JavaScript program with 159-nucleotide chunks of single stranded genetic code" (Dvorsky). Developing the DNA barcode is equally feasible.

"Assuming the clones were intentionally modified to be sterile, there are two ways their infertility could have been engineered. The first involves what is called 'germline' gene therapy, the second so-called 'somatic cell' gene therapy" (Dvorsky). Neither existed in the 1980s, and it's more likely the second was used during the cloning and/or in vitro stage. Somatic cell therapy is "similar to a new technique by which the genetic information of three parents is used to replace faulty mitochondrial DNA in an egg or embryo with healthy DNA from a female donor" (Dvorsky). These changes would be heritable, as seen in Kira.

> In the *Helsinki* comic issue #4 ("False Positive Error"), self-aware Finnish clone Veera Suominen meets clones who have been held for experimentation by Dr. Dmitri Volkov. These comics take place circa 2001, so these are probably the earliest known sick clones. Volkov was part of projects at the Cold River Institute in the 1970s (around the same time that Ethan Duncan would have been working there), and his research focused on mapping genetic diseases in isolated groups. When we encounter him in the comics, he has at least nine Leda clones in his lab receiving mysterious treatments. Veera steals a hard drive with information about injections, stem cells, target genes, and cancer, suggesting that Volkov was using the clones for gene therapy experiments [Griffin and Nesseth].

As they kidnap the clones, imprison them, and experiment on them to the point of death, their work is criminally unethical ... as well as ineffective.

Even in the Neolutionists' rigid planning, love and biology have thwarted them. "The moms of *Orphan Black* help us think about who controls women's reproduction and the limits of that control," explains Sarah K. Donovan in her *Orphan Black* essay "Not Why but Who" (134). The Duncans try to monitor all clones from birth, but still must use surrogates like Amelia, who flee. Their experiment goes wrong, in the genetic disorder that's killing the clones and in Sarah and Helena's unexpected fertility. Meanwhile, the healing ability they tried to create doesn't manifest until the second, unplanned generation.

In the real world, the Canadian Assisted Human Reproduction Act bans the creation of human clones, but this only came into effect in 2004—significantly after Projects Leda and Castor, but at least one year before Charlotte was born. Still, cloning was not advanced enough to create surviving clone babies in 1984, and arguably isn't advanced enough now. Jennifer Doudna, a prominent genetic scientist at the University of California, Berkeley, protests that "nuclear transfers are just incredibly technically challenging and the resulting embryos don't survive, and if they do they have defects that lead to early death" (Lepore).

Further, humanity at the time of this writing has not perfected creating a healthy clone. "It is widely believed by scientists that any human clone would have a multitude of health concerns" ("Clonaid Says"). Obviously, these don't include having scientists deliberately destroy their reproductive systems, which would be unethical. However, Dolly the sheep aged rapidly, a problem which has not been solved. Some researchers report that an unusually large number of cloned animals have a predisposition to arthritis and ailments with the lungs and liver. Embryologist Stewart Newman protests that it is unlikely "that a human created from the union of two damaged cells' (an enucleated egg and a nucleus removed from a somatic cell) could ever be healthy" (qtd. in Tong 248).

To produce Dolly, Dr. Ian Wilmut and his colleagues used 277 enucleated eggs. 29 of these advanced to the blastocyst stage, and only one was brought to term successfully. "According to many experts, producing a viable human clone would require scores of women to donate eggs and carry embryos, most of which would either not come to term or be born with major deformities" (Tong 248).

> "All sorts of things go wrong," said George Seidel, a cloning researcher at Colorado State University. Cloned cattle and sheep are often born dangerously large. "Normally you might expect a 100-pound birthweight in a calf, but with a clone, you might get 160 pounds," said Seidel. Because such outsize calves don't have room to wriggle around in the uterus, they can be born lame or with limb deformities. "Sometimes the kidneys aren't right, they're just plain put together wrong—or the

heart is, or the lungs, or the immune system," he added. "It can be a unique abnormality in each case. They can die within a few days after birth, or sometimes they just can't make it after you cut the umbilical cord." Nobody really knows why. Only if such problems are surmounted, said Seidel, would experimenting with human cloning be ethical: "We shouldn't be deliberately producing babies with abnormalities. We're talking about an abnormality rate of maybe 30 percent in cloned animals. In human babies, the normal rate of congenital defects is about 2 percent, and we wouldn't tolerate a jump to 3 percent" [Talbot].

The real Cosima adds, "We can do therapeutic cloning, we do it all the time with all kinds of animals. Your cells clone themselves all the time, but reproductive cloning,—cloning meant for the reproduction of humanity—that's not legal—at least not in North America. Whether that's being researched in other areas, I have very little doubt that it is. We're not allowed to hear about it, because we're not allowed to do it. But we do clone other species, mammals. So, conceivably it's not impossible that human beings could be" ("Q&A with Cosima").

Cloning and related advances in human biology have a complex history, arming the show's creators with rich scientific studies. As early as 1901, scientists could transfer embryo rabbits from one female to another. "The Cold River Institute was founded by Progressive Era eugenicists; its real-world counterparts were, too. The Eugenics Record Office was founded in Cold Spring Harbor, New York, in 1910" (Lepore). Mice were the first genes cloned, and the first genome decoded. After claiming in 1934 to have achieved in vitro fertilization with a rabbit, Hudson Hoagland and Gregory Pincus founded the Worcester Foundation for Experimental Biology, and there, Pincus and his colleagues invented the pill. At last, women could control their own reproduction. Thus, while female animals were the subjects of many experiments, the final result was increased freedom for human women.

Kendall, it turns out, is the source for both Castor and Leda DNA, as she possesses both. Finding a woman with such a unique biology has worked before. Historically, HeLa cells were taken from a tumor in Henrietta Lacks in 1951 and became the first immortal human cells grown in culture. These were the first human cells successfully cloned. Manson explains, "That was our concept, a woman whose cells make the cloning easy by pure mathematical chance" (Bernstein 99).

The ability to extract human eggs arrived in the 1950s, followed by the birth of Louise Brown, the first human in vitro birth, in 1978. The Human Genome Project began in 1990, and scientists finished sequencing the human genome in 2003. The first historical experiment for gene therapy occurred in 1991 for adenoise deaminase, the same disease that so ruined the life of Brightborn CEO Evie Cho. She gives a speech on being cured through an experimental gene-therapy program of her compromised "bubble girl" immune system. This use would of course be benevolent, but the show extends the treatment into creating "better" children, and producing many horrific failures. Thus, Brightborn shows off the best and worst of genetic manipulation. Today, many gene therapy trials and treatments are underway, but progress is slow. There is much science fiction about "designer babies" but the technology is a long way off, even if one discounts the ethical questions.

> In February 1997, Ian Wilmut and his colleagues at the Roslin Institute in Scotland announced that they had successfully used a technique called somatic cell nuclear transfer to create a cloned sheep they named Dolly, after Dolly Parton. (It was a geek's joke: Dolly was cloned from a mammary cell.) Wilmut and his team had transferred the DNA-containing nucleus from the cell of an adult ewe to a donor egg whose own nucleus had been removed, leaving only the outer membranes and the cytoplasm. To fuse the adult nucleus and the hollowed egg together and to activate development of the embryo, a process usually set in motion by the helpful sperm, the researchers applied an electrical pulse, essentially shocking it to life. The hard part—what Wilmut managed that had been thought impossible before Dolly—was to show that the DNA in the adult nucleus, which was already serving its mature, specialized purpose, could essentially be tricked into dividing and otherwise behaving like a brand-new fertilized egg. The next, not particularly complicated step, was to implant the embryo in the uterus of yet another sheep, which served as a surrogate mother. (It could have been implanted in the adult ewe who contributed the nucleus, but in this case, that ewe was by then dead.) Since the nucleus of each cell in the body contains the genetic instructions for the whole, the resulting offspring, Dolly, was one that shared an identical genotype with the original—a clone. Human cloning by somatic cell nuclear transfer would work essentially the same way [Talbot].

As soon as Dolly was announced, speculation on human cloning took off and "most people were disturbed by the idea of making genetic copies. If a woman cloned herself and reared the child, she would be her own daughter's identical twin. If she had a husband, he would eventually find himself with a daughter who uncannily resembled his wife. Would this lead to confusion, even incest? And how could a cloned child live out his life freely, knowing he was the recipient of a preworn, consciously selected genotype?" (Talbot). Many believed the clone would suffer from predestination—the expectation to share the original's personality and skills or the fears of health problems and conditions. Cloning in many stories suggests a child being designed for a particular purpose—the skills of Einstein or Van Gogh. This is especially evident with the show's Castors—bred soldiers programmed with logic tests. While the Ledas are mostly left free, Rachel the corporate clone was deliberately created by Westmorland and the Duncans, and then trained by Leekie for her role.

Some of these issues are addressed in the show as specifically feminine issues, or ones with feminine solutions. Cosima's horror at Neolution patenting them represents the patriarchal corporation owning the young women—reflecting a tyrannical relationship against traditionally depowered members of society. Having their boyfriends and husbands monitor them sets up a feudal system with the women at the bottom.

Family relationships do get confusing, as the Ledas are technically sisters to Charlotte (whom Susan calls Rachel's adopted daughter) and Kendall (making S. Sarah's biological niece as well as foster-mother, and making Kira Kendall's niece as well as great-granddaughter; Kira and Mrs. S could be considered genetic siblings).

> Kendall had her own child, Mrs. S, and as is normal for a biological mother and child, they share roughly 50 percent of their DNA from Kendall's XX genome. We know this because Kendall's contribution to Mrs. S was through an ovum, which can only be formed from an XX genome—Mrs. S was not formed from Kendall's sibling's cells. Mrs. S also shares the same amount of DNA (50 percent) with the Leda clones, since they are clones of the XX genome. On the other hand, Mrs. S shares only 25 percent of her genes with the Castor clones. Because of this, they are biological uncles to Mrs. S—clones of her mother's brother [Griffin and Nesseth].

However, the clones deal with this smoothly, lovingly calling each other sister rather than worrying overly about which role model Charlotte will grow into or redefining S. and Sarah's firmly-set relationship. In fact, as Helena (arguably the most loving) responds to pregnancy by naming S. the babies' grandmother and poor lost Gracie their aunt (though she's no biological relation), she creates a circle of caring instead of devoting herself to labels. Further, Helena invites the men into the circle, calling Felix "brother-sestra" and naming her twins for Donnie and Art.

Another common criticism is uniqueness—that the child will feel burdened by knowing she's the same as others or by seeing who she could be. Mistaken identity and identity theft could also become newly possible. Aside from the fact that twins have the identical challenge (producing many books on twin psychology and surmounting the difficulties), *Orphan Black* answers this with example. Sarah's impersonation of Beth is quickly discovered, and the clones mostly imitate each other imperfectly, emphasizing their wide range of differences. Admittedly, the clones are often burdened by lost opportunities—Alison envies Helena her pregnancy, and Sarah, Beth's career success. Nonetheless, they model and borrow these strengths by slipping into each other's roles and growing, rather than being consumed by despair. Further, all of the clones welcome the growing family as Helena, driven insane at the thought of false copies, instead finds love and peace on discovering she has a twin. This story, focusing on personal autonomy, dismisses the question of whether these women—even played by the same actress—are the same, partly because they're so different. Each is seen shaping herself through choice as well as upbringing—to the point at which Krystal chooses not to believe she's a clone, even facing the truth.

Despite all these concerns, many would be interested in creating them. "I could imagine three main groups who'd be interested in cloning," said Ronald Green, a professor of ethics at Dartmouth (and an adviser to the biotech company Advanced Cell Technologies). The first, infertile couples, would want to create a child genetically related to one of them. Likewise, gay and lesbian couples could reproduce without introducing another parent as donor, who might try to claim the child. The third group is "people with serious genetic disorders that are not amenable to other modes of prevention like genetic screening—because maybe the specific mutation isn't known or many different genes are involved—and who still want to have their own biological child" (Talbot). While some interviews have discovered egotistical people wishing to clone themselves and have perfect copies, the uses described would empower couples, offering them increased reproductive options, much as in vitro once did.

> In the years since Dolly, public discussions of cloning have shifted away from the specter of multiple human replicants to less disturbing possibilities, like the creation of genetically identical tissue grown for people with Parkinson's and other diseases. The initial revulsion at the very notion of cloning—what bioethicists call the "yuck factor"—has dwindled as more mammals have been cloned and as the prospect of someday replicating household pets seems to render the whole concept somehow cuter and more benign. Legislative efforts to ban cloning for reproductive purposes have stalled—only four states (California, Rhode Island, Louisiana, and Michigan) have passed laws against it—and the federal moratorium merely precludes government money from going to it [Talbot].

Artificially cloning really does represent a world in which women would be needed to bear the children, but men would be wholly unnecessary. Not everyone sees this as a triumph. Stephen Garrard Post, author of "The Judeo-Christian Ethic Opposes Cloning," argues that his religion emphasizes moral growth through experience, and fears cloning would place too much emphasis on genetics. There's also mankind's obsession with "designer babies" (156). He worries that children would be regarded as less miraculous and that men would become obsolete: "Removing male impregnators from the procreative DYAD would simply drive the nail into the coffin of fatherhood, unless one thinks that biological and social fatherhood are utterly disconnected. Social fatherhood would still be possible in a world of clones, but this will lack the feature of participation in a continued biological lineage that seems to strengthen social fatherhood in general" (Post 155).

Further, people might steal DNA from celebrities and use it without consent. In fact, cloning is tied to eugenics—creating a superior child while leaving nothing to chance. "There is the power of one generation over the external form of another, imposing the vicissitudes of one generation's fleeting image of the good upon the nature and destiny of the next. One need only peruse the innumerable texts on eugenics written by American geneticists in the 1920s to understand the arrogance of such visions" (Post 155). Certainly, Brightborn and DYAD's ruthlessness reveal the worst of the process, while Kira's miraculous healing represents the best. The scientists' deliberate alteration of the Ledas to make them infertile also leaves them terminally ill—emphasizing the hubris of playing God and the unforeseen problems that result.

Science, pure discovery, fueled the creation of the Ledas on the show, as Ethan Duncan describes the reason for their creation as proof of concept. Of course, he made his daughters infertile under the best of intentions—containing his experiment. This revelation emphasizes scientists' ethical duties, though his have terribly harmed his subjects. "The impression sometimes created among the public is that scientists are working away in their labs and maybe they're not always thinking about the implications of their work," Jennifer Doudna, a prominent genetic scientist at the University of California, Berkeley, says. "But we are" (Lepore).

> Understandably, it bothers Doudna that, in science fiction, scientists are very often sinister. That's not entirely true of *Orphan Black*, where there are big-hearted scientists and evil scientists, in roughly equal number. Still, what's most startling about the show isn't its interest in science; it's its interest in women. "You began menstruation very young," a DYAD doctor tells Sarah, who submits to a medical examination after DYAD captures her daughter. Sarah, alone among the clones, is fertile. "You are all barren by design," Ethan Duncan explains to Cosima. The series, which takes as its subject a field of research that led to the development both of several forms of contraception and of infertility treatment, is obsessed with female reproductive organs. On television, women don't usually play grownup human beings; they play slightly oversize children, helpless and pouty, driven by appetites they can't possibly understand. At the show's surfeit of interesting, adult females, the mind reels [Lepore].

Building a flaw into the clones so they can't reproduce represents the patriarchy's cruel control over their subjects. It can also stress how artificial humanity is becoming: "By the late twentieth century ... we are all chimeras, theorized and fabricated hybrids of machine and organism" (Haraway 150). Though Rachel analytically responds that the experiment needs to be limited, she's obviously deeply hurt that her father so destroyed her life. Of course, the accidental flaw that's killing the Ledas emphasizes that one shouldn't mess with Mother Nature—one small change can have surprising side effects.

Science versus Religion

Cosima Herter, the science advisor, offers insights intended to refine and deepen the themes and the narrative, showing how science interacts with society, and discouraging simplistic dualities—pointing out, for example, "that religion and science are constantly intermingled throughout history" (Newton). She adds that having Clone Cosima, the "most hard-boiled empiricist" undergo "what may be a near-death experience" at season two's end was a way of allowing the character to "step back from her belief that hard science is the only method of revealing the mysteries of life and existence" and of encouraging everyone to consider "whether there is more to our existence than mere biochemical configurations" (Newton). She comments:

> Another avenue we explored this season [three] had to do with whether or not science and spirituality (or religion) necessarily operate in entirely separate domains of human activity. That is to say, if science is generally described as the domain of facts and rationality, then spirituality is often hostilely described as an exercise in irrational leaps of faith. But when confronted with grave illness and death, it's not uncommon for the lines between these two domains to become blurred. In these scenarios staunch defenders of a "science-only" approach to understanding the nature of humanity and health often begin to question whether or not science can actually offer answers to the more mystical questions about life and meaning more generally. So while science is indeed a required component in healing the Clones' bodies, it does not necessarily provide a salve to soothe the ruptures in their understanding of themselves as living beings who are clearly more than a simple sum of their biological parts [Herter, "Nature vs. Nurture"].

Though an atheist, Herter is critical of the science-religion duality that's emerged in Western culture. Many early scientific practices emerged from religion, and even now many scientists have deep-seated beliefs. Some of their faith-based questions about identity and truth have driven many great discoveries. She too understands the issues, "especially as somebody who is not religious, who is very much an atheist. At the end of the day I will put my faith in science more than I will put my faith in God, but I will also recognize that it doesn't have all the answers" (Newton).

Science and religion pull at each other through the show. Helena is raised by religious fundamentalists who see all the Neolutionists do as sacrilege. The Proletheans appear a force of evil themselves, brainwashing Helena with pure lies and religious dogma. Under their care, she becomes a murderer in the name of God, quoting Bible verses as she slaughters her sisters. Tomas the true believer has lied to her, insisting she's a monster yet using her as his instrument. By contrast, Henrik is portrayed as more of a hypocrite, quoting and rewriting stories to his own ends. Using this dogma, he forces all the women of the compound to carry his children, including his own daughter. His sect of Proletheans actually blend science and religion. Real Cosima notes, "I loved the Johanssen character—his religion is steered through the science at MIT. Because again, religion and science are not separate. There are very, very, very religious people who are also brilliant scientists" (Newton).

His status as a cult leader emphasizes that he uses both science and religion to fuel his personal power—in the wrong hands, both are immoral.

> In January 1998, Richard Seed, a physicist in Chicago, announced that he planned to open a clinic to clone humans. He wasn't affiliated with any sort of reputable research facility and had no funding. If you dig into Seed's history you'll find that, outside of his Ph.D. in physics from Harvard, he had founded a company in the 1970s that specialized in transferring embryos in cattle, and later attempted and failed to found a venture using the same technique in humans. If this doesn't remind you in the slightest of *Orphan Black*'s Henrik Johanssen, the Prolethean religious extremist whose first episode shows him artificially inseminating a cow, then allow us to direct you to what Seed said in an NPR interview in 1997: "God intended for man to become one with God. Cloning is the first serious step in becoming one with God" [Griffin and Nesseth].

Henrik similarly pronounces, "You see, I steered my faith through science at MIT, and what I see here is God opening a whole new door" ("Governed by Sound Reason and True Religion" 202) While Richard Seed made a few big media appearances, nothing appeared to come of his claims.

All religion is not condemned, however. "Nearer My God to Thee" plays for Mark and Gracie's sweet chapel wedding. Interspersed with this are scenes of Helena entering a military plane and seeing her second Castor, while Sarah sees another training. All three scenes are framed as moments of enlightenment, connection, initiation into secrets. The song, echoing religious salvation, can also be ironic as someone has played God to make the clones. Gracie herself is framed as a good person as she prays and cares for others—it's her love for Mark that makes her vulnerable to exploitation. Later, Helena finds her way to her surrogate mother Sister Irina for sanctuary when she's pregnant. For several episodes, she lives in the convent in peace and contentment until the Neolutionists tear her away.

Kira is framed as the angel of the series, bringing divine intervention to save Cosima from death at the end of season two, and to save Sarah midway through season three and at the beginning of season five. Both women, like Alison in the fourth season, suffer from a lack of faith. However, Kira's appearance, surrounded by a warm golden aura, reaffirms that there is more to life than material experience. Helena, who shares Kira's sensitivity, actually arrives in response to Alison's prayer and vanquishes her enemies with a bow and arrow. Likewise, when Alison's sisters save Donnie from death in prison, she throws herself into her performance of *Jesus Christ: Superstar* with a new heartfelt devotion and joy—her prayers have literally been answered. All these moments highlight the importance of faith and the unknowable, even as the woman surmount their creators' original plan and imposed limitations.

Just as religion on the show isn't purely exploitative, science isn't purely altruistic. The real Cosima explains that religion has wrought intolerance and violence, but "we are equally and often as oppressed and exploited and done violence to by science. We forget that anything that we give explicit and uncontrollable authority to has a power to be oppressive and violent and is often used for these purposes. Science is not neutral and we endow it with authority by calling something that is science neutral because then you give it a power to be whatever anybody wants it to be. You've invested it with its own supernatural status" (Newton). Through the five-year arc, corporations work with the cloners, adapting the technology to create vast fortunes, even as the armed forces militarize the Castors. Rachel and Ferdinand want power; the Duncans, scientific acclaim; Westmorland, a personal cure; Henrik, superior children; and Evie, basically all of these. Through their selfish approach to advancement, all become the story's villains.

Following the path of corruption, Leekie has his own disciples, as he comments, "Oh, my "freaky-Leekies" as they've been dubbed in the media. It was once asked what my perfect human would look like. I offhandedly suggested silver-gray hair and one white eye" ("Variations Under Domestication" 106). He need only mention a whim and all his devotees rush to modify their bodies to match it. Similarly, Westmorland's island is revealed as a cult of science, one that has true believers as murderous and misguided as the Proletheans—religion is not the only path to giving away one's power of reason. True science is less about cultism, but, like religion, comes from a place of not knowing the answers. It's the individuals who must decide whether to use it to benefit others or to exploit them.

Characters as Feminist Embodiments

Sarah the Punk

"Sisterhood, as understood in the Seventies, is truly dead when *Orphan Black* begins. Women are not there to help each other anymore" (Berns and Aguilar 148). The only friend Sarah has is her foster brother, and soon a clueless Art and Raj at the precinct. Angie, meanwhile, regards her with deep suspicion. When a woman in the restroom offers to help Sarah with her gun, she's actually joking. "This scene, together with the initial complete distrust among the clones at the beginning of the same episode when meeting each other, formulates a scenario of total individualism among women" (Berns and Aguilar 148). Sarah, however, reaches out to the other clones and slowly creates a true sisterhood, far beyond Beth's distant alliance.

> Sarah and her sisters form a bond which resembles the sisterhood of the 1970s, even with their many differences (of class of sexuality and nationhood), the different clones bond together to battle oppression, here metamorphosized in those who want to imprison or kill them all as a way to interrupt this confederacy of female clones. As can be seen, years have passed since the Seventies but society is still trying to interrupt or backlash sisterhood [Berns and Aguilar 145].

Her first line is "shit," after which she must apologize to the family sitting near her, a way of signaling the audience that this won't be a child-friendly program. "We really wanted an antihero. An ass-kicking antihero. Someone with a lot of armor," the creators explain ("Send in the Clones"). As female punks mocked romance, suburbia, masculinity, and society's expectations of young women, Sarah does the same. She and Felix say rude things about Alison's sphere whenever they approach it. The men she knows are thuggish "Vic the Dick," whom she gets the better of in every encounter, and rebellious, nontraditional Felix. She always takes the lead as the tough one, rejecting Paul's attempts to rescue her.

The real punk inspiration goes to Sarah's mother. Graeme Manson told Maria Doyle Kennedy (Siobhan), that punk icon Patti Smith was the "original inspiration" for her complicated and controversial character. "She's a huge beacon for me, so that sealed the deal," the actress notes (Gelman, "*Orphan Black* Preview"). "We grew up during the 'peace and love' of the 1960s, only to discover that there are wars everywhere and love and romance is a con," Viv Albertine, once the guitarist for British punk band the Slits, writes (qtd. in Jaffe).

Still, Siobhan's battle is largely done, until threats to Kira and Sarah make her reclaim the mantle. It's Sarah who's the angry rebel. Sarah's clash with her mother also echoes the clash between second and the next generation's third wave feminism. As a 1989 *Time Magazine* article explained: "To the young, the movement that loudly rejected female stereotypes seems hopelessly dated. The long, ill-fated battle for the Equal Rights Amendment means nothing to young women who already assume they will be treated as equals. Feminist leaders like Gloria Steinem and Molly Yard, president of the National Organization for Women, are dismissed as out of touch" (Wallis). Teens of the nineties took the previous generation's struggle for granted. "The third wave pushed back against their 'mothers' (with grudging gratitude) the way children push away from their parents in order to achieve much needed independence. This wave supports equal rights, but does not have a term like feminism to articulate that notion. For third wavers, struggles are more individual: 'We don't need feminism anymore'" (Rampton).

One proud third-waver, interviewed in *The F-Word: Feminism in Jeopardy: Women, Politics, and the Future*, notes, "We thought the second wave was boring and dull for 'fighting the patriarchy' but maybe we should be keeping our eye more on the 'patriarchy,' particularly with all the changes coming from the White House" (Rowe-Finkbeiner 105). To Sarah, battling the corporations that claim power over her is a constant struggle. "Embodying the hard-won successes of previous generations, the third wave expands the fight against social hierarchies, moving it past American borders, with a focus on global feminism" (Rowe-Finkbeiner 90). Fighting these hierarchies is Sarah's fundamental goal through the series.

Sarah Jaffe describes the movement in her "Why Feminism Needs Punk": "They sang about being young, broke, and frustrated as the welfare state crumbled around them; the world owed them a living, but it thought they ought to be grateful for scraps. They wanted more and made do with less." Indeed, Sarah's quest through the first few episodes is money—enough for a new life with Kira. She's willing to deal coke and cheat mobsters, to say nothing of taking over another woman's life. Sarah's never had a university education, a real house of her own, a nuclear family. Like many punk rockers, she's edgy and angry at all life hasn't granted her.

Punk in the United Kingdom was born on the edge of Thatcherism, in that transitional time when you could still survive on art-school grants and the dole, and live in a squat and spend all your spare money on guitars and artfully destroyed clothing made by Vivienne Westwood. Although at the time punk roared across the country and beyond, the conditions that caused it to thrive no longer exist either in the United Kingdom or the United States—cities have grown more expensive, the welfare state has shriveled—and the world looks even crueler now than it did when punks spat at it in the seventies. At the end of the "peace and love" years, Albertine writes, it seemed like everything was a con, that politics didn't serve the working class, that "success" was a scam and that the best response was to try to shock the world into action. Today, austerity policies and rapid gentrification in New York, London, and other big cities have left working-class kids struggling to survive; post–Reagan/Thatcher politics is mostly filled with bipartisan debates about what to slash. Rebellion remains necessary [Jaffe].

Sarah grew up in the foster system, adopted by S. at age eight and brought to Canada at age twelve. The term "orphan black" refers to a "child in the black," or an orphan in hiding from the black market. This was Sarah's childhood as Neolution searched for her, and though she doesn't know it, they still seek to control her. She's never had roots or (it's implied) a steady relationship. Feeling abandoned, she abandons her family in turn.

Her actress explains, "What's central to her is this inner conflict she has about motherhood: her daughter Kira is her entire life and yet she doesn't feel like she's fit to be a mother. It's key that Sarah is adopted, too. She was never really part of a family, so she sees herself as a solo act. She has difficulty being intimate with people and she always feels like an outsider" (Elan). This certainly comes out in her relationships. In episode one she aggressively seduces Paul, climbing on top of him. In the next episode, Paul charms and teases her but she refuses to confide in him. Later, Paul apologizes for scaring her and Sarah turns on the aggressive charm. "How sorry are you?" she asks archly. Referencing the shower, she tells him "get in" ("Conditions of Existence" 105). She'll respond to flirtation but not to real intimacy. In fact, she spends most of the season avoiding telling Paul the truth, wanting to trust him but holding back. Her actress explains, "Every part of her distrusts what a family is, what intimacy is, what somebody loving you unconditionally is. It just doesn't compute for her" ("Send in the Clones").

Maslany explains, "I love playing her most; she's my homegirl. There's something primal about her, and listening to the Prodigy's 'Breathe' helped me get into character" (Elan). In the nineties, when Sarah would have been a teen, there were other punk inspirations beyond "Breathe": Riot Grrrl bands were "bursting out of an alternative music scene with a 'do-it-yourself' ethos that was anticorporate and pro-grrrl" (Rowe-Finkbeiner 85). A new generation was rebelling, emphasizing a new third wave feminist spirit. "The more recent incarnations of punk—scenes in places like Boston and Minneapolis with ties to activist communities in the 1990s and 2000s—helped keep left ideas alive in dark times, helped bring a (perhaps smaller) generation of activists to causes like the fight against the World Trade Organization, and helped lay the groundwork for the explosive movements of the past few years" (Jaffe).

Of course, when she joins the Clone Club, she transforms it. Though Beth and Cosima were quietly running investigations while Helena murdered clones and Alison refused to participate, Sarah the matriarch and rebel forges her three new sisters into a fighting force and confronts DYAD's leaders directly. Manson adds, "What I really dig is the spark of Sarah. The spark of Sarah is that amid all of this marshaling of the science, amid all of this control, all of this projection of power, to create a world in your vision or that serves you, that Sarah is chance, Sarah is contingency. That nature in its diversity can adapt, can mutate, and it can bring you down" (Griffin and Nesseth). She shakes up the existing dynamic, even as the punk movement did. Jaffe explains, "Feminism today could use a punk moment. It has become buttoned-up and sanitized, in thrall to capitalist ideals of success and the endless rehashing of narrow debates." Like the clones before Sarah, modern feminism is nonconfrontational, awaiting a jolt.

In fact, Sarah's anti-corporate stance is very third-wave, as she fixes problems through leverage and subversion, not legalities. "The essence of third-wave philosophy, though hard to pin down, is that real social change is achieved indirectly through cultural action, or simply carried out through pop culture twists and transformations, instead of through an overtly political, electoral, and legislative agenda" (Rowe-Finkbeiner 88). Engaged in a private war with DYAD, she blackmails, extorts, and threatens, and then finally reveals their crimes to the public. She ends the series by beating Westmorland, the ultimate patriarch, with a fire hydrant, killing him.

> From the beginning of the series, John and Graeme did not want Sarah to be a killer. And if you think about the five seasons, she does not murder anyone directly. They were saving that moment for PTW and for the finale. They didn't want us rooting for a killer during the show's time on-air and they succeeded. And really, once he started to shoot up and kill random doctors at whim, it was time he was put to rest [BBC Staff, "Episode 10"].

This conflict propels Sarah onto an older path—not only a rebel but a woman struggling for freedom. In "By Means Which Have Never Yet Been Tried" (210), Cosima tells her, "You're the wild type, Sarah. You propagate against all odds. You know, you're restless. You survive." In this way, she echoes the classic woman of science fiction. Sarah breaks gender stereotypes, and as she does, she aligns herself firmly with Haraway's boundary-shattering cyborg. Haraway's cyborg is not a rejection of nature, but an augmentation of it—the rebellious rule-breaker. "Nature herself becomes a coyote trickster figure, an active participant in humanity's technoscientific investigations and not at all the passive resource and recipient of human construction previously presumed" (Thweatt-Bates 29). In Haraway's view, "cyborg women refuse to stay neatly put in their appointed universal category of Woman, universal Man's Other" (Thweatt-Bates 89).

While she shatters boundaries, Sarah also accepts responsibility. At first, Sarah doesn't dream of suburbia, but flight—taking her daughter and Felix (but not her mother) and running off into the wilderness or to an exotic location. Her actress says, "She's lived really hard, she's had to survive, she's had to manipulate people, she's had to hurt people knowingly, she's had to leave people, leave her daughter, she runs away from everything" ("Send in the Clones"). Nonetheless, season one sees her finally accepting responsibility and staying. When Cal offers to flee to Reykjavik with their little family, Sarah resists, telling him "it's not that easy" because "there are other people involved" ("Knowledge of Causes, and Secret Motion of Things" 207). She's become part of a family and society. She sends her daughter there in season three but stays behind herself to fight in London. Fawcett says, "She's a character who has made a lot of wrong choices and is now trying to set things straight, make amends, and trying to be a better mother to her daughter" ("Send in the Clones").

The final season has her following this pattern once again—sending Kira away but taking the fight to the enemy. In the final episode, she considers her first season plan, but at last chooses to stay with her extended family and build a stable life. Manson concludes: "We were asking that question, 'Well, what does freedom look like to Sarah?' And freedom to Sarah is accepting her role as a mother, it's accepting the death of her mother, it's accepting this family, and it's the ability to stay in place" (Ross, "Series Finale"). Fawcett adds that in an unusually happy moment for the show, "The last thing that they're going to do is they're going to go as a family down to the beach, and actually just go to the beach and enjoy the day" (Ross, "Series Finale"). Maslany concludes:

> I think in that moment where they're going to the beach, she's maybe shedding some of the guilt of her past, and this pain, and these things that have held her down, and have made her also want to run, and not be part of this family, and kind of abandon everybody. Not that I think she's going to be perfect, by any means, but she's let a little bit of happiness into her life, and I think that's a huge success for Sarah [Ross, "Tatiana Maslany"].

Notably, she does not end the series with a conventional marriage. "There can be severe formal constraints, as in paranormal romance or epic fantasy, where even relatively empowered/active female characters are relegated to traditional heteronormative endings and/or subjected to the dictates of the male gaze" (Helford et al.). Both she and Helena end safely, raising their children among a support network of sisters, cousins, and loved ones, open to their romantic interests returning, but hardly requiring them. This stresses their independence and validates nontraditional family groupings. Sarah may have settled down but she's hardly a conformist. Swearing, toting a stack of beers, and intending to fish in the wildlife-free "Shite Lake," she takes Kira and Felix on an outing that's less than family-friendly but perfectly herself.

Sarah's Matrifocal Family

Sarah was the mother of the Judeo-Christian religion. Now the show's Sarah is almost the only clone who can reproduce, who quickly becomes the defender of her people. The Old Testament Sarah was thought to be barren but eventually bore a son. Since she shattered biological rules by having a child at ninety, Sarah Manning, her namesake, echoes her equally magical biology. Her last name, Manning, suggests strength and her mission—to "man up" and assume responsibility. It also emphasizes her hybrid nature. Manson says of Sarah, "We always knew that she was the outside, the black sheep, that she would be the one who's different from the others somehow" (Bernstein 35).

A family lives together and has ties of blood or adoption (more than Sarah originally suspected!) and interacts based on their social positions like mother and daughter. The nuclear family of Siobhan, Felix, Sarah, and Kira does this, with their family roles governing their social interactions and larger arcs in the story, as S. and Sarah face down villains to protect Kira, and Felix supports all of Sarah's risky investigations. Sarah begins the story having run away but spends much of it hiding and fleeing with Siobhan or Felix, forced to move back in with them for protection.

Felix's flat is artsy and unconventional, a celebration of sex and inner-city creativity. S.'s home has warm golden light, old furniture with knick-knacks, toys and hand-me-downs, photos on the fridge—all suggest a safe welcoming place filled with history. The clones find a refuge there, as they behave like actual sisters. Siobhan mothers and comforts Alison, and Felix supports his new batch of sisters' crazy schemes. Grace retreats there for comfort, and Kira grows up in its space, as Felix and Sarah once did.

Sarah, Siobhan, Felix, and Kira live in a fatherless family that's very modern, some observers might remark. Anthropologists, however, might tie it to the oldest of matriarchal clan groupings. In these societies, a few of which still exist around the world, women "can have sex with a variety of partners of their choosing—but conversely, they're not treated as 'sluts.'" (Hamilton). Sarah in particular shows off this freedom.

Kira's father is immaterial—in fact, S. and Felix have given up hope of ever knowing. They, the grandmother and the matriarchal uncle, are the ones to help raise the child, not the biological father. Further, when Cal appears, no one, including him, pressures Sarah to marry him or references Kira's illegitimacy. He does not end the series with Sarah (though they could potentially reunite). Manson concludes of both Sarah and Helena's unfulfilled romances, "At the end of the day, when we were boiling it down with Tatiana [Maslany], it was like, these girls' story does not need to be supported by a male romantic interest. The tightening and the closing down and the finishing of these women, it's about a sisterhood, motherhood and family" (Gelman, "*Orphan Black* Boss").

"Among the Khasi of northeast India, matrilocality (the practice of children living with the mother's family or clan) eliminates economic free fall or a jarring move if parents divorce. "No matter how many times the woman marries, her children will always remain with her," says Patricia Mukhim, a Khasi and editor of *The Shillong Times*. "And even if a man abandons a woman he has impregnated, the children are never 'illegitimate'" (Hamilton). "Often the terms matrilineal (descent through the mother's rather than the father's line) or matrifocal (a family structure centered on a woman and her adult daughters) are used rather than matriarchal, because few scholars assert that women historically subordinated men" (Crosby 241). While Sarah and Felix don't take their foster mother's name, Kira takes Sarah's, and they all live with Siobhan. They soon induct new family members—not only Cosima, Alison, and Helena, but also, to lesser degrees, Gracie, Charlotte, Rachel, Tony, M.K., and Krystal.

> In many ways, the Clone Club throughout *Orphan Black* functions as a tribe. There are rites of initiation of sorts (the giving of the phone, the introduction to the others, and the common experience of the unraveling of identity; this last "rite" is one of the reasons that Rachel will always be other than the tribe, as a self-aware clone she never experienced this unraveling), as well as fierce loyalty and sacrifice for the other members of the tribe [Heuslein 79].

Sarah and Kira drift from S.'s home to Felix's—more matriarchal culture based in communal living. Likewise, Alison and Donnie have adopted their own children. Helena appoints S. her babies' grandmother, Gracie their aunt, and Felix her own brother-sestra, emphasizing the legitimacy of created bonds. "Ultimately, the blood and chosen family units created by the clones queer the normative family structure that does not appear in *Orphan Black*. Instead, they repeatedly create and re-create their own non-normative structures" (Wright 118).

Another nonnormative, non-hierarchical power appears in Sarah's daughter. Little Kira's emerging magic of a sort—healing and an intuitive connection that binds the sisters, is the opposite of the scientific DYAD, always monitoring and quantifying. Since she is the miracle child of this matriarchy, unexpected and unplanned by DYAD, she represents the feminine power of love and togetherness defying the system. Her powers are innate, childlike, unquantifiable, feminine. Over and over, Kira argues for love and sympathy between the clone sisters, even Rachel, as she warns of danger with her heightened intuition.

"The name 'Kira' returns us to the word 'kyriarchy' and the sovereign role that childbearing is forced to play in the lives of women. To retain her status as a woman, as mother, Sarah *must* try to retain Kira in what almost seems like an expression of ideology" (Keegan). The term emphasizes the patriarchy's restricting minorities in many categories (ableism, racism...), and certainly, Sarah's five-year quest involves battling the corporation that has wounded all the Ledas, treats them as property, and oppresses them with their full corporate and legal might. Using legal trickery, force of arms, and extortion, DYAD tries to operate on and imprison the Ledas, as well as stealing Kira away. They most value Sarah and Helena for their ability to bear children in a patriarchal dismissal of all their skills, save that one. Only by defeating the Kyriarchy can Sarah fulfil her destiny and create the family she chooses.

> The message *Orphan Black* conveys about familial structures is simple: blood families are abusive and chosen families are full of love. The few examples of blood families are either violent (Kendall Malone murdered Siobhan's husband) or remove the child's agency (Henrik Johanssen implanting Gracie with Helena's eggs without their consent). The chosen families are met with favor even if they are violent in nature [Wright 126].

When Cal offers Sarah his own home and a nuclear family arrangement, she's tempted, but they soon go on the run again and all falls apart. Among the Trobriand Islanders, the word "father" translates something like "outsider"—the mother's husband brought into the clan from outside (Reed 347). Many matriarchal cultures include segregation between the nursing mother and child and the father, who might leave them alone for as much as five years (Reed 140). In this way, Cal, though not by choice, is banished from Kira's formative years, leaving her to Sarah to raise. It's implied the Jesse-Helena relationship will run a similar course, after Helena has killed Henrik, the biological father of her babies.

While the Ledas are instantly welcomed as sisters, boyfriends Paul, Jesse, and Cal are kept at more of a distance, as the dance party, imagined baby shower, dinner party, gallery opening, and final baby shower are reserved for the sisters and those belonging to Sarah's matriarchal family—Kira, Felix, and S. first and soon the additions of Art, Scott, Hell-Wizard, Adele, Delphine, and Donnie—all of whom support the women's storylines and quests. Even Donnie adopts his wife's family name and shop and finally helps raise Helena's babies, emphasizing his acceptance of matriarchal culture.

Felix and Art: Cultural Feminists

> The emerging fourth wavers are not just reincarnations of their second wave grandmothers; they bring to the discussion important perspectives taught by third wave feminism. They speak in terms of intersectionality whereby women's suppression can only fully be understood in a context of the marginalization of other groups and genders—feminism is part of a larger consciousness of oppression along with racism, ageism, classism, abelism, and sexual orientation (no "ism" to go with that). Among the third wave's bequests is the importance of inclusion, an acceptance of the sexualized human body as non-threatening, and the role the internet can play in gender-bending and leveling hierarchies.—Rampton.

"The supposed 'first rule' of Clone Club is that outsiders are not welcome, a situation that resembles traditional sisterhood. Sisterhood was very suspicious of those considered as not-feminists, especially men, because they were viewed as part of the oppression" (Berns and Aguilar 148). However, Felix is gay, Art is Black, and Raj is Indian. "As minorities, they are closer to the feelings of the sisterhood as oppressed women" (Berns and Aguilar 149). All become confidantes of the Clone Club. Scott, though white and heterosexual, is a geeky misfit. In "Guillotines Decide" (508), as the series ends, Cosima tells Felix, "You are one of our best guys. Along with Donnie and Scott and Art."

Felix is the cultural feminist, who supports women's path to power. "It was cool to feel so unselfconscious in my own femininity," said Gavaris (Nguyen, "Orphan Black Cast"). This movement emerged in the 1980s, in part as a reaction to popular liberal feminism, which emphasized the similarities between genders in order to argue for equal treatment and make the law gender-neutral. Cultural, or cultural difference feminism, fought for equality, but emphasized the differences between the sexes. It held that gender-neutrality harmed women "whether by impelling them to imitate men, by depriving society of their distinctive contributions, or by letting them participate in society only on terms that favor men" (Grande 3).

> Cultural feminists claimed the existence of an "essential" female culture that was fundamentally different from and at odds with male culture. According to many radical feminists, as cultural feminism became "the dominant tendency within the women's liberation movement," it "threatened to transform feminism from a political movement to a lifestyle movement." The rise of cultural feminism also disturbed many equal rights feminists who objected to any definition of feminism that promoted the concept of "innate differences" between women and men. As many an equal rights feminist understood and feared, a previous generation of

social feminists had embraced this view of womanhood and had used it to justify the passage of protective labor legislation that equal rights feminists had fought long and hard to overturn [Berkeley 103].

Carol Gilligan, especially, advocated for women and men receiving different treatment based on different skills and value systems. According to Gilligan, women's morality is shaped by an "ethic of care" as opposed to more traditional and masculine principles of justice and rights. Cultural feminism suggests the importance of equity, not necessarily equality, whether "entirely imposed on women by nature or culture or entirely chosen by women through creative political exertions" (Jensen 2). The Clone Club certainly devotes itself to care and comfort, based on each of their different needs. The main provider of this is Felix, who finds a date for lovelorn Cosima, reconnects Sarah with her family, convinces Helena to trust the team, and supports Alison through catty friends, rehab, and theater. His boundary-breaking allows him to shatter the clones' self-delusions. "He gets all the best lines and he provides a bit of levity to an otherwise very dark script," his actor Jordan Gavaris notes ("Insiders: Felix"). When Alison is horrified by an intervention, Felix proves he can play catty with the best of them:

> ALISON: Felix, what am I gonna do?
> FELIX: Put your chin up, be a woman. This is backstabbing 101.
> ALISON: I cannot go back out there.
> FELIX: Of course you can. You're gonna face the music, eat some humble pie, hug it out, play possum, Aynsley's gonna think she's won, and you are gonna live to fight another day ["Unconscious Selection" 109].

Garvis comments, "The Alison/Felix relationship is shiny. It's attractive because it's funny and light, and it's a reprieve from the heavy scenes that are recurrent in the show" (Bernstein 52). He soon becomes a brother to each of the clones in his own way. Felix's place becomes the default hideout for anyone in trouble—Sarah fleeing her family, Alison fleeing suburbia, Cosima fleeing heartbreak, all of them fleeing the police. His unconventional lifestyle (down to bead curtain, art, and sliding door) emphasizes that the women needn't be normal or perfect around him—they can simply be. Her actor adds:

> They all offer me something different. Alison offers me the opportunity to showcase the comedic side of Felix, the lighter side that has silliness. He finds her quite amusing and the situations that she gets herself into are often quite amusing. I think Sarah offers the opportunity to be very raw and real and the theatrics. She talks in a different register. Cosima offers a new relationship, which is always exciting [Ross, "Jordan Gavaris"].

He connects with Rachel quite differently—at their first meeting, she attacks him while dressed as Sarah. In their second, Fawcett considers how far Felix has been pushed to threaten Rachel the frightening matriarch in

"Community of Dreadful Fear and Hate" (307): "Everyone's wound up—Sarah's been missing. We don't normally do this, but we came into this episode five or six days later, and Sarah's been missing. And Felix is very distraught about that and really feels like he's at the end of his rope. I think for Jordan, it was just a good chance to show how close he is to his sister and how much he cares about Sarah and how far he's willing to go" (Ross, "Twerktastic Episode"). Felix is the one to run interference one last time in the finale, meeting her outside Helena's baby shower to give her news of her sisters and wish her a good life, such as it is. While he appears to forgive her for Siobhan's death, he draws clear lines for her interaction with the others, warning her she must remain apart for the good of them all. Maslany adds: "The two of them are on such opposite sides. One of them always seeking to protect the clones, and the other always seeking to control and own them. But there's something about Felix's empathy for her and Rachel's openness in that moment that it's kind of leveling" (Ross, "Tatiana Maslany").

While he can also relate well to Siobhan, he's the only one Sarah completely trusts. "Used to look out for Felix when we were kids ... after a fashion," Sarah thinks in the comics (*The Clone Club* #1: Sarah). Manson explains, "Felix is Sarah's rock. And they're the closest either of them have to real family" ("Insiders: Felix"). Felix and Sarah understand each other, to the point where they're tolerant and supportive of the worst behavior—drugs, casual hookups, and harmful relationships. They learn to support each other through it all, since they are each other's closest family. "She drives him crazy, as she drives anyone crazy, but he's fiercely loyal. And he'll stand up for her to anybody," his actor explains ("Insiders: Felix"). Wil Wheaton describes him as "the best brother a girl could have, especially if you're the type of girl who needs a body identified at the morgue ... or a place to hide from an abusive drug dealer boyfriend, or a babysitter slash bartender, or a person to infiltrate a club of body augmentation enthusiasts."

As the series goes on, Felix is called in to handle many of the clones—especially outsiders Tony and Krystal—using his communication skills. In fact, he finds ways to relate to each, instantly seeing through Krystal's conspiracy theories or Tony's confrontational posturing. Surprisingly quickly, he gains each of their trust, though both are more hesitant about Sarah and her Clone Club. In the circumstances, Felix is "Clone Club light," a way to help without fully committing. Since the Ledas offer the new clones such an option, they emphasize alternate paths to safety and autonomy. This celebration of difference lies at the heart of cultural feminism. "A new feminism would expand the notion of equality of rights to encompass the equality or sameness that makes more intensive unions possible and would remind us that difference is secured by freedom, grounding the notion of difference in the spirit of differentiation that protects it" (Jensen 8).

"Even the arguments made by early liberals on behalf of community as an association of equals take into account the thirst for distinction as part and parcel of our lives" (Jensen 5). This distinction also applies to himself as Felix frames himself as unique. Felix means happy but is linked with the sneaky, clever Felix the Cat. "That sort of hottie attitude is how he survives," Garvis adds ("Clone Club Insiders"). His art-filled home in downtown is the perfect representation of counter-culture, contrasted with Alison, Beth, and Siobhan's tidy "normal" homes where they bring up families. Signs proclaim "Steam Baths" and skewed crowned men's heads stress personal autonomy. A smiling cuddly figure popping from a stereo likewise suggests a happy good time. A figure who might be Sarah watches it all in mild amusement. Inside is exposed brick, lots of light, a corkboard covered in pictures. Felix can often be found unapologetically underdressed or engaged in unusual activities (like cooking in only an apron while flirting with his latest fling). Manson explains, "He's an outsider. He's not a character that you get to see portrayed on TV very much" ("Insiders: Felix"). He adds, "Gavaris found that playing Felix Dawkins wasn't only about putting on a really great accent. He also was able to let go of his preconceived notions of how he was supposed to act, feel or like, according to his gender."

The transgression of gothic can be used to explore gay, lesbian, and transgender lifestyles. "Its tendency to interrogate mainstream conventions and versions of reality make it admirably suited" (394). Felix's clubbing takes him into the dark underbelly of society, and even to a party with surgically altered believers. It suggests the forbidden, the relationship one must hide from the everyday world. "As long as the gothic continues to be an ambivalent cultural form, one that half-opens the closet door to the dark social anxieties relating to sexual desire, it will always be queer" (537). Ironically, Felix is welcome to introduce himself as gay, even in front of the church group—it's Alison's clones who must be kept hidden.

"The common culture of rights teaches human beings to respect each other and to accommodate themselves to one another" (Jensen 8). This Felix does constantly, though he finally reaches a breaking point. When they meet Cal, Kira's father, Felix loses his cool, accepting attitude. He's always been Kira's only father figure, and now he doesn't fit into the nuclear family Sarah briefly creates. "But Uncle Felix isn't going to be babysitting while you negotiate custody," he tells her, then actually breaks down in tears. "There's no place for me here" ("Mingling Its Own Nature with It" 203). He goes instead to Alison, who says she needs him.

In season four, Felix insists he's looking for his biological family—he wants more than being the sidekick and tagalong as Sarah discovers S. is her biological relation and she forms a nuclear family with Cal. In "The Stigmata of Progress" (403), Sarah meets Adele, who has a Southern accent and was hoping Sarah was the drug seller. "She is so bloody cool! Okay, you are gonna think she's amazing. She's a lawyer. Or she was, but there's some kind of, like, 'disbarment' situation or something, so she's…" Felix babbles. Sarah is less impressed. Worse yet, Felix refuses to help Clone Club since he's bonding with his new sister. Nonetheless, Felix the intermediary and Siobhan the matriarch induct Adele into Clone Club too. In "Let the Children & the Childbearers Toil" (504), Adele and Felix head to Switzerland to work on her specialty—tracking patent-hoarding corporations and global profit flows. With this, they find a vital piece of the puzzle.

They return triumphantly in "Guillotines Decide" (508) just in time for Felix's gallery show. "This is my first show in two years; I'm not gonna have any kind of sestra shenanigans," he insists. Once again, he's doing something that's all about him … but once again, it's tied up in the clone drama as his paintings are of them all. As Donnie and Alison help set up, Felix insists he wants her gone before "something cloney happens." Since Felix and Alison are at the center of this scene, his worries certainly seem justified—all their other teamups have had zany clone switching and invasions by killers and annoying relatives, usually simultaneously. In response, Alison gazes at his portraits and points out that "based on the room, it's already happening." He's let Clone Club into the most personal parts of his life, consciously or not.

She and her sisters follow Felix's dictates, though when he's on the spot, Felix introduces Alison as Sarah to Colin the morgue attendant—who tries to get an answer as to why he performed her autopsy. Nonetheless, Felix is pulling off his illusion … all until Ezra Lue, a gallerist from Geneva whom he wants to impress, looks bored. Felix realizes that he can use the power of the clones—for once, not taking each other's places but reveling in their individuality as distinct people—to wow the audience. He introduces Alison (as Hestia the hearth goddess), Cosima (as Metis, goddess of wisdom), and Sarah (first as Athena, goddess of war, and then later as his sister). Showing off his spectrum of clone sisters makes the party truly stand out as he emphasizes his love for their uniqueness. He ends it by giving a touching speech about how he and Sarah have prospered by S. finding and adopting them so long ago, making them a family:

> My sister and I are orphans, you see, and, uh, we could have ended up anywhere. We could have ended up in any family. And if we had, we would have been entirely different people. But my mom—Siobhan. This woman … she chose us as her own. We are who we are because she carried two little London urchins on her wings to Canada. Watching her raise my sister, watching my sister raise her own daughter finding my biological sister, it's quite mad. It's taught me that we are all mysterious works of chance. A choice of nature versus nurture. So, to my galaxy of women, thank you for the nurture.

Arthur Bell is the other cultural feminist, supporting and hiding the Clone Club. He, like Felix, must babysit Helena, tell Tony and Krystal the truth of their origins, hide Alison's shenanigans—even those that involve drugs and murder. His support begins before the series, as he helps Beth cover her shooting of Maggie Chen while strung out on pills. In the first episode, he does everything he can to help his partner Beth (as he thinks) get reinstated and continues to help her through what he thinks is her trauma. As he insists she call him names and drags her to the gun range, he's trying to make her more herself—an irony as Sarah is stealing her identity. However accidental, his training in being Beth helps Sarah manage her charade. He also confiscates the money Sarah is stealing from Beth to make her face her demons instead of running from them. He doesn't know how right he is, since this moment actually makes Sarah stay and help her sisters. In season one, he's an antagonist as he investigates Katja's murder, which Sarah is hiding. However, he's also a loyal friend.

In season three, Sarah calls on Art, and they form a better relationship as they drive through the countryside seeking Mark and through him, Helena. Art reveals he loved Beth, though he couldn't be more to her than a friend. Season four flashbacks show him comforting her as her life deteriorates, and they even spend a night together. He also runs interference with Detective Duko, and shockingly abandons his fellow cop to be killed by Siobhan, since Duko killed Beth. With this gesture, he gives his loyalty completely to the clone sisters and their agenda.

Like Felix, he gets held as hostage as season five begins, thanks to his new partner Detective Enger. Since she serves Neolution, she's like a monitor, linking him with the clones once again. When Neolution rounds up all the Clone Club, pressuring them to negotiate, they treat him as one, and he urges Alison to surrender. He provides a safe haven for more clones as he sends Charlotte and Kira to his ex-wife and daughter in "Guillotines Decide" (508). During the following episode, Enger informs Lieutenant Hardcastle he's mixed up in hiding the Clone Club's crimes. Art in turn approaches the lieutenant, urging him in Beth's name to serve the side of integrity. Art succeeds in being convincing. Eventually he defeats Enger and handcuffs her, as the good cop taking down the bad one by the book.

The finale gives him a harder task, as he rushes into DYAD to rescue Helena and be the hero, only to find himself assisting at Helena's birthing bed while Coady holds him at gunpoint. He resists her order to sexually assault Helena, and works with Helena to outwit Coady and lure her close—though even in labor, Helena deals the death blow, not the male cop. Art holds Helena through the birth, physically and emotionally supporting her so Sarah can deliver the twins. He ends the series celebrating the birth, his own daughter in tow, as Helena names one of her sons for the man who protected them all.

Vic the Bully

Men around the world oppress women through patriarchal social structures and have throughout history. Clearly, along with financial and power-related benefits, there are universal psychological causes. But what? "The male child, the argument goes, perceives his mother and his predominantly female elementary school teachers as dominating and controlling.... As a result, men feel a lifelong psychological need to free themselves from or prevent their domination by women. The argument is, in effect, that men oppress women as adults because they experienced women as oppressing them as children" (Pleck 58). While there may be some truth here, this argument notably blames the victim for creating the dynamic. Analyst Joseph H. Pleck more sees men competing with each other, requiring women to mediate their struggles, as well as provide a bottom social class—however far down the men sink through the hierarchy, at least they will not end up there! Women also provide refuge and comfort while validating the men's masculinity and power. At the same time, men's roles as breadwinner give them pride and satisfaction, even if their job seems soulless and repetitive. For all these reasons, institutionalized masculinity through history has dominated womankind.

Of course, bullies famously crumple when their victims stand up to them. Vic tries to oppress Felix the gay man as he does Sarah the woman. Both, however, completely dismiss his harassment. In the first episode, Felix realizes Vic is frustrated at keeping his emotions bottled up and at Vic's insistence, arranges a funeral for Sarah and a drunken wake to follow. Through this, Vic is allowed to release his repressed grief and move beyond it. Other times when he attacks with physical force, Sarah clobbers him and Alison pepper-sprays him—both asserting that they won't be controlled. Physically mastered, he has no choice but to slink off into the shadows.

When Sarah reveals herself as alive, Vic whimpers and cries, disarmed by his own feelings. "How did you do it?" he asks, low and fierce. "Lying there in that morgue? Holding your breath, Sarah, while I am bawling? I'm crying like a goddamn child. You know what's crazy? You know how stupid I am? I'm standing here looking at you, and all I keep thinking about is Myrtle Beach" ("Conditions of Existence" 105).

As with many stories, the bully is revealed as weak and soft underneath. Vic is desperately glad to see Sarah is alive and yet terribly hurt at how she played him and escaped him. After Sarah stole his cocaine, the mobsters have cut off his finger, in a castration metaphor. To comfort him, Sarah gives him money (emphasizing that she and Alison are bailing him out) but refuses to take him back. "It's not over Sarah," he promises as he shuffles out, but it basically is. A few times after this, he manages to blackmail her into listening to him, but she gives him no more than this before leaving him once again. Vic is her starting relationship, but Sarah soon outgrows him, as does the series, which makes him no more than a initial villain. The clones soon have much more to deal with than a blustering thug.

Helena: From Cultist to Pagan Guide

The penultimate episode takes viewers through Helena's journey from a pawn of the church to a woman seeking redemption and enlightenment. Captured by Coady, Helena recalls her defining moments. Co-producer Alex Levine explains:

> The Helena flashbacks were challenging but so fun to dig into. The genesis of the early convent scenes was a scene from a classic Faulkner novel, *Light in August*. There's a killer in that story who has a seminal event in his childhood. So I riffed on that, and with Tat's help, created a visceral early moment in Helena's childhood where we see that she isn't just an evil child, she's a victim. The other scenes were key moments of her past we knew we wanted to explore, and it was about choosing the moments we felt would resonate with Helena's current predicament [Wilson].

Her name signifies her as a Leda, as Helen of Troy was Leda's daughter and Castor's sister. The mythological character, like her mother, is a pawn. After Zeus raped Leda, Helena grew up the most beautiful woman in the world. Her entire life, she was fought over by kings, finally inspiring an epic war. The name, meaning "shining," actually belonged to an ancient pre-patriarchal goddess soon absorbed into Greek mythology. The show's Helena follows this pattern at first, falling under the control of one group then another. However, she reclaims the legend, turning from pawn to the one who savagely revenges herself on every patriarch and becomes the Clone Club's fiercest warrior.

First, she's about twelve and hiding in a nun's office sneaking chocolates. A nun sneaks in to masturbate, emphasizing organized religion's hypocrisy. She's on the edge of adolescence, with her own body pushing her to break free of the nuns' restrictions. This growth may explain the nuns' harshness:

> In truth, few things in this world provoke such profound feelings of fear and revulsion as the pubescent girl. With her bodily emissions, engendered sexuality and hunger for forbidden knowledge, this feminine grotesque is all things dark and dangerous. The adolescent girl is historically "unhinged"—or, as psychoanalysis would have it, burdened with penial lack and driven frantic with self-loathing. She grubs in wastelands, joins in with the Wild Hunt, outwits fire, survives frost, unlocks doors, and straddles and crosses borders [Lakin-Smith].

Adolescence is a symbolic time of emerging magic, but to the restrictive enemy, a time when they must curb the girl's wildness. Helena is developing a monstrous side, that demands chocolate and speculates about sex, but the nuns don't sympathize with her changes. Instead, the head sister condemns her as a devil, marking her hair with bleach so all can witness her outward monstrosity. Thus, her angelic halo of light-colored hair comes from the church's rejection of her.

When she's finally released from the confessional where they stash her, Tomas is waiting, saying, "My dear child. So this is where I finally find you. I've been searching for so long. My name is Tomas, and I'm going to take care of you. You don't know how special you are." However, this first father figure beats her and calls her an abomination, teaching her to cut herself. He too condemns her monstrous side as evil instead of nurturing it. His manipulations grow from here. Brainwashing truly takes place when the victim is isolated and wholly dependent on her tormentors. Tomas and Maggie Chen are her only teachers and friends. "Tomas was Helena's only source of food, shelter, and other basic needs for survival, assisting in the success of brainwashing her" (Griffin and Nesseth).

In her prequel comic, Helena is shown being forced to kill a dog and dropped in a dark well. Her parent figures are pushing her towards violence, desensitizing and shaping her. There, her imaginary scorpion friend Pupok appears and taunts her: "You like cages very much, yes? You spend a lot of time in them" (*The Clone Club #2: Helena*). He advises her to "sting" her oppressors and promises she will have such a sting someday.

Maggie and Tomas continue to nurture the dysfunctional view of sexuality the nuns have already established. In the flashback episode, she locks her Barbies up, and as she bangs naked dolls together, demands, "Filthy dirty copulators. Do you touch yourself too?" Apart from these is a single doll worshipping in God's house who longs to be different than all the others. Dolls as a reflection of adolescence are significant in many works of fiction, as in real life. However, they teach girls passivity—that being female means being a voiceless pretty form. Simone de Beauvoir explains:

> It is a figurine with a human face—or a corn husk or even a piece of wood—that will most satisfyingly replace this double, this natural toy, this penis. The great difference is that, on the one hand, the doll represents the whole body and, on the other hand, it is a passive thing. As such, the little girl will be encouraged to alienate herself in her person as a whole and to consider it an inert given. While the boy seeks himself in his penis as an autonomous subject, the little girl pampers her doll and dresses her as she dreams of being dressed and pampered; inversely, she thinks of herself as a marvelous doll [340].

Helena is lesser because she is female and more so because she is a clone—an abomination and construct. Tomas, with his gift of Barbies, encourages her to thus alienate herself, identifying with an inert hunk of plastic. Her obsession with the Barbies continues, as she uses one to model each of her victims. Repeating the lessons of her foster parents, Helena treats the other clones as objects ready to be dismantled and unmade.

In the comic, Helena begins with Tomas instructing Helena to be the flood and, for God, to cleanse the unworthy from the earth. The imagery is interesting here, as the flood destroyed the forbidden byproduct of "the sons of God" and "the daughters of man," leading to much speculation about the children of angels. In fact, the clones Helena is destroying are not the ordinary descendants of humans, but creations of patriarchs playing God with unnatural science. Arguably, however, the clones are miraculous prototypes, not monsters.

Tomas's saint name and Helena's use of the Bible set this as a sect of Christianity, though they don't specify this onscreen. Christianity has a long tradition of misogyny, starting with the lesson that Eve was created from Adam to comfort and help him, and then her eating of the apple was the original sin that doomed everyone. Some Christians venerate the Virgin Mary, but many focus on Father, Son, and Holy Spirit, leaving women out of the theology entirely. Many one-sided practices about modesty, chastity, and independence persist to this day in some Christian cultures.

Helena's trauma comes from the repeated insistence that she is evil and that only through murdering the others can she become good, during her most vulnerable formative years. Her childlike id is nurtured, but not the adult ego. Maslany adds, "She has this monster rage inside and yet she also has this child-like thing, because she's not lived in society, so she sees it with a very naïve, open perspective" (Bernstein 62). With this, she comes to believe all she's been told.

> To demarcate the bleeding edge, as it were, of female adolescence, it is helpful to refer to child psychologist, David Elkind's theory of "Adolescent Egocentrism." Centring on the 11-to-13-year-old age group, Elkind describes a phenomenon where young adolescents display an inability to distinguish between their perception of what others think about them and what people think in reality (1967). This psychosis gives rise to two mental constructs—the Imaginary Audience, whereby the adolescent anticipates the reactions of those around him/her in current or impending situations and avoids this fantasy of scrutiny, and Personal Fable, where the individual takes on the belief that his/her feelings are unique and that they are therefore unique and special. It is this duality, posits Elkind, which shapes the young adolescent's sense of self [Lakin-Smith].

Helena's damage comes from both these lenses—her new parents tell her she is unique as the original clone and that she can be worthy of love through doing God's holy work—murder. A comic book scene shows Helena cutting herself while apologizing to Maggie, her other Prolethean parent, for failing her (*The Clone Club #2: Helena*). Maggie cares for her, and tells her, "You are our light," offering her the carrot as well as Tomas's stick. She claims

Helena is special, on a divine mission. Maggie reminds her, "You are a blessing born out of great sin. But the others, they are abominations. They must be cleansed." She gives her a fish-shaped knife, a religious symbol, and adds, "It has been used in the service of God for a long time. To execute his will on earth by the most holy of soldiers" (*The Clone Club #2: Helena*).

In the flashback episode, Helena bursts into a church and stabs a fellow clone who's wrapped in a shawl and praying. In fact, she is closest of all the clones to the devout figure who wants to be near God—Helen'a stabbing her could even resemble an attack on organized religion itself. When Helena sees the woman's face, however, she's shaken. By killing her, Helena turns onto a path of darkness in the service of the Proletheans. "They look like me—I am a copy," she worries, and cuddles in bed, sobbing and shaking. Co-producer Alex Levine comments: "John [Fawcett] was always eager to show her first kill, and the twist of her not knowing she's a clone really made it sing" (Wilson). Tomas soothes her by telling her she's the original. That night, struggling for control and self-definition, Helena begins carving wings into her back. These offer suffering and penance while nodding to her hope for religious salvation even as she fears she cannot be worthy. Helena's actress calls her a "beautiful, hideous collision" ("Send in the Clones").

Stephen Lynch, key makeup artist, invented the concept of "cutter angel wings" ("Send in the Clones"). "It's such a horrifying image of self-loathing and everything else that comes with self-harming," he explains (Bernstein 65). Tomas has taught her to hate herself, so she's treated her body with violence. Of course, they blend her evangelical cause with murder and self-abuse. She is a created woman—far moreso than her sisters. Her actress adds: "We called her 'the little monster' on set. She's part-child, part-trained killer; a saint and a demon at the same time. She's not socialized. Like, she wouldn't know that it's not okay just to burp in someone's face at the dinner table, which allowed me to play her with a measure of black comedy" (Elan).

The Proletheans brainwash Helena with lies, sending her to murder the innocent clones because they deny their right to exist. They also teach Helena their doctrine—that clones are an abomination, less than human. Of course, fanatics have said this about many groups through history, all of whom were biologically no different than they. This works as a metaphor for the Church's many scapegoats, like Jews and Muslims in the days of the Inquisition. In episode nine, Dr. Leekie gives his own take on the situation: "Tomas opposes us, science in general. They're religious extremists. Proletheans, they call themselves.... Years ago, one of their agents infiltrated our project. Maggie Chen.... She and Tomas found Helena in a convent. Then trained the clone to kill clones." He insists he wants charge of Helena so he can de-program her and help her.

Commonly, cults tell their recruits the world can be divided into two kinds of people: those who are inside the group and those outside—lost and unworthy. Helena is the "blessed clone," doing God's work, while all other clones are forsaken. Believers base their identity on group affiliation and keep their distance from those outside. In turn, cults call followers to entrench themselves in the group and obey its doctrine completely. Those under such control read the Bible constantly and fill their houses with Biblical themed merchandise. Concentrating on the Bible in every aspect of their lives makes church followers give over their minds completely.

"We can imagine that Helena's relationship with Tomas is an example of an Oedipus complex gone wrong. Helena was raised in a convent and was clearly abused both by guardians in the convent and by Tomas, her father figure" (Donovan 130). Of course, Tomas's greatest crime is teaching Helena all the clones are abominations that she must murder one by one. "You are no creature of God's," Helena thinks in the comic, pursuing Sarah into the ally (*The Clone Club #2: Helena*). Calling the station, Helena riddles, "She was just one of a few, unfit for family, horse glue." This parallels Cosima's gentler riddle, "Just one. I'm a few. No family, too. Who am I?" but specifically rejects the victim she killed as unworthy.

In episode two, Sarah finds that Helena has left behind a Bible in Katja's room, with the word TRUTH written across the page. Of course, this underscores that the religious cult has not fed Helena truth but lies and manipulations. Searching Helena's lair in the next episode, Sarah and Art find the Bible quote "For you formed my inward parts; You knitted me together in my..." Art finishes it: "Mother's womb. I praise you, for I am fearfully and wonderfully made." There's heavy irony here, for the clones' maker isn't God. As Art concludes, gazing around the room, "This perp's got some deep-seated spiritual problems" ("Variation Under Nature" 103).

Cosima notes, "You know, when I'm seeing this branded onto Maggie Chen, I'm thinking that she's not a lone warrior. To extreme creationist types we would be abominations. Like not God's children but Satan's.... And she's killing us even though she is identical to us."

Sarah instantly understands: "Well, but if you were a messed up, abused, loner whose faith compels you to belong and somebody that you trusted told you that this was the way to redeem yourself in the eyes of God, I mean, yeah, I might become an angry angel too" ("Effects of External Conditions" 104).

To create her, Lynch and Sokolowski referred to religious imagery: Sokolowski was inspired by Eastern European Orthodox images of the Virgin Mary. "We really drew off of that directly," he explains. "We had a little photo shoot where we were presenting [the look] to the producers and [we had Helena] kind of looking up at God with blood running down her eyes" (Miller).

Adds Lynch, "We looked through religious icons and some great frescoes of the Madonna. With Sandy, we thought, Let's show both kind of biblical sides … the sublime or saintly and evil, both sides of the yin and yang. That is why I think Sarah has darker hair and Helena has the opposite and almost angelic hair… "She's been so damaged," Lynch continues. "We wanted to see if we could bring some light into her. One of the first images we created of Helena had her with a halo. We didn't want her just to be evil. And that I think paid off, as you see her love of family and children depicted in more recent episodes…. If you look closely, Tatiana and I just throw continuity out the window. We want to see Helena's inner toil reflected in her face so we change her [makeup slightly] every single time" [Miller].

As the series begins, Helena murders the other clones, targeting two in Europe and then following Katja and killing her when she meets Sarah. Next, she targets Sarah-as-Beth, but when Sarah shrieks "I'm not Beth!" Helena realizes her assumptions have been wrong. Further, she feels a connection, a stirring instinct competing with all she's been taught. However, Sarah stabs her with a piece of rebar, halting Helena's attack and forcing her to withdraw and reconsider.

Her fundamentalism has left her deranged, as she follows the Proletheans' agenda to destroy the sisters she should be protecting. When Sarah tracks her down, Helena waits in a bloodstained white shift with dyed blonde hair—she resembles a corrupted angel, one rejected from heaven. "It's a little bit Virgin Mary, a little bit Joan of Arc, a little bit an archangel, a little bit a fresco…" Lynch explains ("Send in the Clones").

Sarah enters and confronts her sister. "Kneel," she orders. "I'm guessing you know how." As they ask each other, "Where did you come from?" Sarah says she's from the atheist-inspired "out of the woodwork," while Helena says, "God sent me."

"Right. So you don't know either," Sarah retorts, tearing apart Helena's carefully built fundamentalism. The angry, skeptical punk throws out all the patriarchy's attempts to dictate to her. Meanwhile, Helena clings to Sarah's knees and tries to break through and share her religious beliefs. When Helena offers to save her, Sarah knocks Helena's hand from her knee, rejecting her. "Right, because we have a connection," she says tightly. She presses her gun to Helena's head, as Helena whispers that she can see a light in Sarah, her new potential savior.

"There's a light in all of us," Sarah says emotionally.

"No!" Helena shouts. "The others. Poor copies of God's image of human beings!"

Sarah realizes, "They told you you were the original, didn't they?" ("Effects of External Conditions" 104).

After this, Helena becomes obsessed with Sarah, contacting her repeatedly and insisting she has something special about her. At the end of episode four, she collapses from the injury Sarah gave her and Tomas carries her off. He berates and comforts her alternatingly, insisting Sarah and her connection are "nothing. Just one of your fingernail clippings, like the rest of them." Helena repeats Sarah's revelation that Helena is not the original. However, when Tomas presses her with "How could you believe such a thing?" and tortures her, she cowers and he cradles and forgives her. Vowing to be strong, she repeats after him phrases of self-hypnosis and compliance, giving her mind and will over to him. He tells her and she repeats, "I am the original. I am the light" ("Parts Developed in an Unusual Manner" 107).

At cult services, the charismatic leader convinces his followers he has more spiritual authority than they do and that they are unworthy in the eyes of God. The only path to salvation is to do whatever the cult asks of them. With this, the followers trust him completely. There's often an ultimatum—be saved and give money, pledge a new level of devotion or prove oneself a sinner. Tomas confronts Helena with just such a choice.

Tomas urges her to flagellate herself, leaving hideous scars, mirroring the ones he bears himself. Later, he wrestles her into a cage while she sobs and rages. He's an evil person who molds her into another, bringing her down to the level of an animal. By contrast, Kira shows Helena unfettered kindness and sympathy as she embraces her "aunt" in an alley and asks "What happened to you?" Helena doesn't know.

Trembling, Helena holds the little girl, confronting her pain at last. Calling her "angel" suggests Helena is opening herself to a new doctrine, one of love for her new sisters and niece rather than hate. Manson recalls, "She was desperate for connection, it was the thing that was missing from her. All her violence was from never having love. Helena yearns for family. So that humanized the monster for us—she has an innocent quality that we were then able to write for" (Bernstein 62).

When Tomas demands Helena capture Sarah for him and take Kira for herself, Helena finally snaps. "You cannot harm her child!" Helena shouts. Sarah and Tomas stand before her, urging her to make a permanent choice. Tomas twists their words and structures arguments on the theology of lies he's fed Helena. "The child is innocent," he says, mimicking Helena's earlier words to emphasize that he's on her side. He reminds Helena that she's the original, as he's taught her. "You know what that means. The child is rightfully your daughter."

> SARAH: He's lying! Helena, Helena! There's no original. I told you, we're the same. Neither of us is the original.
> TOMAS: Put it down. Go bring your child home, to her real mother.
> SARAH: Helena, Helena! Look, look You know that connection you feel? I feel it, too. It's us.
> TOMAS: She'll say anything to save herself.

SARAH: He locked you in a cage! He lied to you your entire life. He's going to do that to Kira! He's going to hurt Kira like he hurt you.

With this, Helena tries to tear Tomas to pieces, breaking with the cult at last.

In "Endless Forms Most Beautiful" (110), Helena stabs their newly-returned birth mother, Amelia. "You gave me to them! You let them make me this way." Amelia was the one to give her to the church, giving her a life condemned as a "devil child" and monster. Further, she lost her twin: "She separated us," Helena says. "She tore us apart." It's true that Amelia's giving her to the church allowed the Proletheans to torture her. There's also a suggestion that Helena still lashes out at the innocent women who only want to love her with murder—so deep is the Proletheans' conditioning. After she commits matricide, Sarah returns and shoots her, once again stopping Helena from continuing her murderous agenda and emphasizing that violence will be met with deadly force each time. In this moment, she rejects Helena, to the maddened woman's despair. Helena near-miraculously survives, dragging herself to the hospital. However, another cult of Proletheans only waits to kidnap her as well.

In season two, Helena is captured by a different sect, one that's more traditionally cultist. Cults have hierarchical leadership, with followers who revere the leaders and do their will unquestioningly. Cult leaders achieve this by insisting they are envoys of God. At Henrik "Hank" Johanssen's farm, of course, all obey him. Even his wife Bonnie has no objection to his implanting their daughter with his baby, since he uses words like "God's will." When his eighteen-year-old daughter Gracie disobeys him, he has her mouth sewn shut. The most effective way to control the minds of a group of followers is to trap them in an isolated compound where the charismatic leader controls every aspect of their lives. Of course, their farm is far in the countryside—"fourteen hundred acres supporting forty souls."

Religion, as embodied by the Proletheans, is not treated kindly on the show. The name suggests Prometheus, the titan who sought forbidden science and brought fire to man. Since he went against the gods' will, he was eternally punished. The syllable "Lethe" suggests the river of forgetfulness in Greek mythology. Some versions of the myth Leda and the Swan have Hypnos, the god of sleep, drugging her with water from the River Lethe, echoing Helena's drugged egg-stealing scene. This is a story of male gods conspiring to prey on a young goddess, a perfect parallel for *Orphan Black*. Manson notes, "It's safe to say that our Proletheans continue to be the bad guys. The religion side of the divide between religion and science is very much alive this season and it becomes a broader, more interesting world, populated by more characters with more agendas" (Ross, "Sarah Was Not Originally British").

This competing group acknowledges science. Henrik explains to Tomas, "You see, I steered my faith through science at MIT, and what I see here—

what I see here is God opening a whole new door" ("Governed by Sound Reason and True Religion" 202). Both believe her cloning will create a new war for creation. In his black cowboy hat, he's a literal black hat and villain. Meanwhile as Hank supervises cow inseminations on his countrified farm, he and Tomas compare philosophies. He also speculates that Helena, like her twin, might be able to conceive a child.

> HENRIK: Well, farmers pray more than most, but it's not worth the breath without hard work and basic biology, agro-sciences. Helena's been with you for quite some time now, hasn't she?
> TOMAS: Since she was twelve years old.
> HENRIK: I wonder, Tomas, if you've ever considered the fact that, seeing as she's the twin of a fertile clone, well, maybe, uh, maybe Helena can conceive as well.
> TOMAS: Impossible. She's defective and dangerous. Any child of hers would be a monster.
> HENRIK: Well, you know her best. You know a wise man once said science without religion is lame. Religion without science is blind.
> TOMAS: Einstein didn't believe in God.
> HENRIK: It's a brand-new day ["Governed by Sound Reason and True Religion" 202].

Johanssen marries Helena while she's recovering from her injuries and lies feverishly in bed. "Although we are small in rank, we have broken away from the old world because we know what they do not. Man's work is God's work, as long as you do it in God's name. Helena was created by man, not in his name, but God shone his light down upon her," he says. He carries Helena off, and while rape may have occurred, it's replaced onscreen with a disturbing medical procedure. In fact, Johanssen has decided to create life with her by harvesting her eggs. "She is not aware of the egg harvesting procedure Johanssen has subjected her to, nor does she give consent in her barely conscious state" (Wright 126). His eagerness to implant Gracie suggests his biological imperative to be the only patriarch of the family. In fact, everyone at the compound is shown having a tie to his of obligation or biology. The children, all raised together, may be largely or even entirely his. He also has Tomas, his competitor, killed.

After the egg theft, Helena escapes to Sarah and pleads, "Please, sestra. I need your help. Don't send me back. I was married. I think he took something from inside of me" ("Governed as It Were by Chance" 204). After she's welcomed and finds a haven, she goes on a goofy road trip with Sarah, bonding with the other woman. For a single episode, she's given the chance to have a real sister, squabbling over snacks and radio channels. When Helena is arrested after starting a bar fight, she waits, full of faith in her "sestra." Sarah, however, has found higher priorities and abandoned her to be taken by the Protheans. With her new family ignoring her, Helena soon reverts to her cultist status. When instead of her sister, Gracie comes and tells her,

"She's not coming back for you" and "We want to take you to your children," Helena finally succumbs. The true believers see something beautiful in her and will give her the pregnancy she's longed for. "It's a bittersweet decision, but a sadly understandable one. Helena has been so egregiously dehumanized since birth that she's now willing to compromise everything simply to become a religious cult's broodmare. In her eyes, pregnancy is the closest she'll get to what she's always wanted but was taught she never deserved: a chance to feel human and to have value in society" (Gennis).

Henrik is likely planning to impregnate all of the Prolethean women, considering how many zygotes he's prepared. Nonetheless, Helena allows him to father her children and implant the fertilized eggs. On the farm, after, she protects the children, including teenage Gracie. In all of them, she sees something of herself. However, when she finds that Henrik has implanted more of her children in Gracie against her will, Helena turns savage. She brutally kills him with his own fertilization equipment, emphasizing that he is the farm animal, not her. She also takes back the canister of eggs.

Many might expect religious organizations to protest cloning, as an unnatural subversion of God's will. Thus, Helena's early training, by Proletheans who call her a monster and brainwash her with lies to track down and murder the other clones is all too believable. The second season Proletheans, who want to breed her, are a bit stranger.

In fact, they have a real-world parallel in a religious sect claiming to have produced the first human clones. "Raëlians believe that humans are all cloned from alien scientists who visited earth. The movement was started by Claude Vorilhon, following a spiritual experience in 1973. He changed his name to Raël and founded the cult" (Dixon). He advocates cloning as a form of immortality, believing this is the aliens' ultimate intension for humanity. Humans could download themselves into body after body, and thus live forever.

> In 1973, Raël says, he had an encounter with a four-foot-tall alien ("his skin was white with a slightly greenish tinge, a bit like someone with liver trouble") whose flying saucer had landed atop a volcano in southern France. From this creature, he heard the message that humans had been created in a laboratory by advanced beings from another planet who had mastered genetics and cell biology. Subsequent visits to the spacecraft, during which Raël enjoyed the sensual attentions of six "voluptuous and bewitching" female robots, convinced the fun-loving prophet that the aliens did indeed have a superior civilization [Talbot].

Margaret Talbot of *The New York Times*, who toured their headquarters, notes, "You could see them not as bizarros inflamed by a singular vision but simply as the most fervent proponents of a genetic essentialism that is fairly widely shared these days. To put it another way, the Raëlians are just a bunch of people who took literally the cliché that science is replacing religion." The

Proletheans, with their pro-cloning cult, mirror this concept. Their leader has, in the words of researcher Charles Cameron, "done an extremely good job of placing himself astride a powerful tide of hope and fear—the longings of people who want to find emotional and religious meaning in science and biotechnology" (Talbot).

Clonaid was founded by the Raëlians sect. Its head, Brigitte Boisselier (born 1956), also known as Brigitte Roehr, is a French chemist and Raëlian religious leader who claims to have overseen the creation of the first human clone, Eve. The catch is that her company has never provided proof that she and subsequent children were cloned, so the claim is regarded with widespread skepticism. Clonaid claims they carried out 3,000 trials using cow eggs and human cells. "The worrying thing about such a claim is the mystery of the missing "monster" babies: the ones so malformed that they were destroyed in the womb, aborted or which died after premature births. These are the kinds of things we see in animal cloning and there is a disturbing silence from Clonaid" (Dixon). There are other ethical problems, if the claim is true. One of the fundamental objects to cloning is that "virtually every nation agrees that children should not be commodified like barnyard animals or pets" (Annas 26). Of course, Helena and Gracie typify this objection, as they're literally shut in a barn to gestate like broodmares. Soon, however, a new path will open for them.

Helena is kidnapped by the Castors, sending her on an ancient underworld journey like Persephone's in Greek myth. Accompanying her as her spirit guide is Pupok (bellybutton) the imaginary scorpion. "It's been a long time. You're being tested again," it tells her ("The Weight of This Combination" 301). The scorpion embodies the bridging of fluid depths and firm ground, even as it protects its babies with a fierce stinger. Joining motherhood and death, it's an image of the power of rebirth, advising Helena to let the weak parts of herself die and emerge with a new consciousness before giving birth.

Helena faces off with Virginia Coady, the tyrant of the underworld, who sends her sons out to murder innocent women. "She embodies what Freud calls 'the Phallic' mother—domineering, intimidating, and ruthless" (Donovan 129). Even as she tortures Parsons, keeping him in a state of near-death, Helena discovers compassion for her new brother and puts him out of his pain. When Sarah comes to save her, however, Helena charges her with betrayal and escapes without her. In the desert, a place of emptiness, the heroine has nothing to distract her and can hear her own inner voices. "It's not exhaustion that stops you, you regret leaving Sarah behind," Pupok tells her ("Certain Agony of the Battlefield" 306). Though he taunts her with the power of selfishness, she finally chooses love and dispenses with his advice—by swallowing him. She then listens to her heart and goes back for Sarah. She returns from her underworld journey tougher, with a new mission to protect those in danger.

Marcella Althaus-Reid begins her description of feminist theology with the tale of Charles Darwin's daughter Hetty who "was distressed because she wanted to be so good that God would accept her amongst the male angels" (qtd. in Thweatt-Bates 161). Althaus-Reid explains that being born as the Other to the dominant religion and God began the start of feminist rebellion and the quest for inclusivity. "This feeling of 'strangeness' yielded to the realization that inclusion in an essentially patriarchal system was not sufficient, and prompted a search for 'a god who is one of us: for women she was the Goddess'" (Thweatt-Bates 162).

Many women today become Neo-Pagans, worshipping older goddess traditions found around the world. They discover the lost all-powerful goddesses of China, Egypt, and many more, finding feminist pathways to spirituality. Ruth Mantin rebelliously claims "Goddesses like Medusa, Lilith, and Tiamat would be happy to converse with cyborgs about the subversive power of monstrous hybrids" (qtd. in Thweatt-Bates 163). The Clones are not the new Eves, wimpy scapegoats of the church—they are the patriarchy-shattering goddesses of the old world, born anew.

"The gynocentric branch concerns the search for or creation of spiritual practices centering around women and female power, thus appealing to women disaffected with mainstream traditions who yearn for a spiritual practice that meshes with their feminist values," Janice C. Crosby, author of "Feminist Spirituality," adds. Women scour the world, bringing back the goddesses of African, Asian, and Native American religions, seeking pre-patriarchal heroines. "Drawing from archaeology, anthropology, art, oral tradition, and other disciplines, feminists have sought to find evidence of cultures and time periods where women were not spiritually subordinate, and may even have held primacy" (Crosby 241).

Neo-Paganism is specifically nonhierarchical, most often welcoming a circle of equals instead of a church with a male spokesman for the divine. "Wicca defies singular definition; while elements of pre-Christian European paganism are predominant, some of its main characteristics include eclecticism and borrowing from other traditions. Key variants of the concept of the centrality of the Goddess and the democratization of spiritual leadership result in a range of practices. For example, a group may be led by a High Priestess, but all women are considered priestesses" (Crosby 242).

Following this tradition, Helena's journey emphasizes her growth from the child raised by a cult to the independent woman finding her own spirituality. In season four, she journeys alone into the wilderness. Dressed as a shaman in deerskins, she symbolically claims the power of the natural world. Deer, who lose and regain antlers, represent regeneration and the magic of the forest. Dressed thus, she's a conduit to the spirits, seeking their guidance. Her rough hut is likewise a link with nature. Helena has made a capable home for herself in Beavertail National Park and her own clothes, even with a touch of fashion. Skilled at the bow, she feeds herself too. Clearly she's at home in the wilderness. There, her pregnancy swells. Even when she's attacked, she recovers almost instantly, with the fetus healing miraculously in her womb. She's like a fertility goddess, and even an answer to prayer: Alison, in danger of her life, prays for salvation, and Helena, like ancient Artemis, slays the evil thugs with her bow.

Maslany says, "I love being Helena. She's actually quite soft and beautiful and … pure" ("Send in the Clones"). She soon retreats to the convent run by her beloved protector, Sister Irina. It's a peaceful, safe quiet place, so the action leaves her there to develop. On one occasion, Sarah comes to visit to entreat advice on how to connect with Kira. Helena tells her, "You should share our horrors with her" to pass on the Ledas' hard-won wisdom, adding that Kira will have to face all the clones are doing someday ("Let the Children & the Childbearers Toil" 504). Further, Helena reveals that she shares Kira's sensitivity—the connection she felt with Sarah is part of the same miraculous empathy. In this scene, she functions as Sarah's wise mentor, guiding her to reconnect with her daughter.

In "One Fettered Slave" (509), Coady captures Helena and induces labor to take her stem cells for Westmorland. Coady, of course, is the woman fully in service to the patriarchy, a disciple as Helena once was. Drugged and shackled, Helena flashes through her life as labor begins. After Coady kills the last Castor at Westmorland's insistence, Helena begs, "You let him take your babies. Please. Not mine. They need their mother."

Coady retorts, "Well, that's just not true, Helena. You forget, I know who you are. Dumped at birth. A killer. You killed your own sisters. You stink like an animal. What kind of mother could you possibly make?"

As Helena labors, she knows her babies will have a life of experimentation as she did, convinced they're subhuman. Like the Castors and herself, they may be brainwashed into killing innocents. Lying there, she gropes for a scissors and makes the single decision she can to save her babies from torment. There is only one way to protect innocents like the sister she killed. Surrounded by light and choral music, emphasizing her saintliness, she slits her wrist. Co-producer Alex Levine explains, "We had a number of discussions about this choice. We know it's a very dark choice, that it's almost anathema to lots of people, specifically mothers. But we saw it as a heroic choice. Helena saw that these children would end up being tortured, being used and manipulated, being twisted and corrupted as she was corrupted as a child. And she believed by making this choice that she was saving them from a lifetime of horrors" (Wilson).

Coady gets Helena a transfusion from Sarah—while Coady prepares for a Caesarian that will kill Helena, Sarah begs her sister to return, and Helena finally does. The power of sisterhood has saved her from her martyrdom. Awake, she rescues herself as she asks Coady for water, and when the woman approaches she takes her unrestrained hand and slams Coady's head repeatedly against the exam table. "You are shit mother," she tells her. The sainted mother has defeated her and won the day. With Coady bloody and unconscious, Sarah and Helena can escape. However, as they stand, Helena's water breaks. "Babies coming."

The next episode has Helena at her most helpless. Unable to walk, she lies in the DYAD basement struggling to birth her babies. There, Coady finds her and gloats, "Ah, Helena. Let's try this again. This is more your style, isn't it? Down here in the filth and garbage." Symbolically, this is the underworld with the monster-mother, killer of innocents, presiding over the birth. This is Helena's ultimate quest, to emerge into the world of life, magical babies safe in her arms.

When Art comes in, Coady orders him to play midwife while she stands over him with the gun. However, even as Helena grunts through a contraction, she draws his eye to her screwdriver. Art lures Coady in by playing up Helena's weaknesses, insisting she's hemorrhaging. With this, Helena stabs her nemesis in the throat. The evil queen perishes.

Sarah rushes in to help Helena deliver. As the women crouch opposite each other, Sarah talks Helena through it, guiding her sister through the ancient magics. Maslany explains: "It's this culmination of this love between these two sisters, and Art, and Mrs. S, who have been there since the beginning. And they have fought so hard for that relationship, and the whole arc of the show has been the fight for it" (Ross, "Tatiana Maslany"). As she aids Helena, Sarah continues to recall her own birth scenes, with S. coaxing her. It's a primal, desperate moment, far from the sterile birth suite. Maslany says: "To express it in the most raw visceral way—which is very true of both of these characters since Sarah and Helena are both very animalistic and very raw—to have them screaming into each other's faces felt right" (Ross, "Tatiana Maslany").

S.'s presence blesses them, symbolically passing on women's secret lore to the next generation. With her protection, Sarah guides her sister to give birth. As Helena cradles her new twins, a heavenly white light surrounds them. It fades into angel mobiles made of feathers and sticks. They're a bit weird, a bit primitive, but aside from the guiding angel motif through the series, they suggest Helena's forest connection. They bring the ancient magic to Helena's new home, as she lives with the Hendrixes she saved and they all raise the babies together. This, like Sarah's family, is a matrifocal living space as Helena dwells with her sister and her older children, letting Donnie, her brother-in-law, play father. She finally names the twins Donald and Arthur—mythic heroes from ancient pagan lore.

Donna Haraway declared God dead, as well as the Goddess (162). Instead of the ruling man and submissive "natural" woman—Zeus and Demeter or Aphrodite, she saw the cyborg, the glittering hybrid, as the new model. Following this image, Helena completely rejects the Proletheans' teachings, keeping only the hybrid twins they gave her. She will be a loving, nurturing mother, but also still a warrior defending her family. As she reveals when she sits among her sisters, Helena has finished her book, retelling their entire journey. It begins with four stick figures and a drawing of the earth, emphasizing how they have expanded from four separate women in the earliest episodes to a worldwide sisterhood. With this, Helena blesses and affirms them all.

Amelia and Kendra: Black Feminism

Amelia (Melanie Nicholls-King), hunted in South Africa, comes to Sarah's country to meet her and Helena. Just as she's not part of the Clone Club, she's separate from their struggles, though her own parallels and anticipates theirs for autonomy over her body and her children. This split is also one seen in feminism:

> The (implicit) imperialism of *Western* feminism, in its presuming to speak for Third World women (as though they were themselves a unitary category), became an issue of contention in the qumquennial conferences of the UN Decade for Women. But it had already provoked deep lacerations among American feminists, when black women found themselves profoundly alienated from white women and the feminism they espoused. In the words of one black feminist describing a common reaction to feminism among black women: "a lot of black women would say … feminism belongs to white women, they originated it as a form of analysis, it is a form of analysis that only takes into account their experience. Therefore, we shouldn't be involved with it" [Phillips and Cree].

Sarah and Helena's birth mother is a refugee fleeing South Africa after DYAD finds her. Sitting in Siobhan's house, Amelia tells Sarah how she was only 22 and new to England. In her vulnerable state, a wealthy couple asked her to be their surrogate in return for money and help settling in. She adds, "But something was off. The medical tests were extensive. And I overheard the couple talking to the doctor about a child unfettered by tradition. An advanced…" she struggles for the right word, "evolution of some kind" ("Endless Forms Most Beautiful" 110). She fled with her babies and hid them away.

With her colorful scarf and large earrings, she's a friendly, comforting presence. Sarah sees her own struggle with DYAD in this other woman, so different from herself. "It is precisely the chimeric quality of women's commonality, of their sharing a firm collective identity, that contemporary feminism has highlighted, even as it has struggled to overcome the divisions and fragmentations of the female subject. And this legacy of ambivalence continues today, as feminists uneasily but insistently turn to the issue of the plurality of female selves" (Ergas 547). Amelia's other daughter, Helena, has been brainwashed by organized religion to set herself above others. She sees no commonality, only blame, and murders her. Helena shows no understanding of young Amelia's desperation at being a single mother or her bravery in saving her twins from a life of DYAD control. All Helena can see is the woman who abandoned her.

The fact that Amelia is basically the sole Black woman on the show to this point and that she has such a brief appearance before being murdered is problematic. A disproportionate number of characters of color die in television shows, while the white characters survive. Further, her death serves entirely to affect Sarah and change her dynamic with her twin. Thus, Amelia brings more tokenism than diversity before falling into stereotypes.

Sadly, the Ledas' struggle for freedom does not save Amelia. This imbalance also characterized much of second and even third wave feminism. Poor and minority women felt feminism, which grew out of middle-class white women's discontent, did little to improve their lives. "Most women of color say their primary concerns—access to education, health care and safe neighborhoods for their children—were not priorities for the women's movement. As for getting out into the workplace, well, poor women have always been there, mopping floors, slinging hash, raising other people's children" (Wallis). Since they didn't have the luxury to stay home with the children, they weren't freed from it, and their job situations weren't improved. The show's sacrifice of Amelia mirrors this lack of consciousness.

A similar working-class single mother oppressed by the system is Kendra Dupree (Lisa Codrington). Evie Cho, powerful CEO of the sinister fertility clinic Brightborn, recruits her as a surrogate. However, she does not tell Kendra that the child implanted in her is genetically damaged, created for experimental purposes. Such children, often born with defects, are euthanized. Kendra, who already has a child, is desperate for money enough to lend out her body. However, she is far from an oblivious pawn. After she discovers and even films the horrors of Brightborn, she and her friend Tabitha flee to a homeless shelter. The corporate goons invade and murder the heavily-pregnant Tabitha. Knowing she's their next target, Kendra sends her son into hiding and then escapes with her limited funds. She soon has her new child, Jacob, whom she loves. As she explains, "They put this beautiful baby in me, but he was born blind. If they find him, they'll put him down, too." His blindness, her other child's youth, and her poverty all emphasize the small family's total vulnerability.

Black feminism is intersectional—race, gender, class oppression, racism, and sexism are bound together. This describes Kendra and Amelia—marginalized and abused by the corporation who stalks them both through the series. They are corporate prey because they're the most defenseless members of society, friendless and unprotected. If they disappear, few will even notice. The show doesn't specify whether this status comes from their race, class, immigrant status, poverty, or gender—it appears to be a combination of all these.

Sarah and Art try persuading Kendra to help them, but they're oblivious to her desperation to stay out of the fight. Sarah offers, "If you're willing to come forward with this, we could expose them. We could end all this." This is her mission, the opportunity *she's* been seeking through the series. However, this is not what Kendra, who's in a far different place, seeks. Even as Sarah tries to connect, insisting they're both mothers and that they can both rely on Art's police protection, she's ignoring the decades of fear and oppression that have left Kendra terrified.

Kendra replies, "Look what they did to Tabitha. I have another son. They'll hurt us, I know they will." She knows the power a massive corporation can wield against an unprotected poor woman of color and her two small children. In fact, she's right, as Rachel seizes the opportunity to threaten Kendra's other son unless she goes with them. As it turns out, Rachel does not harm Kendra or her children, only uses them as leverage for her battle with Evie. However, the show emphasizes that she could murder all three of them, as they have no recourse in the massive corporate battle. Sarah and Art fail the sensitivity test, trying to win her to their cause even as they fail to notice Kendra's desperate danger from within their own team. She survives but flees with her children and never again seeks out Clone Club.

Other significant Black characters besides Art include the next generation: Art's daughter Maya and Alison's adopted children Gemma and Oscar. These children are middle class, protected through the show by their more privileged parents. As they all play together with the clones' biological children in the finale, they nod towards a hopeful future with brother- and sisterhood for all.

Alison: Back to the Gothic Home

In the seventies, Phyllis Schlafly and the more than 50,000 American women who formally joined her cause campaigned for a return to the nuclear family and its religious values, halting and slowing the acceptance of key social issues—the Equal Rights Amendment, abortion, homosexuality, affirmative action. Wrote Schlafly: "Just as humanism is based on atheism and the notion that man is at the center of the universe, feminism puts woman at the center of the universe. They [feminists] chose the word 'liberation' because they mean liberation from home, husband, family, and children" (qtd. in Berkeley 88). By the late 1970s, this "New Right" was controlling the Republican party.

Postfeminism was "characterized in the 1980s in responses to New Right backlash against feminism and liberalism" (Helford 293). Many eighties women declared the war had been won, so they went back to the homes as traditional mothers. They were characterized by three elements: "Rejection of radical feminist sexual politics, emphasis on individual efforts over group activism, and a profamily stance—the last two as backlash against feminism " (Helford 293). Many subscribed to conservative religion. "Members of the New Right were convinced that American society was on the verge of losing its public virtue as 'secular values' replaced 'religious values'" (Berkeley 87).

Alison Hendrix personifies post-feminism, as she chooses to stay home raising the kids and doing craft projects as a literal soccer mom in her perfect, boring suburban world, Bailey Downs. She goes to university but studies kinesiology, a caregiving skill training her in physical therapy (in fact, there's no evidence she's now or ever practiced professionally, though she coaches children's skating and soccer and works out herself). Sarah smirks in "Entangled Bank" (108) and compares it to massage.

However, in her first moments, Alison presents herself as very tightly wound. Blending suburbia and psychosis, she threatens Sarah with her knife from slicing the kids' oranges. Later she's often found around scissors and guns, though she also tortures Donnie with hot glue. A total control freak, she gives constant orders. She also appears quite self-centered and unsympathetic: She rejects Sarah's introduction with "I don't care who you are. Why, Lord? Why me? I never wanted any part of this. Do I wear a huge 'kick me' sign on my back?" All this suggests she's inherently unhappy, pretending to find fulfillment by overcontrolling everything. The actress says of Alison, "She was somebody who sees her life as cookie-cutter and it was going to be perfect and then, as things fall apart, she just tries to hang on to them even stronger" (Bernstein 52).

Stephen Lynch, key makeup artist, describes Alison. "She has to be sort of impeccable. In her workout gear, and she's quick-walking or coaching soccer. She's quite rigid. And her idea of keeping this front always—'Okay, everything's fine'..." ("Send in the Clones"). In "Nature Under Constraint and Vexed" (201), Alison defends herself quite ably with rape whistle and pepper spray. She learns to shoot from Beth and buys an unregistered gun through her own drug connections. She's a yuppie, but not a pushover. This uptight determination also appears in her role as the figure skating coach—it's a sport suitable for the ice queen, requiring total precision and control.

Rather than finding the truth, Alison's goal is the happiness that comes from not suffering—in her case, this means that her family isn't threatened and that anyone interested in her as a clone stays far away. She also doesn't see the need for anyone else to look for answers, preferring everything to stay on a need-to-know basis. When Sarah seeks her out for the first time, Alison refuses to tell her anything about the situation, saying that it isn't her responsibility. Instead, she becomes furious that Sarah showed up in her territory: "This is my neighborhood, you wait for a call" ("Instinct") [Wolfert and Barkman 30].

Suburban Gothic is defined by Bernice M. Murphy as "a subgenre of the wider American Gothic tradition which dramatizes anxieties arising from the mass urbanization of the United States and usually features suburban settings, preoccupations and protagonists" (2). There's a message that horror shouldn't occur in nice neighborhoods (though of course, it does).

Buffy the Vampire Slayer sometimes faces prosaic problems like bursting water pipes and fast food mystery meat, but on *Desperate Housewives* "the overt supernaturalism and apocalyptic tendencies of BTVS are avoided in favor of a wry depiction of the suburban locale as a place of quiet desperation and festering secrets" (Murphy 168). The heroines solve mysteries about their neighbors, a current also present in *Orphan Black* as Alison contends with Aynsley and Angie.

"In both, the *idea* of suburbia becomes more important than the physical space itself" (Murphy 168). Bailey Downs is "Where Friends Are Family," according to the creepy sign with the maniacally smiling family of four. Felix and Sarah mock the place for the kind of lifestyle it implies, and Alison in turn judges and cleans while staying in Felix's downtown flat. Of course, she also struggles with drinking and drugs. *Desperate Housewives* deals with alcoholism and *Buffy*, drug and magic addiction, stressing the private pain hidden in suburbia. *True Blood* has these and others as many community members are drawn into addictive behavior.

Big Love shows the patriarch Bill Henrikson concealing his three wives and their families from the judgmental community. "It is this contrast between Bill's seemingly normal suburban life and the secrets which he and his family must conceal from mainstream society which provides one of the main conflicts" (Murphy 169). *Weeds* has a determined widow, Nancy Botwin, who starts dealing drugs to support her upscale lifestyle. She soon discovers everyone in her society is corrupted in one way or another. Echoing her, Alison buys drugs and handguns in her clean, cheery local superstore, asking the young supplier about his mother in friendly fashion. Soon she too is selling them on the pleasant-looking sidewalks. "As in *Weeds,* and in many other suburban-set texts, both gothic and non-gothic, upper middle-class suburbia is seen as a place of moral compromise and material entrapment for women" (Murphy 171).

Even as Alison loves her life and family, she hates her new secret world of Clone Club, and in season one, resists with all that she is. "So my bottom line is my children can't know their mother is a freak. Things have to stay on a need-to-know basis," Alison insists ("Variation Under Nature" 103). She uses this self-hating language through the first season, calling Sarah "ugly" in a disturbing moment of loathing. Her inability to have the children so central to her life seems one of the triggers here. Her actress comments:

> She was the most daunting clone for me to play. At first, I couldn't get a sense of her beyond the soccer mom cliché. John Fawcett told me that she's the most feminine character on the show and I just thought: "I don't know what that means!" I ended up listening to a lot of musicals to get into her headspace. There's something about them that suggests repressed emotions and that connects with her: she's got this "perfect life" and yet she is a ball of simmering anger ready to explode. Now, weirdly, she's the character I connect with most because I feel like we're all waiting to be found out [Elan].

She plays Alison holding herself very stiffly and yet in constant movement, anxiously checking her hair and touching her face. She's so tightly wound that she can't ever be still. Her voice is higher-pitched than her sisters' and she cuts her words off in a staccato rhythm. When Alison sends her kids to the neighbor's or rushes them to the car, she excuses it as "a race" or "it's gonna be fun," weak frantic lies the children likely see through. Maslany adds, "I love Alison 'cause she's like all these parts of me that I want to pretend I don't have in me" ("Send in the Clones").

Co-creator Graeme Manson says, "To have the most paranoid of them all as the most normal of them all is pretty rich" ("Send in the Clones"). Alison's tightly-wound nature appears in her relationship with her husband. When he asks why she's suddenly sent the kids away, she retorts snappishly, "You have your usual Thursday night drinks with clients, right? ... So I'll see you when you come crashing in at 3:00 a.m., now, won't I?"

He can only respond, "I don't crash in ... one time" ("Effects of External Conditions" 104). Their marriage is strained, especially in how they connect. "There is an enormous bitterness among contemporary heterosexual women toward men, whom they blame for not understanding them, for not communicating well, for shirking responsibility, for exchanging their aging wives at midlife for young trophy wives" (Paglia 141). While Donnie is kind and certainly shows no signs of doing the last of these, Alison harbors deep suspicions of him. It finally is revealed that he is in fact keeping deep secrets capable of destroying their marriage.

Trapped with her husband as her monitor, Alison reenacts still older story patterns. Gothic involves the uncanny, which Freud described as "that class of the frightening which leads back to what is known of old and long familiar" (qtd, in Hughes et al. 529). The heroine, trapped in the home, discovers it's a monstrous place of hidden dangers. Bluebeard plotlines appear—the jealous husband who spies on and murders his wife as she investigates his past crimes. Further, on the show, homes are not really safe places—police, thugs, and criminals burst into Alison's but also Felix's and Mrs. S's homes constantly. People from drug dealers to nosy neighbors spy in Donnie and Alison's windows, and police destroy their daughter's slumber party. The suburban nightmare house has neighbors with terrible secrets or it traps the characters in claustrophobic unhappiness. Abuse and dysfunctional families are common here. The basements and garages hide frightening menaces. Finally, it's "a place in which the most dangerous threats come from *within*, not from without" (Murphy 3).

In Alison's ridiculously frivolous craft room, she's bound him to a chair with her latest knitting project and tapes down his arms with red and black striped packing tape. There, she interrogates him, demanding he share his one secret, a locked box. He demands she untie him but Alison calmly refuses and spins a Lazy Susan of color-coded scissors with implied threat, then selects one. "Don't worry, honey," she patronizes deliberately. "It's all good. Isn't that what you always tell me?" She snips the scissors in the air with a direct look at Donnie's groin. With this, she actually resembles mad Helena. As she taunts Donnie, she flips the Bluebeard story, becoming the persecutor, not the persecuted. Further, she brings in suburban gothic—a world that looks overly normal but is filled with dark, violent secrets. Even her colorful household scissors are a weapon.

Next, she threatens Donnie with the hot glue gun and advises he think about what he might want to get off his chest. "Or what?" Donnie sneers. "You're going to stick sequins on me?" She drips some hot glue on his furry chest and Donnie screams in pain. Alison leaps back, shocked by her own behavior, and perhaps the fact that she's enjoying hurting her husband. Donnie.... You perform medical examinations on me in my sleep," she insists. She pops her hot pink sleep mask over his eyes, adds her hot pink headphones to block his hearing, and stuffs cloth in his mouth as a gag. This makes the scene more ludicrously suburban as her weapons are so cheerful and bright.

Of course, he's enraged, but appears innocent as he protests to the more rational Sarah, standing in for his out-of-control wife: "Alison, would you listen to yourself? I got up in the middle of the night to watch cricket! Cricket? The South African games start at 4:00 a.m. Is there nothing in my life left unexamined by you? Now take off the GD blindfold! The whole neighborhood is here? What kind of irrational nonsense is going through that head of yours!" ("Variations Under Domestication" 106). Sarah retorts that he needs to respect his wife, who's holding the family together. As the episode ends, he confesses his sins to Alison in bed—he was writing flirty letters with an old girlfriend and wanted to keep a single secret to himself. When Donnie confesses, Alison of the comics thinks, "Dirty letters and secret feelings. I know I should be furious about it. But it's just so much ... smaller than I thought. I don't even know what to feel" (*The Clone Club* #3: Alison).

She forgives him and they go to a marriage retreat, though in the comics, Alison drinks heavily there, appalling Donnie who worries the kids might see her this way (*The Clone Club* #3: Alison). After the retreat, Alison decides on divorce. On hearing this, Sarah is quite concerned.

> ALISON: Oh, I'm fine. It's my decision. Everything is under control.
> SARAH: Okay, now I'm worried.
> ALISON: Well, don't be. I can take care of myself and I don't need you helping me clear my deck of liars and spies.
> SARAH: Alison, you don't know who your monitor is, okay?
> ALISON: Don't fixate. I'm reclaiming my life, Sarah. Please respect that.

Moments later, Aynsley walks in, claiming she "just came to water the plants" ("Entangled Bank" 108). Alison is instantly suspicious. When Aynsley tries to take coaching the skating team, Alison, suspecting she's the watcher, seduces her husband Chad. For the first time in her arc, the uptight heroine actually relaxes as she smokes marijuana with Chad in the parking lot and notes, "This is the first hit I've had since *Godspell* in college" ("Entangled Bank" 108). Moments later, she announces, "I'm objectifying you, sexually, to get back at Donnie," and seduces him, right in the van that rocks blatantly in front of everyone. Her secrets are hidden no longer. The two women find themselves fighting, after. "Postfeminism, based as it is upon competition, guarantees that a power and privilege imbalance will exist among women" (Helford 293). If the women identify foremost as wives, a threat to each other's husbands compromises their identities.

Societal critic Camille Paglia blames women's frigidity on "bourgeois propriety" (183). She explains, "As respectability became the central middle-class value, censorship and repression became the norm" (183). Certainly, this describes the suburban heroine. Maslany says of Alison, "She wants to project perfection, so everything about her clothing says, 'I'm proper, I'm a good woman, and I don't have sex.' And these are all lies. She's a murderer, she's pretty sexual, and quite vicious. She's done so many horrible things, and yet she continues to put out this image of herself (Bernstein 52). The intervention of episode nine horrifies Alison—confronted with the public judgement of neighbors, church and mother in law, she retreats into the bathroom and will only speak with Felix. In contrast with the minister's judgmental comment than Felix is welcome among them, unconventional Felix offers a real safe space. He even shares her pills instead of judging. "There's a lot of common ground there, that they don't even realize exists," Felix's actor says of himself and Alison ("Clone Club Insiders").

Her denial features heavily in her interaction with her sisters. There, she's the least involved, as she insists, "I don't want to know anything, leave me out of it ... plausible deniability ("Nature Under Constraint and Vexed" 201). She disguises as them when pressured and she even agrees to take her turn fostering Helena. "However, she's not actively involved in DYAD; we never see her helping decode Professor Duncan's book or hinting down people who might have more information. The closest she gets is chucking Clone Club some money in case of sketchy transactions" (Wolfert and Barkman 31). At the first season's end, she signs a contract with Neolution so they'll leave her alone—all she's ever wanted. "Alison knows that Leekie and DYAD are far from trustworthy, but the promise of privacy and security is too much for her to resist. Barely a few hours later, she signs the contract and faxes it in" (Wolfert and Barkman 31–32).

Alison's defining moment appears at the end of season one. While confronting Aynsley about monitoring her, Aynsley stuffs a handmade angel from Alison down the disposal. She gets her scarf caught and chokes, begging for help as Alison silently watches. This moment echoes one from *Breaking Bad* season three, as Walter White watches Jane choke on her own heroin vomit. Both are moments of suburbia turned brutal.

After, Donnie offers to reconcile and she's comforted. However, at the next season's start, she discovers he's her monitor. With the knowledge that she murdered her best friend and has no one to trust, she falls apart and returns to the drugs and drinking she'd given up. The actress describes Alison's sense of denial after the destruction of season one. "there's no way to get it back but she'll pretend everything's good" ("Clone Club Insiders"). She's filled with "paranoia, fear, everything that makes Alison Alison" ("Clone Club Insiders").

Meanwhile, she's given Aynsley's part in the play. The decision to have Alison take over Aynsley's role, however, was a late addition. "Having Aynsley originally in the musical was a great way to doubly up the stakes because it meant that her murder is literally on stage," Manson said. "That's the fortuitous thing going on with this musical that eerily paralleled the storyline. It added this other layer of psychological complexity to Alison's slow unwinding" (Wieselman).

In gothic tradition, her community musical is a play of guts, gore, and secrets that perfectly matches her arc. She and her fellow performers dance with mops and buckets while singing about cleaning up blood. Bringing truth to suburban gothic, *Blood Ties* is a real musical. Developed in 2009 by Toronto-based duo Anika Johnson and Barbara Johnston, *Blood Ties* follows three friends participating in a wedding only to find themselves forced to clean up after the apparent suicide of the bride's uncle. "It was a real jaw-dropping moment," Manson recalled of discovering just how perfectly *Blood Ties* echoed the guilt Alison was facing. "We worried a little bit at first that it might be too on the nose, but ended up deciding this twisted little show was on the nose in the right way" (Wieselman). The showrunners "bumped up the camp" and asked them to "give the script a real *Waiting for Guffman* style of excellent amateurism, and encouraged us to create dance moves, staging, and vocal arrangements that were as corny and over-the-top as possible." With this, they had a musical (Maloney).

By the time of the play, as Alison looks in the mirror "she's unraveling completely" ("Behind the Scenes: Hair and Makeup"). "We knew that Alison's breakdown was going to come to a head on opening night because, psychologically, there's nothing more perfect for Alison than to have that breakdown on stage, in front of everyone," Manson said. "It's her deepest fears realized" (Wieselman). She reaches catharsis and tumbles drunkenly off the stage.

"Alison really hit rock bottom and will have to pick herself up and dust herself off now. And she's going to have to do it in a very isolated way," Manson teases (Wieselman). The next episode she finds herself in rehab, where Felix urges her to stay a while and get settled. There, Alison is shocked by Vic, now cleaned up and reformed. Insisting that he's found inner peace with Buddha, he tells her, "Anger is a tool, and we use it on problems, not people" ("To Hound Nature in Her Wanderings" 206). As he stands up for her and encourages her to confide in him, she finds him a surprisingly sympathetic friend as they shoot hoops (badly) and make crafts together. As with Felix, he's unconventional, but she finds him more sympathetic than her suburban friends. However, Vic, as it turns out, is spying on Alison for Detective Angie, who has promised to drop the charges against him. When Alison tells him about killing Aynsley, he finally has enough dirt.

She sends for Felix and Sarah, and Donnie finally discovers the truth about the clones and how Doctor Leekie has used him. He confronts Leekie and accidentally shoots him. In the next episode, "Variable and Full of Perturbation" (208), a guilty, miserable, drunken Donnie tries to leave, but Alison insists they talk honestly. She asks directly if he loves her, addressing their central conflict after two seasons of berating him.

> "The whole relationship with Donnie was just so wonderful this season," says Maslany. "It was so intense. We got to show that love between the two of them again for the first time and some rebuilding of trust. That's such an important thing for the two of them because they do love each other so much, and we have to care about that relationship so that we care about the rest of the storylines. And Kristian [Bruun, who plays Donnie] is so fantastic to work with. He's so funny and so sweet and a great actor" [Orphan Black Season 2].

As they finally confide in each other, each confesses their murder, and Alison helps Donnie clean up his. Their body-hiding scenes are laughably disgusting, involving a chest freezer, giant drill, and attempts not to vomit. The ludicrous scene is complete suburban gothic with their horrors hidden beneath their perfect home. "Do we have a boat?! Have you ever seen *Dexter*? I mean, random scuba divers are finding everything! We can't risk transporting him, Donnie," she protests ("Things Which Have Never Yet Been Done" 209). Meanwhile, they're interrupted by their own kids, Vic, and of course, the police. At this last, Donnie blows up. "You don't want to know what we know and, if you come near my home or my family again, I will bury you" ("Things Which Have Never Yet Been Done" 209). Alison has never been so turned on, and they have sex right on the chest freezer. John Fawcett smiles, "We get a lot of dark comedy and paranoia and suburban shenanigans out of Alison" ("Clone Club Insiders").

The article "Gothic Possibilities" by Norman Holland and Leona Sherman called female gothic "the image of woman-plus-habitation and the plot of mysterious sexual and supernatural threats in an atmosphere of dynastic mysteries" (qtd. in Hughes et al. 233). This pattern, appearing in Radcliffe, Austen, Shelley, and the Brontës, along with more modern works all offer "a central concern with female identity, particularly the conflict with an all-encompassing mother within a patriarchal culture where women's bodies become prisons because women are defined as motherless and defective" (Hughes et al. 234). Certainly, the clones (some of whom are terminally ill) are damaged. All have deep-seated issues of one sort or another. Further, they are crippled by the pain of knowing they cannot be proper mothers and that their own mothers willingly participated in the program.

The gothic trope of doubles fits perfectly here—looking at another woman, especially a despairing suicidal one like Beth, a dead one like Katja, or a monster like Helena, and seeing oneself. In this vein, the Madwoman in the Attic is a "mad monstrous, and fiercely independent figure who act as the author's double within the text, articulating their repressed desire to escape from male houses and male texts" (Hughes et al. 233). Sarah fills this role for Alison, and then in the later seasons, Helena takes over.

In a historical time in which Mary Shelley and the Brontë sisters were nearly barred from being authors, their take on the gothic channeled their rage and subversion against the patriarchy that restricted them. Their melodramatic characters act on their subversive impulses, battling for freedom and succumbing to madness in a world that offered women so few outlets. Caught in a similar web, Alison is the character who has a breakdown and actually goes to rehab, unable to express her pain and rage.

"Alison is very determined this year to carve out a little normalcy in her suburban community," Manson says of season three (Nguyen, "Here's Everything"). She begins campaigning for school trustee. Course, this only postpones her problems instead of healing them: "Defensive behavior, bodily symptoms, and neurotic habits give us something—anything—to do, and we often do these things with a compulsiveness that is religious in nature. But because it is unconscious religiosity it can only stave off the danger and not resolve it" (Nelson 52). When Donnie loses his job, she solves two problems by becoming the new drug seller for her suburban community, campaigning to her clients as she hides her product under fancy homemade soaps (bringing in her love of crafting as well).

Making herself more miserable, she compromises by buying her mother Connie out of Bubbles, a store she's always hated. The place's décor is over the top in pink, purple, and lime. Meanwhile, the name suggests soap, but also the perky denial Alison and her mother share. To enact her plan, Alison must deal with her mother, who makes small jabs over and over and tries to get Alison to ditch Donnie for her old boyfriend Jason the drug dealer ("Community of Dreadful Fear and Hate" 307). Most offensively, she has a poster up endorsing Alison's rival, Marci Coates. Even as her dynamic with her mother pushes her back to her teen years, Alison finds herself literally at the high school, confronting all her choices.

Fawcett says of the episode, "We kind of wanted to just give the audience a breather and change the mood, and really kind of have a chance to be a little bit light and let people laugh … and not have an episode that's really heavy in story and conspiracy" (Towers). Cosima shows up and Felix performs another clumsy switch as he makes her play Alison and smile, smile, smile for the camera. "I think we can get the smiles even bigger than that. I think that we can just drive those cheeks up until it hurts, just a bit," Felix insists. Their entire team resemble perky elves in their pink snow hats. "It's like you're selling bubble gum," Marci chirps. Under all this lurks Alison's sinister funding: The pert school scene is heightened through its contrast with seedy Pouchy, crouched over his drug money in an auto repair place, threatening to slice off Donnie's nose. Alison runs back and forth, juggling this with her mother and her campaign—leaving nothing for herself. At the scene's end, Alison has had enough of the pretense and tells her mother about the clones. Her mother, however, disbelieves and denies everything. Their dynamic hasn't changed. Fawcett adds:

> I think that's kind of what this all comes to: that Alison just realizes that she can't change her mother. And it's kind of like a weird coming to terms with herself and with her mother by the end of the episode, and you feel like maybe Alison will be a little more at peace with her mother, to some degree. Because when you're not like fighting against someone as much, you wind up having a more peaceful relationship. There's this other aspect of it, which is important thematically … which is you can't choose your family [Towers].

Season three ends on Election Day, as Alison campaigns with a bullhorn and free soap. In her rather ridiculously decorated school bus (complete with her picture on the front and cheering inside, Alison appears completely helpless, the naïve domestic heroine. She's far from it, however, as she and Donnie lure the murderous clone Rudy into a trap for Helena to murder. She's like Alison's darker double, the madwoman in the garage who bursts forth to defend their home in Alison's place. At episode end, Alison throws a big dinner for her sisters at Bubbles, then proudly discovers she's won the election. She tells them all, "I know school trustee isn't much, but it's something that we all fought for, a little victory amidst all the bull cookie." Clearly, even as Alison craves normalcy, she's come to terms with her messy secret, dysfunctional family—more loyal than her birth mother.

The next season requires more grotesque scenes as they dig Doctor Leekie back up, then more troubles as Donnie is arrested to pressure the clones to comply. If Alison is the most outwardly normal, she's also the most vulnerable, as the police strike at her repeatedly. The Hendrixes end the season camping with Helena in primitive safety, but Neolution soon comes for them. "The Few Who Dare" (501) offers the incongruous sight of Donnie fleeing with his rolling bag as Alison is kidnapped by masked goons.

In "Beneath Her Heart" (503), Alison returns to her suburban world by trying to manage the Church Fall Fun Fair, only to be confronted with Aynsley's family, as well as judgmental neighbors who know about her drinking. When Donnie takes the drugs she'd meant to use on a rude neighbor, her secrets are finally revealed. Choosing to own them at last, she finally faces down suburbia; she tells the community about her sisterhood, acknowledging her larger world outside her town. Alison insists, "I have atoned for my sins. And I have a life that is so much bigger than Bailey Downs. I am part of a sisterhood that you couldn't even begin to understand." The big issues in suburban gothic are "personal identity and the paradoxical comforts and perils of conformity" (Murphy 4). In this moment, she finally gives up her propriety for love. After this embracing of all she's hidden, Alison decides she wants to discover herself away from husband and home. She bids a brief farewell to Donnie and they sing "Ain't no Mountain" together.

"The female version centralizes a female point of view, culminates in a happy ending, explains the supernatural, and tends toward terror, while the male version uses multiple points of view, more often has a tragic ending or resists closure, includes real ghosts, and favors horror (Hughes et al. 235). The threat of losing autonomy has been the heroines' great demon through the series, though it vanishes when they bring DYAD's many crimes to light. In "Gag or Throttle" (507), Alison returns with a purple bob and tattoo. As she adds, thanks to a Jungian she's "so much better at being present now" instead of living in her panicked headspace. Further, she literally invites the madness into her house in the form of Helena. As Helena murders the thugs terrorizing her family in seasons three and four, and then settles in with her unconventional babies Orange and Purple, Alison finds peace as she lets Helena express all she herself never has. Alison also embraces music and begins to love her dark side, instead of frantically burying it in conventionality.

Donnie: New Man or Family Joke?

In a comic book flashback to young Alison and Donnie at "Hookup point," he asks, anxiously, "That was good, right?" and she responds with "Practice makes perfect." (*The Clone Club* #3: Alison). With women's liberation came a new staple character to the screen. "The new sensitive man stood between the liberated woman and what television suggested were two unattractive extremes, spinsterhood and feminism," explains Judy Kutulas in "Liberated Women and New Sensitive Men" (223).

> The new sensitive men added the final critical touch to the portrait of the liberated woman. He provided the legitimacy that equated her from the feminist. He modeled sensitivity for male viewers, reassuring them that there was still a place for then. in liberated women's lives and teaching them how to treat female coworkers as friends and equals. Perhaps more importantly, off the job, the new sensitive man found his sensitivity rewarded in sexual ways not available to earlier television working singles. More than the cute apartment, new job, and stylish clothes, he promised that being liberated had its own set of payoffs; payoffs that could cycle a working woman into traditional domesticity or, like Mary Richards, keep her proudly careerist.
>
> Together, the liberated woman and the new sensitive man carefully separated the most palatable aspects of feminism and packaged them into a neat consumer-friendly ideal. From the start, television's notion of liberation was fraught with contradictions, but a lot of its appeal was its complexity, which signified its realism. That complexity eased the frustrations and pleasures of real women's lived experiences—their uncertainty, their sense of being trapped between ideologies, their objectification, and their new consumer identities [Kutulas 224].

Kristian Bruun, who plays Alison's doughy husband, Donnie, says that like his wife, he's committed to suburbia: "They love their quiet suburban lifestyle. They really cherish it. They love their family, they love their community, they love being leaders of a sort within their community. And Donnie loves Alison, even though they bicker a lot. I very much think Alison wears the pants, and I think that works for Donnie, he's fine with that" (Bernstein 57).

Paglia adds that this reflects a larger societal problem: "Nor are husbands offering much stimulation in the male display department: visually, American men remain perpetual boys, as shown by the bulky t-shirts, loose shorts, and sneakers they wear from preschool through midlife. The sexes, which used to occupy intriguingly separate worlds, are suffering from over-familiarity, a curse of the mundane. There's no mystery left" (184). Of course, Donnie has some mystery. He's revealed as Alison's monitor in season two but subverts the predatory role because he really is clueless. As he confesses, he was recruited into a study: "Long-term social metrics. They told me it was totally benign but the subjects had to remain completely unaware" ("Knowledge of Causes, and Secret Motion of Things" 207). The comic shows Leekie recruiting Donnie in college, needling him on his lack of success and telling him, "Do you really want your life with Alison to start out mired down with debt? She deserves better" (*The Clone Club #3: Alison*). Leekie promises to pay him and also forgive his student debt. When he protests the invasive tests, Leekie responds, "You're not exactly a doctor, now are you, Donnie," belittling him. On the show, he finally confronts the man who masterminded all this.

> DONNIE: You came into my house and probed my wife.
> LEEKIE: Listen to me, you turnip. In 100 years' time, no one will care in any way about Donnie Hendrix except as a footnote in this experiment.
> DONNIE: You ruined my marriage. My wife hates me.
> LEEKIE: I gave you your wife. Put the gun away and go home to bed, huh?
> ["Knowledge of Causes, and Secret Motion of Things" 207]

Donnie shoots him, fumblingly, apparently by accident. It's a ludicrous moment as "Love is All Around" plays ironically, as it did earlier that episode during the miserable chaos of family day at the rehab center.

"It seems clear enough that there have been recent changes in the constitution of masculinity in advanced capitalist countries, of at least two kinds: a deepening of tensions around relationships with women, and the crisis of a form of heterosexual masculinity that is increasingly felt to be obsolete" (Carrigan et al. 160). In a cut scene from the season two finale, Donnie insists that as the man of the family, he'll defend Alison and her sisters. He tries blackmailing Rachel with Leekie's body, but she responds by showing him photos of his children, extended family, and social circle. "Nobody leave the experiment. Not even you two, the most boring subjects I've ever administered. Not even Aldous, it seems. So go home and monitor your wife. Or I'll drag her in here with the rest of them." With a final plea of "they're your sisters" that falls on deaf ears, he leaves the women to rescue themselves.

Donnie ditches his job, forcing them into another crisis, this one financial. As he tells Alison, "I finally did it, Ali. I finally told Susan Teller what was what.... Oh, it was frickin' glorious. I called her a bitch" ("The Weight of This Combination" 301). The word choice suggests his frustration with a domineering female boss—though ironically, this mirrors his relationship at home. Once again, his interactions at work speak to a larger gender shift: "Some of the familiar economic and cultural changes in contemporary capitalism—the growth of large bureaucratized corporations, the integration of business and government, the shift to technocratic modes of decision making and control—have implications for the character of 'male dominance" (Carrigan et al. 161). Having lost the company car, he must ride the children's bus, which his wife is driving.

Donning the pants for the family, Alison continues showing up Donnie in season three, running for office to protect her children when Donnie can't. As their finances dip, she is the one to find a source of income, selling drugs concealed in ladylike soap boxes to her friends on the street. It's a world in which Donnie has little influence. Not only does Alison take over her mother's business but Donnie does too, working in the garishly feminine shop selling soaps and perfumes. It's revealed that Alison's mother insisted Donnie take Alison's name ... and when he did, she lost all respect for him ("Community of Dreadful Fear and Hate" 307). Alison carries heavy boxes of soap that he can't handle in "Newer Elements of Our Defense" (304) and meets with the drug supplier Jason Kellerman alone. They hit it off ... worse, he's Alison's ex.

In "Certain Agony of the Battlefield" (306), Alison and Donnie wildly dance in their underwear with cash flying everywhere to Dulce and Gabana's "Riff-Raff." It's such a break out for the repressed couple, emphasizing how much they've changed. Fawcett comments: "They're living out their gangsta fantasies. We love the suburban underwear—hey, anytime we can get these two in their underwear, it's pretty good. That was a hilarious evening on set, no question. Kristian and Tat—it's this weird thing because they connect a little bit in this kind of music and in the art form of dance, I have to say. Get these two together at a club ... watch out" (Ross, "Twerktastic Episode"). Alison's radical swings emphasize how lost Donnie feels in the shifting parameters of their marriage, a larger symptom of the transformation of his place in the world. "A good many men feel themselves to be involved in some kind of change having to do with gender, with sexual identity, with what it is to be a man. The 'androgyny' literature of the late 1970s spoke to this in one way, the literature about the importance of fathering in another" (Carrigan et al. 160).

Donnie tries being the man again in "Certain Agony of the Battlefield" (306): He insists on going with her to the latest drug meeting and adds, "I'm not talking about being jealous. Because I am jealous. Your man is savage jealous, Mrs. Hendrix. But paying this debt to Kellerman is business, and if we really are going to take it to the next level, then we do that together." He bursts in on their meeting in a shiny new car—an acquisition that means manpower and wealth, as well as rescuing him from the bus he hates. "10k down in cash! Should have seen the guy's face" ("Certain Agony of the Battlefield" 306). At once, Alison and Jason criticize his ridiculous purchase.

In "Community of Dreadful Fear and Hate" (307), Donnie goes with Jason to meet the boss and gives Alison a long, pointed kiss goodbye. However, his macho moment is undercut by Jason's emasculating "I'll take care of him." Jason is clearly the macho man, leaving Donnie in the weaker role, and both know it.

> JASON: I should have brought Alison.
> DONNIE: Yeah, you've made your preference clear.
> JASON: Look, man, are we having a problem here?
> DONNIE: Not unless you come between me and my family.
> JASON: Consider your territory pissed on ["Community of Dreadful Fear and Hate" 307).

The "New Man" of course is common in sitcoms as the gentle "nice guy" who generally gets the girl. As Kutulas notes, "He was a media creation, a man himself liberated from gender stereotypes and open to his feelings, genuinely interested in women as people, nurturing and warm, a man not afraid to cry" (223). Donnie may try to act tough, but he fits this category. The head drug dealer Pouchy and his family threaten to cut off Donnie's nose, and he waits for Alison to save him. "Big guy, big guy, don't! Por favor, not my nose!" he begs after they ludicrously push him towards the paper cutter. After Alison comes through, he, less than collected, asks to use the bathroom in another humorous moment.

Donnie confronts Jason in "Ruthless in Purpose, and Insidious in Method" (308), but finds Jason is far tougher than he can handle. He retorts, "You work for me now, you understand? If I want your wife, I'll just take her." Donnie slaps him, but as Jason ridicules him for it, he beats him up, adding, "You like that, you boat shoe, chino-wearing bitch?"

Donnie struggles to hide his injuries after, and confronts Pouchy's gang alone, or tries to, insisting to Helena, "It's a dad decision, for the family. And you're part of it now" ("Insolvent Phantom of Tomorrow" 309). However, his negotiations result in his confessing to emasculating low sperm mobility as the dealers joke, and not getting his money back. When they threaten his children, he can do nothing, but the stronger Helena steps in, killing all the drug dealers and getting Donnie's money back, plus a good deal more ("Insolvent Phantom of Tomorrow" 309).

It should be noted that as Helena laughs at his jokes and calls him "strong like baby ox" in "Ruthless in Purpose, and Insidious in Method" (308), Donnie feels strikingly gratified. He's being appreciated as a man in a way Alison usually doesn't bother with. Meanwhile, Felix and the others help Alison cope while Helena provides the muscle. Bruun comments that Donnie "is a better man having met his extended family" (Nguyen, "*Orphan Black* Cast"). "History Yet to Be Written" (310) ends with the dinner at Bubbles. Alison has won her coveted school board position, leaving Donnie as the politician's still-unemployed spouse and support. Mrs. S and Alison are the heads of the table and Donnie seems fine with that as he teases Helena about her pregnancy. Once more, he's in the supportive role.

In season four, he must push his effeminate side further as he plays Felix's husband when they infiltrate fertility clinics. Felix actually tells him he's "mincing" too much and should seriously dial it back. As usual, Alison bosses him around when they must dig up Leekie's corpse and evade police suspicion. Soon Brightborn's police contacts throw him into prison to be a hostage for the Clone Club—once again, he's the damsel with a knife literally to his throat. The women of the club strike back, capturing Duko and then letting Siobhan execute him in her own revenge plot. As Donnie blubbers and begs, the women arrange his release. Near season end, Helena returns to save them all again. While Donnie lies helplessly tied up and Alison prays for deliverance, the stronger sister shoots the Brightborn goon threatening them and leads them off to safety camping in the wilderness.

While Alison is captured early in the fifth season, Donnie runs off into the trees, ridiculously dragging his wheeled suitcase behind him while Alison cries for rescue. Once again, he fails to be her shining knight. Helena rescues him, though he reciprocates and drives her to the hospital when she's injured. He soon gets to make a fool of himself at the Church Fall Fun Fair in "Beneath Her Heart" (503), as he prepares a Highland dance in full kilt. After he drinks the tea Alison has drugged, he wobbles onstage and falls heels over head, apparently giving the audience quite a show. As he lies passed out, Alison stands over him and gives a speech defending them both, coming to his rescue once more.

In the finale, Donnie's gotten a new job and is even the Regional Manager. Ironically after all the escapades with the corpses in the garage, he's found a job creating concrete floors. As he specifies to Alison, "I don't pour them but I do help the clients with the designs." It's a job that's "architectural and creative," but also a souvenir of his Clone Club adventures. Though he's finally the breadwinner again, he also cuddles Helena's babies in the episode, softening his image. He ends the show performing a striptease for Alison (throwing his sweaty clothes straight into the washer in the ultimate woman's fantasy), once more taking the gentler role as she directs his action.

Cosima: Classic Second Wave

Asked who she relates to most, Tatiana Maslany replies that it's Cosima, "She's very focused, she loves what she does so much, she's extremely passionate about what she does. And she makes really dumb decisions sometimes and falls for the wrong person sometimes" (Wheaton).

Cosima Niehaus first appears as a helpful voice on the phone, guiding Sarah through hiding Katja's body and instructing her to find the briefcase. The "PhD student, evolutionary developmental biology at University of

Minnesota" lingers long enough for an introduction, then heads back home ("Variation Under Nature" 103). She begins the first season as the brains, instructing Sarah over the internet in what to do whenever she's stuck or needs something researched. An eager scientist, Cosima's passion for biology often finds her "totally dorking out" ("Entangled Bank" 108) over her various experiments and projects. She seems classic second wave feminist, with a higher education level than all her sisters. From her Birkenstocks to her time at Berkeley to her lesbianism, everything around her emphasizes she can succeed without men.

> "What stands out," wrote one Dutch feminist, "is the *social* side of feminism." In establishing health clinics, rape crisis centers, and centers of advocacy, or more generally creating separate spaces for women to meet in—cafes, bookstores, seminars and study groups—and promoting a specific sociability—parties, dinners, vacations, shared living arrangements—feminists seemed to be realizing the great ambition of female solidarity [Ergas 541].

For important sectors of many feminist movements, lesbianism was seen as the perfect path to independence. Whether or not Cosima believes in this path, her appearance and values sync well with it. "'The Lesbian,'" wrote an American feminist in 1969, "is freed of dependence on men for love, sex, and money." Likewise, feminist theorist Monique Wittig reiterated: "Lesbian societies are not based on women's oppression. Furthermore, what we aim at is not the disappearance of lesbianism, which provides the only social form we can live in, but the destruction of heterosexuality—the political system based on women's oppression" (Ergas 541–542). As Cosima seeks this kind of relationship, she also battles for respect. Queer theology particularly seeks to question "the myth of heterosexuality as a natural or a given" (Thweatt-Bates 163). Knowing this, Cosima tells a critical Rachel that her sexuality is very emphatically not the most interesting thing about her when they meet—she is a person not a deviation from the norm.

Lesbianism has not always been rebellious counterculture. Analyst Lillian Faderman argues that it is not sexual activity that makes lesbianism subversive to the patriarchy. After all, she points out, romantic friendships "had been encouraged or tolerated for centuries" (qtd. in Kulkarni 82). Love between women only became threatening after the emergence of the feminist movement around 1920, when women suddenly gained the opportunity to achieve economic power and independence. It was then that love between women "became potentially threatening to the social order" (qtd. in Kulkarni 82).

Many lesbians preferred not to separate from mainstream society by to unite with other groups to promote change (Ransdell 646). "In queer theology, the cyborg's emphasis on bodily difference is articulated in the ways in which specific bodies transgress the categorical boundaries of gender roles and sexual behavior" (Thweatt-Bates 161). As a young lesbian female scientist investigating secret cloning, Cosima breaks many boundaries. Further, her specialty, Evo-Devo, sounds like Evil Devil, though it also sounds cutesy. However, a more literal artificiality in Cosima is her illness, as the genetic differences in her biology threaten to kill her.

"One vestige of radical feminism that persists to the present day is the network of feminist countercultural institutions and projects that were begun for the purpose of spreading feminist values, providing services to women in a nonoppressive environment and linking localized feminist communities across the country" (Ransdell 649). Cosima, warrior of the counterculture, helps bind the clones together, reassuring each as they form a sisterhood. "Studies of lesbian subcultures speak of these 'women's worlds' as social spaces where women are empowered to define their own experiences" (Ransdell 649). Within the safe space of Felix's flat or Cosima's lab, they form small communities, followed by the hideout under the gaming store in season four.

Further, Cosima is driven by discovery, her greatest passion.

> From the moment we first meet her, Cosima only becomes more deeply invested in the biology of the clones. She can't resist a new opportunity to get closer to the truth, even when it's dangerous. Take her attitude toward Helena, for example. While most of us would agree that a religious fanatic who just killed one of your sisters is typically someone to be avoided—especially when your name is up next on her hit list—Cosima has the opposite idea: "If she's not dead, we need to find her and find out what she knows.... We need to find out who she is, Sarah; she found us, she's got answers" ("Effects of External Conditions") [Wolfert and Barkman 27].

The actress says of playing Cosima, "Her weapons are her intellect and her sense of humor and her fascination with the world" (Bernstein 41).

Meanwhile, her kindness and openness inspires the same behavior in others. Stephen Lynch, key makeup artist, describes Cosima as having "a west coast, maybe Berkeley vibe" ("Send in the Clones"). Maslany adds: "Cosima's sort of a hippy stoner. Personality-wise, she was the lightest of the clones to play. She looks at everyone and everything as being full of possibilities. She's fine with how finding out the truth about the clones involves a lot of theorizing and that there aren't necessarily any answers. Intellectually, she's on another plane. I also love how she falls for Delphine: it's stupid and illogical but I love that." (Elan).

Cosima was born in San Francisco, a bastion of multiculturalism and acceptance (Bernstein 42). With this, she's open and welcoming to all. Maslany adds that the character is "probably being the most well-adjusted and the most loved. I think she's been supported her whole life" (Bernstein 41). "Cosima is the kind of misfit daughter or friend that everyone knows," Lynch explains of the bisexual biology nerd. "The girl who has gone her own way completely since high school. Her perspective is: I am my own person. I am an alternative to all of you" (Miller).

> To get her look, both Lynch and Sokolowski drew inspiration from women they encountered in real life. For Lynch, this was one of his students. "There was a girl in my class whose look I really liked," Lynch tells us. "She would draw on extreme brows that went sky high or they were really arched. It's that heavy eyeliner that is extended inward and outward at the corners." (In a funny twist of fate, the very student appeared on set one day as a background extra. After Lynch introduced her to Maslany, the two had lunch together.) For her hair, Sokolowski looked to a colleague in wardrobe. "This lovely lady who is in wardrobe had her hair white blond with these dreadlocks and she always kind of wore it like that. In my mind she was like Cosima, so I tried my own version of it" [Miller].

In 2013, the comics show Cosima in Berkeley, breaking up with her girlfriend Emi (her monitor of course) and heading off to Minnesota. She switches to Evo-Devo, a change shown to have been requested by Beth, already in touch with her. "Just happy to take one for the team, you know? We need to learn as much about ourselves as we can," she adds (*The Clone Club* #4: Cosima). Leekie watches them interact and suggests to Delphine that they tell Cosima of her origins. Deeply in love, Emi follows Cosima to Minnesota and pursues her until Paul, sent by DYAD, threatens her. When she persists, DYAD has her killed.

Halfway through the season, however, Cosima falls for a fellow student and finds herself worried this woman is her watcher. Thus, she tumbles into the same trap as Sarah, loving the one sent to spy on her. "Though we can't deny that her attraction to her new monitor was a factor, it's also in her insatiable curiosity that Cosima ignores Sarah's emphatic warnings to stay far away from Delphine" (Wolfert and Barkman 27). Of course, the metaphor is one of being emotionally open (a traditional feminine power) versus guarded, the more masculine approach. Cosima is such a nurturer that she falls, even with a scientist's caution and her knowledge of Neolution.

Cosima's new girlfriend, from France, studies immunology, specifically host-parasite relationships ("Conditions of Existence" 105). Since Delphine is indeed a spy and parasite on Cosima's life, the study is apt. The audience discovers she's secretly sleeping with Leekie. However, she introduces Cosima to Neolution and Cosima's soon intrigued. As she goes to meetings, she's skeptical but slowly won over. Sarah is appalled. She insists, "Neolution is bullshit.... Whose bloody side are you on, Cosima? ("Entangled Bank" 108). When she hangs up, Sarah sadly tells Felix, "Cosima drank the purple Kool Aid." They can no longer trust her as an ally.

Symbolically, a lesbian relationship can represent finding a lover who mirrors the self, much as all the clones do. Cosima is thrilled that Delphine is so much like herself. "I just wanna make like, uh, crazy science with you," she smiles, linking the DYAD institute with their relationship ("Entangled Bank" 108). Likewise, Delphine describes it in science terms, noting, "As a scientist I know that sexuality is a spectrum" and allowing Cosima to "coach" her ("Entangled Bank" 108).

Evelyne Brochu (Delphine) observed that her character's romance with Cosima is "one of the most important love stories in the show. I think it's great it's two women and that their main problem isn't that they're two girls." Manson added, "It really speaks to the heart of the show. It's a clone show that is about diversity.... It's just two characters who love each other" (Nguyen, "*Orphan Black* Cast").

On discovering Delphine is monitoring her, Cosima is devastated of course. At the end of season one, Cosima starts coughing up blood and finally confides her condition to Delphine, whom she forgives. She decides to take the Neolutionists' offer. "We have to know our own biology. That's what this is all about. Right? Maybe I can help us best from the inside" ("Endless Forms Most Beautiful" 110). Her fragile health appears to be another motivator.

The actress explains: "Season two picks up with her now facing her mortality. She's facing death and she's facing illness and the degeneration of her body and something very unknown happening inside her" ("Clone Club Insiders"). Even as she struggles with this devastation, she maintains her feminist insistence on autonomy. Meanwhile, her quest for answers is tied up with her romance. In the scene of Cosima's stem cell procedure, Delphine touches her suggestively and kisses her, blending medical care with emotional care ... though this is an insidious moment because she hasn't told her lover the stem cells are from Kira. "Did you ever stop to think once that this is my decision and not yours?" Cosima asks. In a rage, she pushes the other woman from her space. "This is my lab. My body! I'm the science" ("Knowledge of Causes, and Secret Motion of Things" 207). Cosima is the most ethical scientist seen on the show. When she discovers the stolen stem cells, she's horrified. After, she unwillingly requests a second baby tooth but refuses to consider bone marrow, until she falls unconscious. Her curiosity and desire to uncover the truth drives her, as she continues studying, even while dragging an oxygen tank behind her in the lab.

The actress explains of the couple, "There's so much lying from both sides ... at the same time, there's so much love and attraction" ("Clone Club Insiders"). The two women's declaration of love emphasizes their priorities and the lines they're willing to cross:

> DELPHINE: There is something important I want to tell you. Je t'aime [I love you].
> COSIMA: Is that why you didn't tell me that they were Kira's stem cells?
> DELPHINE: Yes.
> COSIMA: Is that why, even before I got here, you gave Dr. Leekie my blood samples, even though I told you not to?

DELPHINE: Cosima, it's your life.
...
COSIMA: If you betray us again, I have enough dirt on you to destroy your career. And I love you, too ["Variable and Full of Perturbation" 208].

Rachel smashes the precious stem cells, putting Cosima's life in further jeopardy. Nonetheless, she dances with her sisters that night, even knowing she may die. In the morning, cuddled in bed with Sarah, she shows her her tattoo, explaining, "So this spiral, this is the golden ratio and it's a mathematical pattern that just repeats itself in nature, in flower petals and honeybees and, you know, the stars in the galaxy and in every molecule of our DNA" ("By Means Which Have Never Yet Been Tried" 210). She's painted with science. Graeme Manson comments that this is his favorite moment and adds, "That is a triumphant scene because it's distilling a whole bunch of science down into a feeling and a tone of mystery and understanding and beauty, and it's really hard to get characters there—to fight them through all this science and plot" (Griffin and Nesseth).

"That was a really lovely moment," says Maslany. "It was just so pared down and no kind of fireworks. It's just two girls talking, and it really drove home that state of sisterhood and how much the clones love each other and need each other" ("Orphan Black Season 2"). She wakes with a revelation. In "The Weight of This Combination" (301), Cosima describes her vision to little Kira: "I was having this dream where I was, like, way above, and I could see below, and then I came back. To you.... I don't really have words for what I'm trying to say." She opens to a new spirituality beyond all science has taught her.

Soon Delphine returns to her and Manson describes it as "a conflicted relationship.... Delphine is forced to make hard choices for the good of Cosima, and Cosima bucks against those choices and fights for her own independence" (Nguyen, "Here's Everything"). Delphine breaks up with her, telling Cosima, "Cosima, I am keeping my promise to love all of your sisters equally. But to do that, I can't do this. Do you understand?" She adds, "Look, we all have our part to play, me, Sarah, Alison, but yours is to cure—yourself, and all of your sisters." They both know it's the right thing to do, as they find themselves declaring loyalty to opposite sides. In this moment, Cosima must choose between love and her mission—in second wave fashion, she claims the latter.

Cosima finds a new girlfriend in Shay, thanks to Felix, who makes her start dating on *Sapphire*. Shay tells Cosima that she is able to "see inside your soul." She's a caregiver, who focuses on spiritual counseling and physical practice, finding out whether people are in balance and helping them get there. She's a comforting, sweet relationship in contrast with Delphine's rise to power at DYAD. Shay's supportive, holistic outlook blends well with Cosima's new spirituality and gets her a little distance from DYAD ... however, she's still working with Delphine there.

Of course, leaving one's old life, like the sixties and seventies women who got divorced, proves problematic as the past won't vanish. Delphine spies on the new couple, popping in at embarrassing moments and then finally threatening to torture Shay, believing she's a spy. Apologetic in "History Yet to Be Written" (310), Delphine visits Shay to give Cosima permission to share the clones' secrets, then she and Cosima meet briefly to find closure and kiss goodbye. After, an unknown assailant catches Delphine in a parking garage and shoots her.

Cosima is devastated, of course. Season four adds further blows—Cosima crumples to the ground sobbing when the vicious Evie Cho shoots Kendall, describes Delphine's death, and destroys Cosima's work on a cure. All the pillars of her life—family, love, and science—are taken, leaving her to die. In desperation, she considers implanting herself with Sarah's cheekbot. Felix, the sympathetic, supportive outsider like herself, stops her by restoring her true love—he tells her Delphine is alive. As she breaks down in tears, Cosima backs away from destroying herself. After, Cosima tells Sarah, who's had a similar breakdown, "I'm proud of you, sestra. We both made it back from the dark side" ("The Redesign of Natural Objects" 408).

Still seeking the cure, no matter the roadblocks, Cosima works with her unethical creator, Susan Duncan. Susan left her own family decades ago and devoted her life to science during the actual second wave era. She made great discoveries, but gave up husband and daughter, as well as her ethics. Living with her, Cosima finds a new unconventional family. Nonetheless, Cosima rejects her ambition and continues to follow the moral path. When Rachel attacks Susan, Cosima grabs what's most precious—the cure she's finally created and the junior Leda clone Charlotte—and flees. With this, she pledges to save her sisterhood and the vulnerable next generation of women, though she soon discovers she's trapped on the great island of the patriarchy.

In the nearby village of Revival, Cosima is rewarded as she reunites with Delphine. While her beloved girlfriend is an ally, she refuses to directly confront their great enemy: Westmorland, the ultimate patriarch, tries to overawe and dominate Cosima as he welcomes her to his house of specimens. His disciples watch her, emphasizing how little autonomy she really has as she lives in the patriarch's kingdom. Nonetheless, Cosima continues to defy Westmorland. When he invites Delphine to dinner, she follows but refuses to wear a Victorian gown preferring instead a Victorian man's white tie attire. "Play along in a dress like this? Frock that," she quips. At the dysfunctional dinner, Cosima drinks heavily, continuing to mock Westmorland. She forces him to face her assertive, genius, gender-bending personality even as she corrects his anecdote about Darwin and reveals that she knows his plans. Alone among

Rachel, Susan, Ira, and Delphine, she bluntly defies the great patriarch, showing that she's more than his specimen or a mere damsel.

He catches her off-guard, however, when he needles Cosima about her parents, Sally and Gene, discussed onscreen for the first time. In response, Cosima speaks honestly, considering the turns their relationship has taken.

> They, uh ... they still think I'm in school in Minnesota. I haven't spoken to them in I don't know how long. Uh, which isn't unusual for us. They're ... they're, uh Professors and they live on a houseboat, so they're pretty remote. Anyway, but ... but, um they're in love. And they love me. But I haven't even told them I'm sick. Because if I did that, then I'd, you know, crack. And I'd have to tell them everything. I'd have to tell them that I'm a clone. And then they would know that everything's a lie.

Her new sisterhood has cost her the most important relationships of her life, even as she struggles to reconcile her new life and old one.

Westmorland also banishes Delphine, strong-arming the couple and suggesting a symbolic disapproval of their lifestyle. Cosima continues to spread love and well-being, caring for the terminally-ill little Aisha and befriending Mud. This teen runaway loves Westmorland and explains, "He saved my life, okay? I'm just a dirtbag junkie. I stole from my parents. I ruined everything. I couldn't even OD properly. I—I was a vegetable for, like, six months. And then I woke up here in his house" ("Manacled Slim Wrists" 506). Her nickname suggests her vanished self-esteem, which motivated her to devote herself to the patriarch. However, Cosima persuades Mud she must not put all her trust in him but should return to her worried family. She protects the young women of the island, even while helping them towards independence.

Soon, Cosima confronts Westmorland, dismantling the lies through which he controls his sycophants—he's not immortal, only a liar. Wielding his power over her in brutal fashion, Westmorland subjects Cosima to the ultimate test. He shows her his caged experiment, the wounded, suffering Yannis. "You want to end the suffering? Here, you can do it.... Go ahead, you do the ethical thing." He presses a gun into her hand.

Cosima hesitates then retorts, "You gave me life. I know you can take that away. You can't take away my humanity." She drops the gun and comforts Yannis. To her horror, however, Westmorland shoots him, barely missing Cosima, and cages her there in the basement. As with the island, this becomes an outward manifestation of the power the patriarchy already holds over her. From behind bars, Cosima pleads to be released so she can save Kira from Neolution's insidious plot. She makes a fragile alliance with Susan, Ira, and Mud—the latter two finally release her. She runs to the village to save the cure and little Charlotte once again. Confronted by the angry villagers, raging after Aisha's sudden death, Cosima calms them with her sympathy, even as she tells them the truth: "I'm sorry, but the fountain isn't real. He deceived you. I know that's really hard to hear, 'cause he deceived me too." She forms ally after ally, telling them all that Westmorland has never cared, cannot cure them, is an emperor with no clothes. This is the path of the revolutionary, mixed with enormous love for all Westmorland's victims. They let her go, and she and Charlotte manage a daring boat escape through the icy waters.

In "Gag or Throttle" (507), Cosima returns with the cure. She and Scott research Westmorland, and track down his real identity, destroying his financial power base. The patriarch is demolished at last. Cosima ends the series telling Scott she has a new mission now: there are 274 Ledas who need curing and she'll travel the world saving them all, with Delphine proudly by her side. She quotes an early boundary-breaker in a man's world, Jane Austen, who wrote, "There is nothing I wouldn't do for my friends. I have no notion of doing things by halves. It's not my nature" ("Guillotines Decide" 508). This total devotion stunningly describes her. As the woman who tears down the patriarchy, keeps her morals, and finally saves her sisterhood the world over, she's the perfect feminist model.

Beth Goes Third Wave

More than Sarah, Beth is third wave—having it all from a gun to posh clothes, and a loving boyfriend as well. This feminist movement from the nineties destabilized notions of "universal womanhood," body, gender, sexuality and heteronormativity. Young women began wearing lipstick, high heels, and tight clothing, despite the previous wave's resistance to this type of dress. Some lived with boyfriends in an increasingly socially acceptable alternative to marriage. At the same time, nineties women insisted on careers.

> In the 1990s, a self-critical, diverse and contradictory feminism came to the fore. This was a feminism that reflected postmodern ideas; it allowed for individual choice, and Social Work Education some of the certainties (the "grand narratives" of second wave feminism) could no longer be taken for granted (Mani, 2013). It accepted fully the idea that there might be different feminisms, and that gender was something, as Judith Butler argued, that was "performed," not innate (Butler, 1990). It also railed against the emerging "Men's Movement," which not only suggested that feminism had gone too far and was no longer needed, but that women who were feminists were "ball-breakers" who were out to get men (Bly, 1991). The book *Working with Men, Feminism and Social Work* (1996) reflects this mood well. The authors argue that feminism must target men and women; that only then will society as a whole change, for the benefit of all, women, men and children [Phillips and Cree].

Beth of course has lipstick, a fancy car, a live-in boyfriend, and a steady job. Her hair is long and straight—groomed, not ignored or cut into a butch style. While a cop, she prefers a more feminine-style gun, as Alison (who also enjoys shooting) explains to Sarah. Beth doesn't just straddle masculinity and femininity, but her choices. The actress describes struggling with Beth, who doesn't have an accent or outrageous clothes to define her: "She's almost the right side of the law, and yet she's a bad cop" (Bernstein 80). In the Clone Club, she did legwork, letting Cosima and Alison support her from behind the scenes. At the same time, she befriended the terribly sweet, vulnerable M.K., calling her Mika and at one point weeping in her arms. The multifaceted heroine could indeed have it all, or so it appeared.

> "We were promised that we could do it all and we would be as successful as men," says Carolyn Lo Galbo Goodfriend, 39, a mother of a five-year-old, who manages more than $300 million worth of accounts for Kraft General Foods in Rye Brook, N.Y. "But the trade-offs and sacrifices a woman has to make are far greater than a man's." Lo Galbo once met Steinem at an awards dinner and demanded to know, "Why didn't you tell us that it was going to be like this?" The matriarch of *Ms. Magazine* answered with admirable candor: "Well, we didn't know." Many mid-career women blame the movement for not knowing and for emphasizing the wrong issues [Wallis].

As it turns out, her relationship with Paul was falling apart and she had a drug addiction, linking her with the party girl pop stars of the nineties—Britney Spears, Christina Aguilera, and the Spice Girls, who promote "girl power." As her drug use endangers both relationship and career, Beth shows that the perfect life third-wavers sought could be a complete sham, an attempt to balance that could implode.

"The 'grrls' of the third wave stepped onto the stage as strong and empowered, eschewing victimization and defining feminine beauty for themselves as subjects, not as objects of a sexist patriarchy. They developed a rhetoric of mimicry, which appropriated derogatory terms like "slut" and "bitch" in order to subvert sexist culture and deprive it of verbal weapons" (Rampton). Beth, who certainly has a mouth on her, calls her beloved partner Dipshit. Beth-as-Sarah gets into character and mocks him for his macho-style gun.

Of course, Sarah's vision of Beth isn't real. As Fawcett says, "Because technically this is Sarah's version of Beth. This is what Sarah thinks Beth was, which was interesting. When we talked about that, I mean that really is the reality. Who knows Beth? The only thing that we've seen of true Beth is the video tapes of her that we saw in Beth's apartment. Beth's still kind of elusive. But I love the feeling that she's communicating with someone who is dead" (Ross, "Twerktastic Episode").

Beth has only moments before suicide, but Sarah comes to know her well, through her husband and partner, through the life she abandoned. At the same time, she offers complex mysteries to unravel. Beth has a second phone, which makes Sarah wonder what kind of double life she's leading. The comic offers a DVD of Beth that Sarah finds hidden. In this last confession, Beth says, "I thought I knew the big picture. Who the enemy was, who to keep an eye on. But I don't. I just don't know anymore." This suggests that she already had discovered DYAD but encountering Helena and the Proletheans after she killed Maggie Chen revealed a new enemy force. She knows Paul's ex-military and she spies on him as he spied on her, but she may be uncertain whom he's working for. "I can't.... I don't want it to be him. I want something we can fix. Just ... normal relationship bullshit. But how can I trust him? How am I supposed to trust anyone ever again?" Likewise, the third wave battle left the public uncertain of the rules—dating, working, bringing up children—all were thrown into chaos. Young women were rebelling but were less clear than the previous generation on what they were actually seeking. Sarah manages to learn from Beth's frustration. Seeking a clearer path, she confides in her sisters with everything she learned and soon trusts Paul as well. Through the five-year show she knows what she wants: a life with Kira and freedom for her sisters. In her mission, Beth, who paved the way, proves a guide.

Feverish and on the edge of death, Sarah confronts her vision of Beth and tries to reconcile her feelings about Paul ("Certain Agony of the Battlefield" 306). In her head, Beth jolts her into maintaining her purpose, adding, "I let myself get consumed by this thing. I killed myself because I couldn't understand it." She gives Sarah good advice, to protect her loved ones and "Stop asking why. Start asking who. Sister." With this, Sarah's inner cop points her in the right direction. Fawcett says, "Part of the emotional feel of a season finale is that it all kind of comes back around, to the train station. It all comes back around at Beth and Paul at the beginning of the series really. And I think it's one of those big contributing factors to make this episode feel so emotional and make it feel like a mid-season climax" (Ross, "Twerktastic Episode").

Season four opens with an entire episode of Beth flashback, introducing her contact, M.K. At last, the actress plays "real Beth," not Sarah's imitation or dreams and videos. Maslany comments, "She's so complicated and has such a darkness to her" ("Closer Looks 401"). She describes her "solitariness" and adds, "her separation is her demise" ("Closer Looks 401"). Certainly, Beth confides little in her sisters. She's a real mess, popping pills constantly on the job and snorting cocaine while waiting for Paul. Her guilt and misery at shooting a civilian may be cover as she knows who Maggie is. Still, her pain is real.

"The Scandal of Altruism" (406) finally reveals the season's tease—the motive behind Beth's suicide. She disguised herself in the wig and went to hold a gun on Susan Duncan, revealing that she's self-aware. However, Susan's pleas of altruism and caring finally reach Beth. Furious, Beth realizes she's been used and tells Evie Cho, who tipped her off, that she won't kill Evie's enemies just so she can get promoted. Responding ruthlessly, Evie threatens to kill all Beth's loved ones if she doesn't kill herself. Out of love for Paul, her sisters, and her parents, Beth does. Thus, her combination of family, boyfriend, and policework that characterized the third-wavers ironically conspire to get her killed. With drugs in the mix, she has no chance. It's Sarah who must spend season four piecing together the clues of Beth's final investigation and continuing her mission. Similarly, the third wave struggle made uncertain and unbalanced strides for equality. It's the next generation's more inclusive fourth wave that must ensure freedom for all.

Siobhan the Rebel

Siobhan Sadler (Maria Doyle Kennedy) is known as Mrs. S or S., suggesting distance and also a codename from her young charges. She brought up Sarah and Felix, and now is continuing with Kira, the next generation. "I always see her main intention as being good," maintains Kennedy. "I think she really loves Sarah. Part of their problem and their relationship is that they're actually so alike. They butt heads against each other all the time.... I think she does love her, but there's issues of trust on both sides" (Gelman, "*Orphan Black* Preview").

Among the archetypes, she is the radical feminist, hailing from the second wave era and willing to blow up buildings with her terrorist network to achieve her goals. Juliet Mitchell and Ann Oakley, two protagonists of the early second wave feminism recall: "At the beginning of this phase of feminism, sometime in the sixties, there were radical feminists and women's liberationists."

> Early radical feminists shared the views of writers such as Shulamith Firestone, whose *The Dialectic of Sex* affirmed the notion that womanhood was an essentially biological condition which provided a natural unity for women. Thus feminism entailed the alliance of women by women for women, on the basis of their belonging to a particular sex. Women's liberationists, on the other hand, as Mitchell herself had argued in two seminal works [*Women: The Longest Revolution*, and *Women's Estate*), rejected the radical feminists' biological claims. They sought, instead, to explicate women's conditions in fundamentally social terms, viewing solidarity among women as historically constructed rather than biologically grounded. Eventually, however, women's liberationists began to identify themselves as feminists and also became identified this way [Ergas 535].

The question of biological destiny versus social feminism is especially important with the discovery of Sarah's clones. While S. gets in a quick dig on finding that Alison (the first of Sarah's sisters she meets) went to college, she doesn't pressure Sarah to be like any of the others. Mostly, S. acts as fierce mother to Felix, Sarah, and Kira, irrespective of biology. From her first appearance, she makes it clear that protecting Kira, even from Sarah's sloppy mothering, is her highest priority. Notably, in the fifth season, she approaches Rachel, she tells her, "You saved my granddaughter. I'm willing to take a gamble on nature over nurture" ("Guillotines Decide" 508). Here she does in fact hope Rachel's biological bond with her sisters will win over Neolution's programming.

Kennedy uses "chicken" as a real-life endearment. That, like her singing (and also Donnie's Highland fling in Season Five, as she puts it, "came from Graeme and John being present when something happens and saying to themselves 'Let's get that in the show'" ("Maria Doyle Kennedy Q&A"). Her chosen family isn't the only way Siobhan ignores biological dictates. Though a woman, she generally dresses androgynously in flannel shirts. She also has a rebellious past, complete with skill at firearms. As Vanessa Farr, a Senior Social Development and Gender Advisor with the United Nations Development Programme (UNDP), notes, women are often "referenced for their capability to make peace as a supposed organic by-product of their ability to mother and nurture. These lines of discourse have tended to promote a simple women = peace: me = war dichotomy" (qtd. in Begoña). Farr goes on to contend that we "have to question the idea that women are always and only victims and men always and only perpetrators of violence" (qtd. in Begoña).

In fact, Siobhan was involved with "The Troubles" in Northern Ireland, lasting from the sixties through 1998. As she explains, "England was burning, Maggie Thatcher firing on all barrels at Ireland, the Falklands. She sacked Social Security, went after the immigrants, the poor, the unions" ("Parts Developed in an Unusual Manner" 107). Siobhan adds later, "I was on Guns for Funds. Running weapons to finance freedom. It made a lot of sense at the time. Not particularly effective, but good times" ("Governed by Sound Reason and True Religion" 202). Even her adoption of Sarah ties in with her rebellion:

> SARAH: What do you remember about Brixton, about my people, then?
> SIOBHAN: Mmm, not much. There were always women around. Kids would come and go, wards of the state. They weren't all wards. We were a, a safe house. Some of us worked in Social Services, helping women and kids, refugees, deportees, radicals on the run, that kind of thing.
> SARAH: And this boy, Carlton.
> SIOBHAN: Yeah, Carlton. I remember him. He was a fine boy. Fine man. Sometimes his pipeline would bring in a child in the black, a child to hide. You were one of them.
> SARAH: Why'd he have to hide me?
> SIOBHAN: We didn't ask what we didn't need to know. I had the chance to legitimize

> a child, so I became your legal guardian. The last time I heard from Carlton, he was about to be arrested and he warned me, he begged me, to move you away, to hide you deeper. So, I left everyone I knew and I brought you and Felix here ["Parts Developed in an Unusual Manner" 107].

"Nobody is all good or all bad," adds Kennedy. "I think she has a very strong moral compass, and sometimes she acts outside the law and sometimes even with force, but always with a sort of old fashioned code of honor. Sometimes, the actions are not great, but she does things to justify a higher cause or to protect the ones she really loves" (Gelman, "*Orphan Black* Preview"). With this history, Siobhan is also established as a warrior woman with a tradition seen over and over in the conflicts of her era. "Every bit as fierce-minded as their men, women have historically played a distinctive role in the troubles of Ireland. From the near legendary Countess Markievicz (Constance Gore-Booth), who was one of the leaders of the 1916 Easter Rising, to the black-bereted Provisional I.R.A. women of today, they have preached belligerence, run guns, helped plant bombs and provided sanctuary," a *Time Magazine* article explained in 1972 ("The Women and the Gunmen").

The violence on the streets in 1969 and 1970 was horrific with many deaths. "From the outbreak of the violence in Northern Ireland in 1969 until the 1994 cease-fires, around 3,400 people were killed and over 20,000 injured" (Begoña). This may seem a small number to be called a "war," but considering the length of the conflict and small size of the country, the effects were devastating. During the Troubles, some women gained membership in the IRA, an organization that had been all male until the early 1970s. They were imprisoned and killed in active service, alongside their male counterparts.

Feminist scholar, researcher, and activist Simona Sharoni argues that "the prevalent view of women as victims of conflict ... tends to overlook, explicitly or implicitly, women's power and agency" (qtd. in Begoña). In popular culture of the time, IRA women were "desexualized," depicted as "girls" in propaganda of the time and "angels of death" or unnatural monsters in the tabloids. Of course, this coincided with women's shifting roles: "The feminist movements of the 1960s and 1970s reflected the political contexts in which they were forged.... In particular, the ideology of the student movement, which sometimes coincided with the interests of working-class trade union and party organizations, contributed to the formation of 'new lefts.' Of such 'new lefts' feminists became important and critical—components" (Ergas 531).

The feminist movement emerged amid prison protests, assassination and war. "The Northern Ireland Women's Rights Movement came into being in 1975 as an umbrella organization to unite and organize women" (Begoña).

Not only did more women's rights emerge, but even the peaceful feminists of the time also had much to fight for, as milestones in England and America mirrored.

> In the United Kingdom, for instance, the Equal Pay Act of 1970 was followed by the Sex Discrimination Act (1975) and the subsequent establishment of the Equal Opportunities Commission. The Employment Protection Act (1975) mandated statutory paid maternity leave and protection from unfair dismissal during pregnancy, the Domestic Violence and Matrimonial Proceedings Act (1976) reinforced women's rights in restraining violent spouses, and the Sexual Offenses (Amendment) Act, also of 1976, improved the protection of rape victims' privacy during trial. In the United States during the 1970s Congress approved 71 items of legislation, or 40 percent of all legislation regarding women's rights approved in this century [Ergas 528].

Siobhan's history as a rebel can be seen in her mothering as well as her resistance to authority, in which she mentors Sarah and the others. When Paul asks her allegiance, Siobhan answers, "I'm a mum, aren't I? If you think you're taking Sarah back, you'll have to kill me" ("To Hound Nature in Her Wanderings" 206). She agrees to investigate Sarah's past for her without question. In the next episode, after she's told of Sarah's death (actually Katja's), Mrs. S agrees to be kept in the dark but not if Kira is in danger. She concludes, "Whatever is going on, if it takes one step towards Kira, you need to yell, 'Fire.' The home we've built for ourselves in this country, we burn it all down if we have to" ("Entangled Bank" 108). She finally finds Sarah's birth mother Amelia, though the woman warns Sarah that Mrs. S isn't what she seems.

Siobhan snatches Kira at season one's end and hides with her fellow rebels in the countryside. After she brings Sarah to her, she appears in drab clothes with a rifle, emphasizing her rebel side. Both these moments leave Sarah uncertain whether she can trust the woman who's held back so much. S. abruptly tells her that she'll be leaving with Kira alone and smuggling her back to England. She also insists that she's on Sarah's side. As Sarah explores the birdwatchers' safehouse, she discovers S.'s past—one she shared in. Sarah recalls coming to the safe house as a child. She also hears about Mrs. S's old life as she describes running "strike kitchens on nothing more than scrap meat and canned veg" and "scrubbing Kalashnikovs" rather than pots and pans ("Governed by Sound Reason and True Religion" 202).

However, S.'s old friends have sold them out for religion and money. A ruthless Mrs. S stabs her friend's hands to the table with kitchen knives and then shoots her. Sarah and Felix are stunned, and he protests, "Our dear old mum's a dead eye with a rifle. It just makes me queasy.... This is insane. It's S, you know? She makes tea and ... and she taught me piano" ("Mingling Its Own Nature with It" 203). Presumably many British young people are equally shocked that their mothers can do far more, as they once did in the tumultuous seventies. S insists, "Just like you, I got caught up in a struggle I didn't ask for. Only I've been at it longer, so I'm better at it than you" ("To Hound Nature in Her Wanderings" 206).

However, in "The Weight of This Combination" (301), she defends her nuclear family by betraying Helena, a choice that appalls Sarah. Covered in bruises, with several broken ribs after Seth has attacked her, Siobhan stands by her choice. She calls it "a wartime decision."

> SIOBHAN: It's what I had to do at the time.
> SARAH: What, betray my sister? Give her to them?
> SIOBHAN: For Kira.
> SARAH: That's not your bloody decision, S, is it?
> ...
> SIOBHAN: I—I had to choose. Sarah, stop. Don't. Please. Don't turn your back on me. Not on your people.
> SARAH: You're not my people.

Sarah falls apart completely at the loss of Helena, and quests to go find her, while Felix stays behind, caring for his foster mother. He understands S.'s decisions, even as he knows Sarah will charge in impetuously and make everything worse.

S. claims her mistake, going to pick up an escaped Helena and Sarah and owning up to what she did. She lets Helena punch her over and over, but embraces her, reaching a turning point in their relationship. In return, Helena names her the baby's grandmother. S. adopts another child that season in lost teen Gracie. She takes her in and sees herself in the younger woman, telling her: "I was married young, too. Eloped, much to the utter disappointment of my mother. My husband, John, was killed. Oh, my goodness. We were going to have a family. When my husband passed, I was adrift. Angry. But I couldn't go back home. My aunt Joan took me in, and she stopped me from self-destructing" ("Scarred by Many Past Frustrations" 305). She tries to set Gracie on a healthy path, as she watches over her as her Aunt Joan once did.

In "Insolvent Phantom of Tomorrow" (309), S's children return to London where they meet her old lover Carlton and tease her about her past. She replies, "These boys were all John's friends. And then after he was killed, they became my family. And, yes, Carlton was ... a little bit more than that." They also discover her picture behind the bar, and she sings in public, revealing a much lighter side while on her old stomping grounds. "Mrs. S is an incredibly strong woman. She's a survivor. You don't get the feeling that anybody would get one over on her," Kennedy teases. "But at the same time, all that commitment and conviction, it does often infer a passionate person" (Gelman, "*Orphan Black* Preview").

A much darker story follows as her old friend is beaten to death and S.

tracks down her mother, Kendall, only to hold a gun on her ("Insolvent Phantom of Tomorrow" 309). She reveals that while she married at seventeen, her mother had no right to kill John. She threatens her mother with death several times, but in this episode and the next, they reach a place where they can share information and vital tissue samples. They end the season going to see Kira together as a family once more.

When Kendall is killed through the Clone Club's plots, an infuriated S. strikes out at Sarah: "You put my mother in the line of fire. Laid your moves without me and then you put me in the middle and you made it my fault. And now I don't even have a body to bury." She brutally adds, "You came to me an orphan. That's all you'll ever be" ("The Antisocialism of Sex" 407). Sarah goes out and spirals out of control with drink, drugs, dancing, and sex, even as the angry S. keeps Kira safe at home. When Sarah finally stumbles in, however, S. forgivingly makes her breakfast. Shortly after, the entire Clone Club unite to help her take revenge on her mother's killer, emphasizing their solidarity.

With dignity and calm Siobhan goes to her death in "Guillotines Decide" (508), accepting that it's worth her life to broadcast Neolution's crimes, dismantling the evil corporation and freeing Kira, Sarah, and her sisters. She even convinces Rachel to ally with them, much as she once must have convinced other young women to choose sisterhood and fight the establishment. Kennedy notes, "I think she understood that Rachel was a product of the life she had lived and the (lack of) real love she had been shown. I think S. began to believe that if she could really get in there, she could affect some change" ("Maria Doyle Kennedy Q&A").

On the death scene, Kennedy remarks that Manson called her to describe the "emotional bomb" they wanted to drop. She adds, "As soon as I heard it, I thought it was exactly the right thing for the show—probably the biggest loss that the core characters could suffer, and something that would make them dig to their very essence in order to survive." ("Maria Doyle Kennedy Q&A"). Of course, she doesn't go quietly. She enters her house gun drawn, and spars with the brutish Ferdinand before he shoots her near the heart. While Ferdinand smirks about her "grit," he denies S.'s calm resigned requests for a "mercy tap" and then the photo of her children. However, the last, disguised as feminine sentimentality, is meant to distract him as she goes for her gun and shoots him in the throat as she threatened. "Quite enough lip out of you," she proclaims. She continues their gender battle as he chokes, smirking, "Do you know as a woman now, I'm 14 percent more likely to survive a gunshot wound than you. Maybe not this one, but okay, it's been a good run." While he dies frantically, with undignified blood spurting everywhere, her death is calm and stately, sitting upright in her easy chair, surrounded by the home she made and the photo of the children she loved. The powerful mom has squashed the sexist abuser and safeguarded all the princesses in the end.

Castors: Military Hierarchy

In season four of *Buffy the Vampire Slayer*, her group of ragtag demon-fighting pals discover a competing military team run by the mysterious Initiative. They're a formal military branch who show what demon-fighting would look like as an organized patriarchal model. They have rules and a budget, weapons and backup teams. At the top of the traditional hierarchy is a motherly woman with power and discipline, who demonstrates to the young heroine a tougher path. However, Buffy rejects this system in preference for her own, which beats theirs and saves the day.

Critic Karen Sayer perceives Buffy's circle as a feminine utopia, based on support and cooperation, a "home and family," as opposed to "the fractured, driven, individualized and consequently masculine world" (112). In *Orphan Black*'s season three, the Ledas' own circle of inclusion is contrasted with competing hierarchal clones living in a system much like Buffy's Initiative. Community and acceptance are central here, in contrast with obedience. These different strategies reflect different purposes. "Although both are originally sourced from the same person, who is genetically chimeric, the projects of Leda and Castor have intentionally different aims: Leda, to explore that science of cloning and the possibilities therein; Castor, to explore the possibility of creating an army of clones" (Heuslein 80).

Maslany comments, "I'm excited for people to see Ari [Millen]'s clones. The 'Castor' clones. Because unlike Sarah's [clones] they were all raised together, instead of separately, so they'll have a different kind of nature, nurture situation. I think it'll be cool for the audience to see. I'm excited for it" (Kavner). Indeed, the men are raised together, so they don't have different accents, and they can't be seen to wear makeup, so their distinctions are subtler than the women's. They appear an armylike mass in truth, and many at the compound are never named or set apart. The sameness nods to military training (which they likewise all share).

In contrast, the women shift who takes charge based on who has the best skillset for each situation. Pamela Grande Jensen adds in her introduction to *Finding a New Feminism: Rethinking the Woman Question for Liberal Democracy*, "In order to contribute to any community, it is necessary to be a self—a person with something to share" (8). This set of contrasts is more evident in the Ledas than Castors; their team is based on love, family, and relationality, not orders. This echoes the gynocentric model of a few world cultures, all of which favor a system not based in rules and hierarchy:

"In matriarchies, mothers are at the center of culture without ruling over other members of society," says Heide Göttner-Abendroth, founder of The International Academy HAGIA for Modern Matriarchal Studies. "The aim is not to have power over others and over nature, but to follow maternal values, i.e. to nurture the natural, social and cultural life based on mutual respect." In other words, if patriarchy is West Point, heavy on the rules and hierarchy, matriarchy is that alternative school where kids call teachers by their first names and play non-competitive games with the parachute [Hamilton].

The Ledas meet cozily in someone's house, often Felix's Bohemian flat or S.'s home with Sarah and Felix's childhood artwork and discarded belongings. Over tea or Alison's crafts, they chat on their colorful phones about how to solve problems by working together. Later they make a home and lab beneath a game store, easily switching from cooking to scientific experiments, while playing a few rounds of the latest adventure game. They have an alternate community of outsiders, all those who cannot fit in for whatever reason: Helena the madwoman, Sarah the punk, Siobhan the rebel, Felix the artist, Kira the mystic, and Cosima the hipster. Even Alison, the ultimate conformist, is struggling for more in her life. Through embracing differences people "develop tolerance and mutual respect—qualities quite capable of being transformed over time into trust and compassion" (Jensen 8).

Their system resembles Buffy's, in which "The Scoobies' contingent, contextualized, functional form of participative management is in strong contrast to the enforced, patriarchal, hierarchical structures which typify the series' evil leaders" (Playdon 138). The villains rule the male hierarchies that only a few females join for power—the Castors, DYAD, Brightborn. Whether dusty military compounds or glamorous offices, their workplaces are cold, off-putting, even violent. The Clone Club by contrast is a club, in which the women dance and eat as well as planning to save one another.

The men are also given more agency and self-awareness in the story, a problematic gender choice. The self-aware Castor clones actively solve the problems of their biology. By contrast, Leda clones (excepting Rachel) are kept in the dark until the series begins. "Treating the males as capable of informed rational participation and treating the females as passive noninformed participants, reinforces the idea that men are expected to fulfil rational and autonomous roles and women are not," explains Darci Doll in the *Orphan Black* essay "Re: Production" (160).

> The genetic illnesses of the Castor and Leda clones symbolically reflect a version of a rational, active, male subject versus a life-giving, passive, female subject. The male clones' defect is neurological and affects their ability to reason as evidenced by the tests on logical syllogisms that they fail when in the grips of neurological deterioration. It is also sexually transmitted so that they actively sterilize any women that they have sex with. The female clones' defect is reproductive and causes their ovaries to deteriorate so that they are unable to have children—except

of course for Sarah Manning, who is so unique that the Neolutionists sought to surgically remove her ovary. The women are passive carriers of their illness and cannot transmit it sexually (as far as we know) [Donovan 132].

Notably, they get eye movement and logic tests rather than internal scans, emphasizing that their minds are more damaged than their bodies. The Castor disease manifests like encephalitis. Ari Millen recalls that the producers thought of it as "mad cow disease for humans" (Bernstein 116). "The illness in female clones originates in the reproductive organs and spreads to the lungs, eventually killing them. The fatal illness in the male clones, however, stays isolated in the brain. This is reinforcing the view that women without reproduction and men without rationality are flawed (and in this case fatally so)" (Doll 159).

They follow the same quest as the women, seeking to repair themselves, though there are significant differences. "Projects Leda and Castor treat the infertility differently in ways that go beyond autonomy and reinforce the reproductive gender roles. Mainly the female clones are treated with passive observation; the male clones are encouraged to copulate with other females to see the extent of their sexually transmitted infertility. Project Castor encourages the males to be active in the acceptance and understanding of their infertility" (Doll 160).

The Castors' damaged minds and the Ledas' damaged bodies once again work as a gender metaphor of how men socially construct women. Emmanuel Reynaud explains in "Holy Virility: The Social Construction of Masculinity":

> Man reproduces the body/mind separation that he creates in himself in his relationships with women. Just as he tends to picture himself as pure mind, so he sees woman as unrestrained flesh, a body over which the head has no control. He likes to consider himself a cultural being, almost completely free of natural contingencies, while he represents woman as a sort of natural being still subject to the obscure forces of nature. On this basis, he defines as "masculine," not only the few characteristics associated with the male sex, but all the human traits in which he acknowledges an ability to combat natural alienation. In the same way, he calls 'feminine' all those characteristics which submit to that alienation. Thus he makes woman into the symbol of his own dependence, and in addition, the further he dissociates himself from her, the more he feels he is his own master; he creates two definitions, femininity and virility, which exacerbate the anatomical differences, increase women's dependence and concentrate everything that seems to represent human strength in himself [142].

When the Castors find their minds are failing, they despair and sometimes require mercy-killing, as without the mind, there is no point to their existence. However, another metaphor can be seen here, one of giving up versus finding a solution: "In his race for power, man is able to separate mind and body: he sees the mind as transcending the human condition, and he turns his body into the place of natural alienation" (Reynaud 141). Strengthening and training the mind then using it to command the body is everything. The women focus on endurance and survival, lasting as long as they can. In fact, Cosima, the most damaged of the heroines seen onscreen, is the one to create a cure where others like Susan fail over many years of trial. The show suggests it's her creativity and insight as well as the desperation to save herself that lets her succeed. Notably, the Ledas are healed specifically through the power of sperm-egg combining—giving birth. The Castors can only hope their "mother" Coady will save them—in fact, she does not, and they all die one by one.

If the man, particularly a soldier in a world of discipline, and particularly a clone created from before birth to be a weapon, trains to rise above his instincts and urges, he is better than humanity. Compassion, like other traits the Ledas prize, is a weakness. "He wants to be strength, rationality and transcendence, whereas woman is weakness, irrationality and immanence. At one fell swoop he imposes 'femininity' on woman and is determined for his part, to be virile, and to differentiate himself clearly from her" (Reynaud 142). Thus, the women have damaged bodies, emphasizing how the Castors see women as little more than wombs, waiting to be injured by the Castors' complex plans.

Since "Castor" was the son of Leda and the Castor clones appear strikingly younger, they're cast as immature, the younger brothers of the Ledas, literally and symbolically. Art tells Sarah of the prostitute that met Rudy and Seth, "She says they have the same tattoo. Left forearm, picture of a two-headed horse" ("Transitory Sacrifices of Crisis" 302). With it, they identify with the ancient legends.

The Castors train with syllogisms; these are sometimes used as a diagnostic tool complete with the eye movement scans: "As a diagnostic tool, syllogisms have been used to identify schizophrenia and brain damage affecting the prefrontal cortex, an area of the brain attributed to decision making, working memory, attention, social behavior, and personality. Syllogisms also reflect the dual-processing model of reasoning, in which two systems interact to help us form conclusions" (Griffin and Nesseth). Their origins seem more symbolically significant. These logic puzzles were part of a traditional education in Ancient Rome. They're patriarchal and ancient, suggesting structure and rigidity ... though if their facts are wrong, the syllogisms become flawed—a metaphor for the Castors themselves. Their entire purpose and training are corrupt, leaving each treacherous and morally dubious.

Mark appears in season two, nearly a year before his brothers, as he's tied into the Proletheans' plot. As Helena and Sarah end season two by meeting more Castors, they're alerted to this new branch of clones. In the season three premiere, Seth and Rudy brutally abduct Krystal Goderitch. Though

Rudy (set apart with his scar and peaked hair) is caught and imprisoned by Marion Bowles, the mustachioed Seth escapes. In the episode, he attacks S. (emphasizing how easily he gives in to violence) and then lovingly rescues his brother. However, Seth is showing signs of serious glitching. In the following episode, they increase their brutality: The pair get the young woman Patty drunk for Rudy to seduce, until he suddenly springs Seth on her and insists she must have sex with him too. It's a shocking, creepy moment. As Patty tells her story later, she adds, "When I tried to leave, Rudy, if that's even his real name, he got this look in his eye and it was like he was angry for the other one, Seth, like I had insulted them by rejecting him."

Further, as she reports the assault, which included going through her purse and yanking out her hair, she adds bitterly, "I consented to the first guy, so that's not rape, right?" Art's face says he understands how unfair the law is, but there's nothing he can do about it. While the episode criticizes the justice system, it's harsher on the Castors' culture of toxic hypermasculinity which raised them to believe they're entitled to do whatever they want with women's bodies. In fact, Rudy describes Sarah as "made of the good stuff," emphasizing how he sees her as a commodity. As the writers tackle gender constructs, they don't pull punches.

Raising the stakes, Rudy takes Kira hostage in Felix's loft. Once again, the men act savagely, preying on innocents. Seth, who's standing guard downstairs, begins glitching. Worried, Rudy rushes down to him and after realizing that Seth is too far gone in his illness, shoots him twice, mercy-killing him. Rudy continues through the season as the clone chosen for the most violent missions.

As far as other Castors, Parsons and Styles are among the named clones at the Castor compound. Styles joins in waterboarding Helena, while Parsons is victimized himself, with Coady performing brutal brain surgery on him to keep his brothers alive. Other unnamed Castors are seen around the camp as well.

Mark, the first clone seen, appears as an obedient sounding board in the religious cult, polite and helpful, respecting Henrik as a mentor and slowly falling for his daughter Gracie. Thus, he's poised between obedience to outside teachings and true love, a struggle that continues after Castor reclaims him. "Modern war is a cyborg orgy" with frightening new technology (Haraway 150). The military of the show have weaponized the Castors, breeding them from birth to fight. However, as Mark falls in love and defects, and then Paul leads a coup, it becomes clear that their loyalty can change. "The main trouble with cyborgs, of course, is that they are the illegitimate offspring of militarism and patriarchal capitalism, not to mention state socialism. But illegitimate offspring are often exceedingly unfaithful to their origins. Their fathers, after all, are inessential" (Haraway 151). Mark grows beyond his training, mostly for love of Gracie, though like the others, he continues struggling for survival.

Sarah must care for Mark, and begins to sympathize with him, even calling him "brother" after she digs a bullet out of him. Sarah tells him of Helena, "She's not a monster, she was just ... trained to be a killer. Does that sound familiar?" ("Newer Elements of Our Defense" 304). Together, the pair find a bit of commonality, though this is short-lived. Meanwhile, the brutal Rudy finds Mark and Sarah and taunts the latter: "How is that sweet little girl of yours, anyway? Hmm? Kira sure is gonna miss her mommy. Mommy? Mommy? Where are you? Mommy! I can't find you! Oh. There you are, mommy." He is the killer, while Mark is more relatable.

When Rudy drags Mark home, Doctor Coady orders him to record his "intimate encounter" with Gracie, but Paul clues him in to a more insidious plot—women who have sex with Castor clones contract a terrible disease. These living weapons prey on innocent women, even as the Ledas try to save those in danger. This makes the Castors enemies of feminism and common decency—symbolic (and sometimes literal) rapists who prey on and destroy women's bodies without consent. "A new feminism would urge that any philosophic consideration of human good would be diminished if it did not raise the question of gender but also that feminism would be diminished if it did not recognize the commonality of all humankind" (Jensen 18).

"When it comes to abolishing patriarchy the problem for men is not for them to create a 'new man,' but, on the contrary, to destroy that 'man' from whom, as males, we have all been created, and who, in one way or another, we have all reproduced" (Reynaud 141). Men like Paul, trained in the patriarchal world of the military, must learn to give it up to earn the love of someone like Sarah. "As for the question which worries some men—knowing what a male who is not a 'man' could be: each man can discover that for himself in a variety of pleasures available when one is relieved of the burden of fitting into a category" (Reynaud 141). Mark finds his answer—falling into a loving mutual relationship with Gracie. Paralleling him, Paul makes a similar journey, sacrificing himself so the stronger Sarah can fight on. The other Castors, however, cling to their old roles and refuse to leave them. Soon enough, they all perish, discarded by a world that has no use for them.

On their way to destroy the Ledas and snatch their source in "History Yet to Be Written" (310), Rudy and Coady meet with David the shady government director. He shows no sympathy for Rudy's terminal illness. Rudy may be a murderer and rapist, but his arc suggests a veteran used and abandoned by his government, trained to be stereotypically masculine but not to return to society. When he attacks the Hendrixes, Helena kills him, though she sympathetically lies beside him as he expires.

In the season finale, Mark agrees to help the Ledas take down his evil mother and plays Rudy to set a trap for her. He, the most adaptable of clones, is learning the clone power shown through the series. After, he and Gracie go off for what little remains of his life. In season five, Mark returns, the last of the Castors. Desperate for a cure, he allies with Coady and sends Gracie in as willing pawn to kidnap Helena. His desire for survival finally outweighs his selflessness. Fawcett says: "The Castors have a ticking clock. He's not somehow biologically different than his brothers. But he has more heart and soul to some degree.... And he's torn. He's got this weird innocence and this emotional core to him. He's fallen in love and he's bonded with Sarah, and he's helped Sarah to some degree" (Ross, "Finale"). Of course, his mother quietly executes him at Westmorland's behest, even while promising him a cure. Mark dies, last victim of the failed experiment.

Paul the Macho Man

Episode one introduces Paul Dierden, the clueless boyfriend Sarah inherits along with everything else of Beth's. When he asks too many questions, she seduces him passionately to distract him, and both find themselves falling in love. However, the image of the duped boyfriend is undercut in episode five when Sarah discovers Paul is letting people run medical experiments on her. She immediately arranges spy equipment and starts checking on him, only to find Beth had already done the same.

Paul is ex-military, and calls Sarah out on her swindling and stealing. As such, he's a matched adversary for her, as well as a tougher balance for softer males like Donnie and Felix. In "Variations Under Domestication" (106), as Vic threatens violence, Paul easily takes him down. "Traditional masculinity is thought to be in crisis. This perceived taste of crisis, and the development of the 'new man,' have resulted in a small programming backlash in which the aim is to reclaim traditional masculinity," notes Buck Clifford Rosenberg, author of "Masculine Makeovers: Lifestyle Television, Metrosexuals and Real Blokes" (145).

Rosenberg sees traditional masculinity "based on physical strength, resourcefulness, stoicism, and pragmatism, and frequently, physical labor" in jeopardy thanks to second wave feminism, which triggered many social changes, and a de-industrialization of jobs in favor of "an increasingly feminized service sector" (146). Thus, to placate viewers who feel thus, many shows have, as well as the sensitive male hero and thuggish villain, "men who are men" filling traditional valiant roles. Paul is a throwback to a more traditional time. Of course, his macho heroism is undercut by the fact that Paul doesn't know about the clones. Cosima comments, "See, it's a double blind. Um, the monitors are unaware of the purpose of the experiment. That way they can't skew the results" ("Variations Under Domestication" 106). This makes Paul more of a pawn than a mastermind.

Paul finally tells Sarah, "You asked me what happened in Afghanistan. I was a private contractor. I killed six marines, friendly fire. They covered it up. That's what they have on me."

"If you were born outside their control, what do they really have on you?" she retorts ("Endless Forms Most Beautiful" 110). With this, she coaches him on breaking away from his masters. More importantly, Sarah risks her life to rescue him in season one rather than the reverse. In "Parts Developed in an Unusual Manner" (107), she gets backup from her stronger, crazier sister Helena, and together the pair drag him to safety. Further, the softer Felix provides the getaway car and a refuge, in which Sarah chooses to sleep with Paul as herself. She has the power and makes the choices.

After, he's further depowered—forced to be Rachel's boy toy and monitor. In "Ipsa Scientia Potestas Est" (205), Rachel informs him that he'll be taking the place of the brutal torturer Daniel, guarding her, reporting on her vitals, and sleeping with her too. Back at her place, she orders him to strip bit by bit, degrading him as she claims power in their relationship. Not only is he given the submissive role, but unbeknownst to him, Sarah and Helena are watching from a distance and judging him even as Helena turns her rifle on Rachel. As Sarah talks Helena down, the pair of them have the power—not Rachel and certainly not Paul.

Paul's position seems clear. This, however, is another fake out. At the end of season two, when Mrs. S meets with the army, it's Paul who shows up.

> S: I didn't peg you for a major, back at Prof Duncan's house.
> PAUL: I wasn't. A lot has changed since I came back in.
> S: But you are still prepared to play double agent?
> PAUL: Like you, I want to know the truth.

Actually a trainer of the Castors, he makes a deal with Mrs. S to give Helena to Castor, all to protect his beloved Sarah. "The cloud of that deal is going to run through the first two-thirds of the season," Manson says. "We get to know his motivation. We've seen Paul make great sacrifices to help Sarah in the past. He certainly has a place in his heart for Sarah" (Nguyen, "Here's Everything").

Paul is horrified when he discovers Coady's weaponization of the Castors. He brings her down by reporting her actions to the military—the man who outranks and supervises her. Only with this disapproval can she be eliminated. Unlike the women, who fight the system, Paul operates within it and can use it to advantage ... or so he thinks. With permission from the hierarchy, Paul tells her: "You're sterilizing women. You are unfit to lead. I am taking charge of this camp, and I will use force." He locks down the base.

However, Paul's bosses in Arlington actually know what Coady's up to and support it, so they alert the clone Rudy to go free her. Rudy returns and manages a coup.

Heroically, Paul gets Sarah out of the base and proclaims his love for her. In this scene, he's no longer gender-flipped, but valiantly, classically masculine. As the love interest, he shows he can save the day, though this will leave Sarah to carry on the quest. Refusing to join Sarah, he goes back to take responsibility for the project. Coady notes, "Your devotion to my boys was pure, Paul" ("Certain Agony of the Battlefield" 306).

In turn, Paul begs her to be a mother not a warrior: "Cure them, Virginia. Drop the rest."

She refuses, noting, "The science in this room could rewrite the very nature of humankind. You ask me to turn my back on it? I'm sorry, Paul. I can't." He blows her up with a grenade, fighting her firepower with greater firepower and removing the head of the program ("Certain Agony of the Battlefield" 306). Fawcett notes, "When Paul finds this information, he has to make a very big moral decision, and he does. He protects Sarah and it was a very emotional ending. To me, that's what's so great about this is we get a lot of answers in this episode" (Ross, "Twerktastic Episode"). With force and weapons, the heroic male destroys the threat, at least for a time.

Cal Goes Off the Grid

Cal, living in the backwoods, is scruffy and completely masculine in his flannel shirts. On seeing Sarah he regards her with loathing. "Last time I saw you, you took ten grand and my car" ("Mingling Its Own Nature with It" 203). However, Sarah reveals Cal is Kira's father. Suddenly, they're thrust into a nuclear family dynamic with Cal, the man who fled civilization, discovering his unknown child. Going off into the woods and leaving behind family responsibilities is a classic male American fantasy, seen in much of nineteenth century literature. However, Sarah and Kira burst into his masculine recluse, shattering the illusion.

Living in the forest as Cal does, he's framed as having a spiritual side, something that can ground the angry Sarah. It also links him closely with Kira. His actor, Michiel Huisman, explains, "There's something in her that he really connects with. Her instinct is stronger than his but he also has that. I wouldn't call it a sixth sense or anything like that but that quality of reading people and being able to go by your gut, Kira has that so he easily feels connected to her" (Ng). This link with intuition, like Kira's, is a traditionally feminine power, giving him a softer side.

Once he ruled the corporate world before he grew disgusted with it. Cal tells Felix his story of creating "Minidrone pollinators, for areas where bee populations have crashed. I designed the microoptics, but my partners forced me out and sold the technology to the military. And, now, they kill people from bases in Virginia with it. But I don't" ("Mingling Its Own Nature with It" 203). It's his morality that made him flee the military and corporate hierarchy to escape all its unjust policies. He's the anti–Paul, the anti–DYAD as he embodies the freedom the clones are fighting for. Huisman adds: "That made him more anti-corporation, maybe even more anti-government-involvement than he already was. I always imagined that he was there [at the cabin] to get inspired for a new plan and a new adventure. I do think he made a lot of money but he wants to press the reset button" (Ng).

He accepts Kira's sudden existence with good grace: He reaches out to both Sarah and Kira, with family card games and fun (with more adult fun for Sarah). Sarah is replacing her nontraditional, matriarchal family with a nuclear one, at least for a few episodes. Suddenly, their happy family unit is shattered when Daniel, Rachel's monitor, bursts in on them and kidnaps Sarah. Cal rescues her in spectacular fashion, crashing his car into theirs. Though his act is impetuous, even foolhardy, he plays the traditional masculine hero during the brief scene.

After this, he's left watching Kira as Sarah continues to fight for clone rights, something else he accepts with good grace. Suddenly, he's not the central action hero, but the babysitter, emphasizing the reversal of gender roles through the show. Like Kira, he figures out the Clone Club's existence intuitively, in fact with help from Kira's drawings.

When things settle down, he invites his new family to move in with him, with a beautiful house in the city. However, they must go on the run once more. Sarah sends him to babysit Kira in Iceland, and after Sarah retrieves Kira, he isn't seen again. Huisman adds that they could all live happily together "if it was on another show with the three of them" (Ng). The Clone Club and its struggles against Neolution take precedence, in a show in which the sister bond is the most important. Sarah and Cal's options remain open, but it's suggested neither of them truly needs the other. They could be together, but it would require major adjustments (to be fair, ones Cal with his house purchase appears prepared to make). Huisman concludes, "Maybe for a split second after the initial shock has come down, maybe he thinks, 'Wow, maybe this is something that would be an option for us to be some sort of family.' But of course, it turns out there's a lot more going on. They're not going to be a happy family anytime soon" (Ng).

Rachel the Gender Traitor

Rachel Duncan comes from Cambridge, a classy institution only a few hours from Sarah's own urban birthplace. Makeup artist Stephen Lynch describes Rachel as "the ultimate high-end woman" with top-line skin and hair products. He comments, "In Rachel's mind, makeup is fun and a class thing. She has to absolutely represent the high end and we think that she would be so disdainful of someone like Sarah.... So we tried to get as far away from Sarah as much as we could. And I thought what would that mean?" Rachel hires people to do her hair and makeup, "trying to look radiant with her expensive look. She can't achieve that kind of radiance, though, because she is kind of dead in her eyes. So I don't think she ever gets the look that she is really going for" (Miller). Her suits are starkly colored. Costume designer Debra Hanson says, "She's so damaged, and you see her struggling withal the things that have happened to her, and struggling with her own conscience. Then later, there are blacks and creams, but it's neutral. It's a sleek simplicity" (Bernstein 69).

This polished, Wall Street Executive type works with Doctor Leekie. She's the wicked establishment clone, the one fully loyal to the evil scientists. As such, she's the gender traitor, willing to serve the male-headed establishment and even betray her fellow sisters and perform brutal surgeries on them, all for the illusion of power.

When Rachel meets Sarah in "Endless Forms Most Beautiful" (110), she makes an offer from the company: "So, my name is Rachel Duncan and we are going to come to terms. The agreement defines mutual disclosure and formalizes contact with what I call Topside." She offers an apparent sisterhood with the words, "You're not an orphan anymore, Sarah. We found you. And my role is to transition you into self-awareness." However, her words suggest the Garden of Eden snake. When she threatens Kira, Sarah decisively rejects her offer. "Rachel didn't feel like a truce, she felt like a gun to the head," she tells the others afterwards.

> Rachel poses the greatest threat to the clones—far more so than the Proletheans or Leekie. While DYAD lives in service to science and the Proletheans to their religion, Rachel only serves herself. She's constantly exerting her own autonomy, dominating Paul sexually and taking Leekie's fate in her hands rather than following Marion's orders. Yet despite all this, it doesn't change the fact that Rachel remains an object. No matter how high in the ranks she rises, Rachel cannot escape the degrading patent embedded in her genetic code which subjects her to the same repressive control as the other clones [Gennis].

Sarah investigates Rachel in "Governed as It Were by Chance" (204). Cosima tells her, "'Six scientists incinerated in lab explosion,' while working on a medical research project spearheaded by Professor Susan and Ethan Duncan." They were her parents, who brought her up as a self-aware clone though also with love and laughter. After the explosion, Rachel is raised by DYAD, where Leekie treats her as his creation, not his daughter.

Rachel thinks in the comic, "Aldous always told me that I was the fortunate one. That I had knowledge and power my 'sisters' never would" (*The Clone Club #5: Rachel*). However, she adds jealously, "They have love; they have family. The very things that were denied to me. What right do they have to that sort of happiness? They're little more than corporate property. I'll rightfully take what's mine" (*The Clone Club #5: Rachel*).

"Gender, race, or class consciousness is an achievement forced on us by the terrible historical experience of the contradictory social realities of patriarchy, colonialism, and capitalism" (Haraway 155). Leekie raises her, but as a scientific subject, not a person. This has given her a skewed concept of relationships. "Rachel's actions have been largely fueled by a cocktail of rage, bitterness and jealousy. Yet when she broke down while watching home movie footage of herself playing with her father as a child it was hard not to be moved. Even proclones have feelings, it appears" (Hughes). Menacing scenes in Rachel's grey home often have the video of her bright, happy outdoor childhood frozen onscreen. The striking contrast between who she is and who she could have been emphasize the character's dark twists. Even as she watches her family videos over and over, seeking connection, she seduces Topside cleaner Ferdinand and her own monitor Daniel, ruling them instead of letting them rule her.

When Helena kills her boy toy, Rachel makes Paul take Daniel's place as handler and lover. "I've been self-aware since I was a child. I'm not exempt from the program. I simply enjoy a unique vantage, one with privilege," she explains coolly, insisting his monitoring her will be a "promotion." She aggressively tells him to take off all his clothes, even checks his teeth, and then straddles him ("Ipsa Scientia Potestas Est" 205).

> "Helen [Shaver, the director] really challenged us to go for it," Maslany remembers. "[She] wanted to explore Rachel's sexuality because she felt there was such a mine field there to play with. You don't get to see that side of Rachel. Like, 'What does that look like?' It can't just be classic missionary. That would be so boring.... To us, it was interesting to explore this idea of her inspecting Paul like a prize horse and denying him pleasure.... The power dynamic was really unusual. I haven't seen that before on camera. Helen was our first female director and really brought that knowledge to the directing" [*Orphan Black Season 2*].

In fact, she doesn't have it all—Rachel's endless viewing of the home videos emphasizes how much she's given up—parents as well as the hope of children. She also lacks romantic love, relying instead on the monitors she coerces to be with her so she can exert some control over her life. In the comics, Rachel thinks of Ferdinand, "I suppose I should be flattered by his interest. But it's mostly convenient. A connection to Topside. Something Aldous always kept from me" (*The Clone Club #5: Rachel*).

Sometimes an adolescent girl with no parental support will "become coldly intellectual, ruthless, power-driven, or functioning without heart"

(Nelson 47). This sort of young woman clings rigidly to justice without mercy. "Rules and laws push past her femininity and lead her with a kind of driven, possessed attitude. Intellectual pursuits may be taken up—and with a mania that destroys relationships and is destructive of everything around her. She is ruled by her masculine side, not guided by it" (Nelson 48). Chillingly, she condemns her foster-father Leekie, taking his place as head of DYAD. Though Leekie expects her to kill him, she spares his life, telling him to run and adding, "It's foolish to spare you. But you raised me. Nurture prevails" ("Knowledge of Causes, and Secret Motion of Things" 207). This is her only concession.

When the Clone Club bring back her long-lost father Ethan Duncan, Rachel insists on distance, insisting, "Our relationship must remain professional for all concerned" ("Variable and Full of Perturbation" 208). Though Ethan approaches her as an emotional father, Rachel remains cold. However, on discovering the clones were deliberately made infertile, though she doesn't react outwardly, she trashes the office in a fit of rage as soon as she's alone. Fawcett explains:

> I think in that moment, though, for Rachel—someone who basically believes herself above all of these other clones—she realizes she's just like everyone else. In fact, Sarah is more special than she is. There is kind of the bottom falling out for Rachel in that scene. And I think that Rachel really wants children somewhere down the line, and being told that this was done to her was part of the design of everything and she is just like those other girls is what really starts to thin Rachel out. And, as a result, we kind of hit a very emotional breakdown from her, which ends that act. It's kind of an intercut where you see Rachel having a very outwardly fury of emotion and smashes a bunch of s—up. She's on an emotional journey here, too, that began with the discovery of the fact that her father is still alive and that she's been betrayed all this time [Ross, "Tony the Transclone"].

Rachel's misery, as she climbs the DYAD hierarchy but must contend with infertility, echoes many women after second wave feminism. "The bitterest complaints come from the growing ranks of women who have reached 40 and find themselves childless, having put their careers first. Is it fair that 90 percent of male executives 40 and under are fathers but only 35 percent of their female counterparts have children?" (Wallis). Elizabeth Mehren, 42, a feature writer for the *Los Angeles Times*, calls her generation a "human sacrifice" and adds, "We believed the rhetoric. We could control our biological destiny. For a lot of us the clock ran out, and we discovered we couldn't control infertility" (Wallis). This is careerist Rachel's great pain—that selling out has left her with nothing.

Her father defiantly kills himself, while condemning her for becoming a monster, someone who, he says, "doesn't deserve" him. Rachel breaks down in tears, sobbing and pleading, but it's pointless. Her father abandons her for the second time, or so she feels. Just watching their family videos makes her laugh and cry maniacally. "I just feel like that's brewing under her all the time, in the same way that Alison's always pushing [down her feelings] with this huge well of panic," describes Maslany. "I feel like so much of [Rachel's] pain is pushed as far down to her toes as she can possibly keep it. And that's what makes it all the more powerful then when it comes out and [all the] more exciting to see a buttoned-up character release their shit." (Orphan Black Season 2)

Rachel kidnaps Kira, plotting to adopt the child nature gave to Sarah not her. She locks her in the disturbing lab-bedroom where DYAD brought her up—the clichéd pink and white with a pile of dolls reflects DYAD's demand for submissive, childish conformity, instead of Rachel or Kira's personalities. "Dear child, I know how frightening this must be for you. But you'll get used to it. You may even grow to like it here. Just as I did," she coos.

Next, she brutally plans to remove Sarah's ovary, taking the other woman's fertility as her own has been taken. In a similar act of spite, she sends Delphine away from her dying girlfriend and smashes Cosima's cure.

> Rachel does this despite knowing that the clone disease is encoded in her DNA just as much as it is in Cosima's, and that finding a cure for Cosima also means finding a cure for a disease that she will likely develop. This behavior could suggest either that Rachel is so highly motivated to hurt Sarah that it trumps finding a cure, or that she is confident that the other scientists at Dyad will develop a cure without Cosima—and she would rather have a solution that doesn't indebt her to a clone [Griffin and Nesseth].

Choosing power and DYAD over her sisters and their biology, Rachel makes a fearsome foe. "Young women often make this choice at a crucial moment of their development, hooking elbows with the Devil and walking off on a power trip—assenting to and joining in the cultural chauvinism that rejects or mutilates feminine values and the unique power of the feminine" (Nelson 48).

In an instant, Sarah hurls a pencil through her eye and into her brain. The very rules on contracts, statistics and "pencil pushing" have destroyed Rachel. She spends season three recovering, but also being stored out of the way like a commodity, until the Ledas discover she has value for her father's codes—not for herself. She finally arranges an escape, though only by sacrificing Krystal, her fellow clone, and leaving her comatose indefinitely, much as she was treated herself. In the world of users and victims where Rachel has grown up, she's determined to be the latter, whoever she must sacrifice.

In "History Yet to Be Written" (310), she finds herself in a strange biology museum, though with luxurious silken comforts. The place suggests soothing isolation and the wealth none of the other clones enjoy. Further, a silver mirror provided reveals how her eye has been replaced. It's a mechanical eye, making her a cyborg in truth. "Modern medicine is also full of cyborgs, of couplings between organism and machine, each conceived as coded devices, in an intimacy and with a power that was not generated in the history of sexuality" (Haraway 150). Rachel in season four has become a small part machine, echoing the maggot plot as well as the new cyborg angle the show takes. Manson notes, "Everybody likes an eyepatch, but y'know, we wanted to do more than just an eyepatch" ("Body Horror"). This is especially appropriate in the season that quotes *The Cyborg Manifesto* for its titles, emphasizing women's liminal status.

She spends an episode hollering for someone to fill her in. Finally, little Charlotte enters to announce Rachel will be her new mother. Following her is Susan Duncan, back from the dead. "Welcome home," she tells her. Rachel has gotten her mother back as well as a daughter—all she's ever wanted. She spends the season discovering her dream isn't all she expected. Her mother admires Cosima, the symbolic good daughter, more than cruel Rachel. "We see important figures in Rachel's life, notably her mother Susan Duncan, vocally expect Rachel to be more than the other clones, downplay any successes, and criticize any perceived failings, all while maintaining Rachel's status as Other, separate from the surviving Leda clones" (Griffin and Nesseth). Further, after abandoning Rachel forever, she chose to raise a Castor clone, Ira, instead, and place him at the center of her world. Rachel feels terribly betrayed.

She also spends the season doing physical therapy, progressing from wheelchair to walker to cane. At season end, Ferdinand (who has finally found her again), tries to help her find what she's lost:

> FERNANDO: I like the cane. Elegant. Multi-purpose.
> RACHEL: I'm not the same. My ... infirmities. I don't feel much of anything anymore.
> FERNANDO: I spent a great deal of time and I lost a great deal of money searching for you. We had plans, you and I. Your eye is magnificent. But your self-pity is repugnant ["From Dancing Mice to Psychopaths" 410].

He goads her into resuming their S&M relationship, which she finally does. Of course, S&M centers on issues of power. Rachel's tying Ferdinand up, hurting him, interrogating him, making him beg for information or "convert" to her worldview, are all nonconsensual methods the patriarchs of DYAD have used on the Ledas. Rachel is making Ferdinand undergo everything the clones must, suggesting she not only wants to dominate him, but show him what her life has been with required examinations and dehumanization. However, he finds this treatment more exciting than educational. S&M often involves haughty dominatrixes who force men to serve them, even making them cross gender lines to wear maid's uniforms and clean the house or wear corsets (Paglia 202). Her sexual outlet stresses Rachel's desperation to be the man, the DYAD insider, not the subject.

She finally conspires to take her mother's place as all-powerful ruler. Having booted out her competitor Evie, Rachel takes over the board, emphasizing that she will be far more brutal than her or Susan—the torturer of the clones she insists she's nothing like: "Evie had no baseline. And Susan has no balls. So let's talk clones, shall we?" Calling clones "wholly patented, farmed and monitored lab animals," she unveils her terrible plan—clones that never leave the lab, never have the childhood she was robbed of. In short, she's creating clones treated even more cruelly than she was. Further, as the exploiter now running the board, she cannot be confused with the subjects. "We operate in countries where human cloning is not illegal. Where our corporation supersedes their citizenship, their personhood. So why grant them this illusion of freedom? If we want to know if our lab rats' tails will grow back, we damn well will cut them off and see!" she crows.

Horrified by this development, Susan rejects all Rachel has become. "Oh, Rachel. All the joy and insight your sisters have given me…. For every Sarah, every Cosima, I regret making you," she says. Further, she insists, "Power does not equal free will, Rachel. You are owned…. You are betraying me. You are betraying your sisters and you are betraying yourself" ("From Dancing Mice to Psychopaths" 410).

However, Rachel retorts, "Now I must do what Neolution raised me to do, make the hard choices." She stabs her mother in the abdomen, rejecting her abandonment. Stabbing Sarah too, Rachel leaves them both to die, even as Sarah pleads that they should be allies. Clone Club and compassion repulse Rachel.

However, her greatest transformation comes as she remakes herself in the next season, as the P. T. Westmorland disciple. The last few episodes of season four have her seeing visions of swans in her remade eye. Cyberpunk stories often feature a hero "torn between the physical and digital worlds to overcome a dilemma which threatens both" (Benjamin 189). This story is not *The Matrix,* and yet Rachel is trying to gain power in the real world even while drawn to the fascinating dream messages. These beckon her towards a richer inner experience.

Of course, the Leda and the Swan myth is one of rape as the woman (once, actually a local mother goddess) is forced to submit the patriarchy. This echoes Rachel's new role. "The power of the cyberpunk protagonist lies in its ability to traverse the fantasy of its social situation by casually manifesting its proportional expression across the individual embedded in both worlds, to confront the irresolvable antagonism of the Virtual and the Real together in a shift of consciousness beyond the human 'extras' in the virtual world" (Benjamin 191). Through her cyborg nature, she can reach a deeper reality and bridge them. However, this nature is making her a corporate slave, like a Borg or Cyberman, not a heroic hybrid.

At season end, she's told her creator is waiting to see her—a new purpose after the disappointment of her mother. After meeting him, he appoints her the new head of DYAD. More than this, however, he gives her a purpose, so much so that she tells Ferdinand in "Clutch of Greed" (502) that she needn't hurt him any more to feel complete (though he's disappointed to hear it). She stops attacking her clone sisters, instead negotiating peace in return for tests on Kira. As it turns out, her pleasantry is all an act, as she intends to harvest little Kira's eggs and implant them in 1300 surrogates. This is Westmorland's plan, and she, once again, is his willing disciple.

Rachel's belief in her own superiority is shattered in "Gag or Throttle" (507). Childhood flashbacks show her raised by Leekie, reciting her serial number to his collaborators, emphasizing her nonpersonhood. Behind her back, her nails are raw and bitten. Now, she perpetuates the cycle, presenting Kira to the board in their stark warehouse and calling her the "modern-day Eve." On his giant screen, Westmorland dominates the room as the ultimate patriarch.

At last, the audience sees what Westmorland has offered Rachel—he calls her his daughter and embraces her, giving her the love Leekie didn't. More importantly, he frees her, vowing that she's no longer property. However, now Westmorland orders her to submit to Coady for an intrusive gynecological exam. Rachel's face goes blank. After, she shows her loathing for this treatment as she demands privacy and wipes herself off. For long moments, she gazes at the file and serial number Westmorland had promised no longer applied.

In a flashback to an intrusive exam, Doctor Nealon reveals the clones are dying, but refuses to give her details, any more than they would to a lab rat. She protests, "I have a right to know" but is told she's still a subject. As he and Leekie deny her information about her own body, they reinforce that she's always been under their control—all her hope of being an equal in their system is a lie. She has no respect and now power, not even over her own biology, like a secretary to a misogynist leader.

After, Rachel discovers Westmorland's tablet in his desk, which he's been using to watch her every move through the artificial eye. She's not just his property, but as he remade her, he controlled every moment. The swan visions, the freedom he offered were all illusions. Now he breaks another promise and demands to keep Kira, whom Rachel is seeing as a younger version of herself. While she cannot save adult-Rachel, she can free the child doomed to follow her pain-filled path.

At last, Rachel rebels, covering the eye Westmorland is using against her with an eyepatch (one that ironically is the costume of a hero, not a villain). She wheels the helpless Kira off, passing her to the Clone Club, and then emails their information about Westmorland's real identity to the board. After, she steels herself and gouges out the false eye. No longer can the patriarchy use her body against her and treat her as a pawn.

Manson and Fawcett joked in a final interview about the ways they considered killing off Rachel—Sarah lopping off Rachel's head with a samurai sword, Rachel driving her wheelchair off the dock and into the lake. However, Manson concludes that he's glad they "did the hard work" of saving her: "How could you redeem Rachel? But slowly chipping away it was a really big arc this year of revealing Rachel to herself first, and then how is Rachel going to react? And through episode eight and nine we played with the tension of not knowing where Rachel was going to land, but then when we do get to the end and Rachel has sided with her sisters" (Ross, "Series Finale").

S. joins her for an unlikely alliance and tells her, "You saved my granddaughter. I'm willing to take a gamble on nature over nurture" ("Guillotines Decide" 508). She asks Rachel to help them bring down Neolution before they can sterilize everyone but the wealthiest, treating earth's population as she was treated. S. adds that they need Rachel's insider knowledge: "You're a smart woman, Rachel. Like any good CEO, you kept a shadow file, a record of where the bodies are buried. Give me the proof I need to back this up. Give yourself a chance to be truly free." Rachel agrees. Instead of ruling Neolution through blackmail, as Ferdinand suggests, she gives S. the files for her to broadcast, depowering DYAD and freeing her sisters and herself. Nearly at the end, she's finally learned the value of freedom.

The final episode has her resigned in her day-to-day humiliation. She tells Felix from the backseat of an ordinary Uber, "I have a glass eye, no friends and no identity unless I want to be found. It's a little late for elitism." Maslany adds:

> I feel like Rachel's entire life has kind of been stripped away from her. Everything that defined her, she's had it physically ripped out of her life. She's this blank slate going into the world, totally unsure of what's next—which I kind of love for her. I think that somebody who has always known what their life was going to be, and has always been in such control but then is thrown into it, and is more vulnerable than any of them, I just think that's such a fantastic arc [Ross, "Tatiana Maslany"].

Rachel asks longingly after Helena's babies but accepts that she'll never be part of Clone Club. In fact, she's discovered freedom in letting go—not ruling, monitoring or controlling her sisters. She adds, "Ever since I was six years old I've compared myself to each and every Leda. The last thing I want to do is see another face like mine" ("To Right the Wrongs of Many" 510). In her final act of the show, she gives Felix her files so the Clone Club can travel the world saving all the Ledas. With this moment of benevolence, Rachel saves her sisters, but only from a deliberate distance.

Tony's Trans Struggle

"In May 2014, *Time Magazine* put Laverne Cox on the cover and proclaimed a Transgender Tipping Point. Since then the mainstream media has developed an obsession with trans people, for both good and ill, but how has speculative fiction dealt with this? Do we have a trans problem?" critic Cheryl Morgan asks, pointing out the dearth of representation. Responding to this concept, Jordan Gavaris, Felix's actor, describes how *Orphan Black* offers "all shades, people you may not always see represented" (Wheaton). Similarly, Kristian Bruun (Donnie) says he wants the show's themes to resonate more in the current political climate: "I really hope that we have the chance to change a few minds toward inclusion, toward acceptance. It's mind-boggling that these things are being questioned today" (Schneider). Tony Sawicki embodies all these wishes as he provides a voice for transgender inclusivity in this saga.

He appears in "Variable and Full of Perturbation" (208), trying to help his monitor Sammy, who's dying after a job gone wrong. Maslany says, "He'd grown up in a different environment, a little more working class, and yet had one great friend in his life who'd supported him. He was very comfortable in his own skin and boldly himself and had no judgment about himself or his gender identity" (Bernstein 78). When Sammy gives Tony a message for Beth, Tony leaves Cleveland and meets with Art, who brings him to Felix. Tony's the first Leda who isn't self-aware, leaving Sarah and Felix the job of telling him. On finding out, Tony doesn't join Clone Club, but drives off on new adventures.

He is the first clone seen who's living with the Leda genome but not engaging in the fight—foreshadowing the hundreds more revealed at series end. In this vein, Fawcett comments, "I think that the biggest thing is that we want to expand the world. We spent a lot of time in season 1 trying to show everyone what our world was.... But now [season 2] we want to expand the world, make the show a little bigger, make the show a little badder, make the show a little more off center. It does feel like the world has grown. There's more cast. There's more mystery. There's more rabbit holes to go into. Now it's time to see it less cloistered" (Ross, "Sarah Was Not Originally British").

Unsurprisingly, Felix is struck by the differences and similarities to Sarah.

"Tony was a collaboration between myself and the writers and the hair and make-up team," notes Maslany. "I did research and reading and dissecting of what that experience might be, but it also came a lot from my own imagination and my own ideas. As far as his background went, we wanted to go with a guy who was raised in hetero-normative society, sort of a small-town situation where his masculinity comes from very hetero guys.... It was important to me that the physical effects of testosterone would be evident. Obviously, I can't change my body too much because I'm playing all the other clones, but there definitely were things I did to try to man up my body a bit, whether it was working on my arms or growing hair" [*Orphan Black Season 2*].

Makeup artist Stephen Lynch took ninety minutes to transform Maslany with a rabbit hair goatee and chest piece tattoo. Maslany also put on ankle weights to walk differently. The makeup artists insist of Tony, "We wanted this to be more than just you know an after school special or a one-week gimmick. It's too important" ("Behind the Scenes: Hair and Makeup"). They call the show "a makeup artist's dream." Likewise, the hair artist, Sandy Sokolowski, built a mullet wig. "I added scalp so there was a crown and everything, but it was really cool," Sokolowski says. "We were just getting rolling. Hopefully Tony might come back" (Miller). Bypassing the angst, confusing, and tortured explanations, Tony simply asks Sarah to be quiet while he studies her.

> FELIX: You all right, mate? It's a lot to take in.
> TONY: Yeah, yeah. Look at us. We're hot. Damn, girl.
> SARAH: Not our usual identity crisis.
> TONY: I did all that work a long time ago. There's only one Tony and you're not me, sucker.

He understands that clone sisters, like his old female identity, are not his true self, and thus feels more comfortable with the clone revelation than the other characters. Tony has already been through a complex journey of deciding who he wants to become—a necessary step in transgender transformation: "The conviction of being really a [man] may grow, rather than being present from the start. It may not be complete; ambiguity and uncertainty are common. Those who push on must negotiate their way out of the social position of being a [woman] and into that of being a [man], a process liable to corrode family relationships, lose jobs, and attract police attention" (Carrigan et al. 159–160). The transgender individual also destabilizes categories, pushing on the boundaries of binary identification. In the fourth wave era, especially, the boundaries of feminism expand to encompass these new categories. Morgan adds:

> At first glance, science fiction at least has always been interested in trans people. The very idea of medically changing sex (and let's glide over what being trans means for now) has a science-fictional feel to it. *The Encyclopedia of Science Fiction* dates stories about gender transformation at least as far back as 1924 (SFE, 2017). Fantasy has an even older tradition of magical transformations, including Ovid's *Metamorphoses* (approx. 8 CE, read in 1986 translation). However, the vast majority of such stories have been told by people who are not trans (cis people). While they may have a (sometimes prurient) interest in trans people, their understanding has often been lacking.

Certainly, the episode emphasizes the Clone Club's reaction *to* Tony more than his own growth and struggles. Still, Felix approaches Tony's situation with sympathy, suggesting a familiarity with trans culture. As he tells Art, "*He's* trans. He's, yeah, just another variation in my sister's skin." Meanwhile, Tony snarks that Felix is "Pretty gay, by the looks of this place." He strips and bathes in front of him, going out of his way to mention his genitals, as Felix retorts that Tony enjoys "Pushing buttons. Testing boundaries." When Tony kisses him, Felix tells him, "Fluidity doesn't shock me, either, Tony," but refuses to go further. Fawcett notes:

> That was one of those parts of the story that really solidified this concept for me. As we were trying to figure out how to use the character, that to me was the pinnacle of what made this so cool—to put Tony and Felix together in a very strange romantic way that left Felix very conflicted. And then the other aspect of these two kisses is that you have to go, "Wait a minute! That's Tat and Jordan!" [Laughs] The reality of it is it's not Tony and Felix, it's Tat and Jordan. And when you go and think that, that's even a bigger mindf—[Ross, "Tony the Transclone"].

A little on Tony's background comes out during the episode. Tony tells Felix, "At least you didn't know your real parents were assholes. You know, mine were so full of shit, it made sense when Beth said we were related." Based on his police records, Art describes Tony as "sketchy as hell." He calls him a convicted thief from Cincinnati, "formerly Antoinette Sawicki."

When he leaves to go on the run, Felix and Tony both observe how capable he is of fending for himself. He kisses Felix goodbye, a moment they both address sarcastically, though with understanding and affection. It "was quite exciting for Jordan and I to shoot the intimate scene between the two of them," admits Maslany. "That was an amazing scene to shoot, too, because Jordan was just so incredible in it. And I felt like we were just touching on territory that we hadn't gotten to explore together yet" ("Orphan Black Season 2").

Meanwhile, Tony's experience reflects the clones' as a whole: Cael Keegan writes in "Horizontal Inheritance: *Orphan Black*'s Transgender Genealogy": "Tony is not the only trans character on *Orphan Black*: all the show's clones are 'trans' bodies who illustrate the scientific construction of sex and gender, the phenomenon of passing, and the history of eugenics embedded in reproductive medicine." This echoes Haraway's cyborg theory that shows the woman as liminal boundary breaker if being male is the standard. Keegan continues:

> *Orphan Black* belongs to a set of science fiction texts—including *The Matrix* (1999), *Avatar* (2009), and *Under the Skin* (2013)—that explore what might be called "transgender" phenomenology without necessarily being about transgender identity. Referencing early sci-fi narratives like *Frankenstein* (1818) and *The Island of Dr. Moreau* (1896), these texts explore the relationship between the body and

subjectivity, investigating how we know our bodies belong to us and how that knowledge is produced and controlled—by kinship, medicine, gender assignment, and the logic of species. Through gender, *Orphan Black* pursues ethical questions about bodily autonomy, medical authority, and the surveillance state that are fundamentally important to transgender studies.

Gender is emphasized as artificial, much like the clones' creation—all becomes constructed, throwing everyone's identities into question. Indeed, the other clones are queered—shown as supporters of nontraditional lifestyles. There's Felix the gay artist. Cosima is a lesbian, but also sports dreadlocks and a nose piercing, as she hails from the counterculture West Coast. Helena, akin to a wild animal as she ignores society's rules—from table manners to murder—is also an outsider. Rachel considers herself set apart from both normal humanity and the clones as she hides safely in DYAD, while autistic M.K. also withdraws from the world. Sarah and Helena's reproductive capacity is "queered" in that it is unexpected—a mutation, and Sarah lives in a female-centric family with no husband or boyfriend. Even Alison, the most traditional seeming, gulps pills and alcohol in secret, to say nothing of her and Donnie's murders and drug-dealing. Tony is only the most blatant expression of the nonconformity they all share.

Gracie the Victim

Gracie Johanssen, the daughter of the cult leader Henrik, has a disturbing life. Brainwashed into obedience (or rather, never experiencing another life) she believes Helena isn't even a person and tries to smother her with a pillow, saying "Go back to hell, where you belong" ("Governed as It Were by Chance" 204). This indifference to any life not belonging to her people emphasizes the dangers of dogma and tribalism. Later, she tells Mrs. S, "I was always taught they were less than human. Abominations" ("Scarred by Many Past Frustrations" 305). Her father barbarically sews her mouth shut as punishment. In "Ipsa Scientia Potestas Est" 205, she protests, emphasizing how he's taught her to condemn unbelievers:

> GRACIE: I was protecting us. Not taking a real life, like killing a coyote that wants to eat our chickens. I'm so sorry, father.
> HENRIK: Just you help us get her back and all will be forgiven.
> BONNIE: And, if you don't … then you will carry the child yourself.

Such a threat from her own mother is particularly chilling, emphasizing her own cult zealotry superseding her daughter. Gracie obeys, tracking Helena and returning her to the farm. However, her obedience endangers her own life, when her father still impregnates her with his and Helena's zygote and her only response is to submit, and then crumple and cry.

Mark Banschick's article in *Psychology Today*, "What Awful Marriages & Cults Have in Common," stresses a person's dependency on the cult leader, one resembling a child being abused by a parent. For Gracie, this is literally true, and with her raised in the cult as well, she feels she has no other choice. Banschick adds, "The fact is that abusive relationships have a lot in common with cults. In both, victims feel completely demoralized, injured and trapped." Further, abusive relationships regress people to a childlike, dependent stage in which they can't break away.

A person trapped in a cult frequently feels there's no way out: "Cults are designed to keep a clear separation between those inside and outside. The more faithful a follower, the more reliant the person is on the group. It becomes everything—family, friends, church, home, work, dwelling, community. Extracting oneself from that after decades is difficult, and sometimes impossible. It is both terrifying and isolating" (Banschick).

Her only possible lifeline to the outside comes from Mark. He is Gracie's handsome prince, rescuing her from her father's farm, wedding her, and vowing to protect her. He carries her off as Helena stays behind to murder her father, something Gracie allows by her inaction. While her love with Mark is real, her paternal relationship is heavily damaged. This is quite believable based on cult psychology: "The cult leader—often a man—will punish your 'disobedience.' He will call you evil and wayward. He is so convincing that a part of you starts to believe him. He may even create a theology that keeps you in place. It's a form of brainwashing. What's good for him is what is good for the religion" (Banschick).

In "Newer Elements of Our Defense" (304), Gracie's mother drags her home. She and the others show no love for Gracie—only for the miracle child she's incubating. When Gracie loses the child, her mother instantly turns against her, blaming Gracie for the miscarriage, saying her elopement angered God. "What happened, Gracie, is that you betrayed your family. God wanted to punish you. So he cursed you, and he took the child. Our legacy. And you lost it!" As childlike Gracie pleads for forgiveness, her mother condemns her: "The only reason our door was open to you again was because of that child, and now it's gone. You ruined the last chance for this family. You will not be welcome back here again." Gracie's only worth to her mother, like to her father, is for her reproductive capability.

However, to her and Mark's horror, sex with him renders her infertile. Like Ferdinand, all promise of the handsome prince is subverted as he's revealed as a monster. Granted, this attack on his beloved is beyond Mark's control. Gracie is even in many ways relieved: "I was supposed to have children. It was expected of me.... Part of me feels relieved, Cosima. Does that make me a monster?" ("Certain Agony of the Battlefield" 306). Cosima reassures her, but she has much more healing to do.

In season three, Siobhan and Felix take her in and try to give her a happy life. She tries to reconcile her abuse, telling Siobhan in a quiet moment, "My father put that baby inside me and my mother let him." Siobhan responds with sympathy and tells her about her own youthful runaway marriage. "I don't blame you for not wanting me here. I wouldn't trust me either," Gracie says. However, in an assertive moment, she tells Felix she refuses to hate him for being gay because of how she was raised. She adds, "Look, all my life I've had doubts, but I just let my parents tell me what to think and what to do. I'm eighteen years old and I've never smoked anything or been to a rock concert or gone skinny-dipping" ("Scarred by Many Past Frustrations" 305). With this, she dresses in Sarah's most revealing old clothes and tries to go out clubbing. S. and Felix intervene to prevent the sheltered girl from going out alone and instead they all drink and dance around the house, giving Gracie a taste of fun and empowerment at last.

Next, she moves into Alison's house and works at soap making. She embraces this new family and is happy to reunite with Helena. However, season end reveals she has betrayed the sisters so she can be with Mark, though she feels very badly about it. She focuses on pleasing the dominant man in her life, endangering the entire community for him, and thus emphasizes how she's still a cultist deep down.

Her role as the victim under the patriarchy's thumb continues. In season five, she finally finds Helena in her convent. She lies that Mark has died two weeks before and says she'd understand if Helena doesn't trust her. She adds, "Thank you for letting me stay. I don't have a family anymore; I didn't know where else to go" ("Guillotines Decide" 508).

As Helena welcomes her and acknowledges her as family, Gracie hesitates, even as a dying Mark calls and insists she turn over Helena to Coady. "Gracie, I'm depending on you. I don't get the cure otherwise," he tells her over the phone. Terribly torn, she tells him she hasn't found Helena yet. However, Coady traces her phone and sends thugs. Still generous, Helena tries to take Gracie with her when they flee. However, Coady's goons arrive and Gracie breaks down, crouching in despair as they capture Helena. She pleads, "I'm sorry" and one tells her, "It's okay. You're forgiven" before he shoots her in the head ("Guillotines Decide" 508). Gracie has never fully escaped her obedience to the patriarchy, a cringing slavery that finally kills her—the show makes her pitiable but far from innocent.

Kendall the Matriarch

Kendall Malone, the wise matriarch and great-grandmother of the series, arrives in "Insolvent Phantom of Tomorrow" (309). Kassov, Sarah's childhood protector, tells Sarah who owns the prison number she's tracking: "Geezer's name is Malone. Went in in '78. Kendall Malone. Aggravated homicide. Paroled 2007. There's an address on here, it's current" ("Insolvent Phantom of Tomorrow" 309).

Mrs. S and Sarah track down the progenitor of the Castors only to discover she's a woman ... technically. She's a chimera, a rare genetic anomaly whose DNA makeup includes two separate genomes—in her case, male and female. While still in the womb, she absorbed her fetal twin into herself. "These cells become integrated into the host twin's developing body, where they may be localized to a certain organ or tissue, like a kidney or specific patches of skin, or distributed throughout the body, creating a patchwork of two genomes in the person" (Griffin and Nesseth). Now she's a hermaphrodite of a sort, a male-female blend once revered as a source of great wisdom and prophecy. Manson describes Kendall: "The science works. We thought it was an intriguing way to put the original as the ultimate goal of both Castor and Leda and put us on a collision path towards our finale. And also, it was important to us to draw, for Sarah, some deep understanding and a little bit of closure with her own past" (Dalton, "Creator").

Kendall is also S.'s mother, imprisoned for killing her husband, John Sadler with garden shears. Kendall claims she only killed him after he attacked her, and anyway he had taken her child from her. Still angry, Siobhan actually points a gun at her, blowing up her house and insisting she'll kill her as needed. With this, their messy, problematic relationship becomes a plot point. As it turns out, she isn't just Sarah's grandmother, but her clone-source. "This varied depiction of motherhood ... shakes up who we think a mother is (which in turn makes us question what role moms out to play in society" (Donovan 134).

"In the old days of the rural village, women gained power by moving into the grandmother role, where they could boss around their sons' young wives from the apex of the extended family. But today aging women are edged off the map. Isolated by the nuclear family, scattered in the suburbs, surrounded by strangers with no sense of their past role or contribution, aging women now experience cultural abandonment" (Paglia 141). Kendall is in truth banished far away, with no connection to her biological and adoptive descendants. While Kira has the structure of a loving grandmother, it's suggested that angry Sarah could have used a wise confidant. Instead, she had the mother she was rebelling against and her tolerant, exasperated brother—without mentoring, she fell into a destructive spiral. Maria Doyle Kennedy (Siobhan) notes:

> I think for S., finding and reconciling with her own mother changed everything for her. She saw how much of her own actions and rebellion as a younger woman were a response to the disconnect and loss of relationship with her family. She also

knows that she won't be around forever, and so she desperately wants to create a network of love and support and friendship around Sarah and Kira and Felix, so that they are able to care for each other and able to carry on without her when she is no longer there ["Maria Doyle Kennedy Q&A"].

After, Siobhan, Kendall, and Sarah convene for a family chat. Siobhan insists Kendall tell her history, for Kira's sake. In fact, five years after his first tissue-collecting visit, Ethan Duncan returned to the prison where he once had found Kendall, riddled with guilt and paranoia. He told her that Neolution had taken over the program, killed his wife, stolen his daughter, and "poisoned the science," and he wanted to escape. Kendall sent him to Siobhan for hiding and insisted Duncan send Siobhan the last clone, the one unregistered in the foster care system. "I couldn't expect forgiveness, but I wanted you to have her—she's your blood, too," Kendall says, poignantly, with tears. "A little piece of me. All I had left of my foul life to give" ("History Yet to Be Written" 310). With this, she altered Sarah's life forever.

Manson says, "I think Kendall has been trying to make amends since we've met her. And, like a lot of characters in the show, she's discovering family for the first time" ("Closer Looks 406"). Kendall's death lets her make those amends, though she keeps her attitude to the end. In "The Scandal of Altruism" (406), Cosima and the Clone Club make a desperate bargain to share Kendall's DNA and all their research with Susan Duncan so she can help find a cure. To their shock, all the research is suddenly wiped, just as Kendall is kidnapped. Evie, the villainess of Brightborn, has decided to murder the Ledas. She and the corrupt cop Duko kidnap Kendall and Cosima and drive them to the deserted countryside.

Cosima begs Kendall for a plan, but all gruff, proud Kendall says is "No tears, Cosima. These shites aren't worth the salt. Tell Siobhan she's done right, always. And tell your sisters I'm proud to have been part of them all." With this, she does her best to comfort Cosima and prepare her to survive. Looking away, Cosima hears the shot and falls to her knees in despair. The clones have lost their progenitor and also their protective grandmother. The fight has become so much harder.

Krystal Goderitch: Girl Power

If Beth was trying to have it all, third-wave style, Krystal embodies the nineties even further as the girl power icon in her pink low-cut tops. She's like Buffy the heroic cheerleader, or Xena in her cleavage armor. Television shows *Charmed*, *The Powerpuff Girls*, and *Sailor Moon*, along with films like *Clueless*, all celebrated being girly yet capable and successful. "Pinkfloor expressed this new position when she said that it's possible to have a push-up bra and a brain at the same time" (Rampton). Continuing to ham up the frivolity, Krystal adores shopping, unlike her more serious sisters. Wardrobe department head Debra Hanson speaks of costuming Krystal by walking around the mall. She describes her as "a typical pretty, young, confident girl. She's not a brain surgeon. She's got a little bit of money, but she's spending it on [shopping] and she watches television, and enjoys the celebrity shows" (Bernstein 74). This matches her up well with girl power, as the '90s media-focused movement was invested in increasing girls' self-esteem and personal empowerment without "sacrificing" preoccupations with beauty, sex, and consumerism.

> This is in keeping with the third wave's celebration of ambiguity and refusal to think in terms of "us-them." Most third-wavers refuse to identify as "feminists" and reject the word that they find limiting and exclusionary. Grrl-feminism tends to be global, multi-cultural, and it shuns simple answers or artificial categories of identity, gender, and sexuality. Its transversal politics means that differences such as those of ethnicity, class, sexual orientation, etc. are celebrated and recognized as dynamic, situational, and provisional. Reality is conceived not so much in terms of fixed structures and power relations, but in terms of performance within contingencies. Third wave feminism breaks boundaries [Rampton].

As far as sex, Krystal appears kissing a Rudy in a short red dress and going into his room since she's in a nonexclusive relationship ("The Weight of This Combination" 301). She needn't be a fighter or a scientist, only a happy, sexy young woman. Her actress notes that some of her mannerisms and accessories further weaken her: the huge nails change how she handles things (Bernstein 74). Graeme Manson comments: "Krystal came about really organically, through this character in season two that Tat would always put on between takes. It was just this funny, sort of airheaded character and we kept joking that maybe she would work her way into a clone, and that's what happened. We're refining it along the way now, of course, but again, that's part of the fun of working through a bunch of seasons with these actors" (Framke). Perky music always highlights Krystal's appearances, from "No Good Woman" by Elise LeGrow when Felix gets his nails done to "Girl, Tell Me Something" when she infiltrates Brightborn. She's the one clone who is consistently objectified, leaning forward in her low-cut top while she does people's nails. Later, in "Human Raw Material" (405), Donnie gives her a massage while staring at her body. She also learns self-defense in skimpy exercise gear.

Krystal enters the story as a victim, once again contrasting her with the other Ledas. Rudy and Seth try to kidnap her, and they kill her monitor Hector, who was rescuing the only Leda wimpy enough to need it. In "Ruthless in Purpose, and Insidious in Method" (308), Delphine meets her to help set up a new monitor. "You" by the Katherines plays perkily as the screen focuses in on the brightly colored fingernails first, and women second—more objectification. Krystal promptly dumps her life story on Delphine while giving her a manicure: "So this guy, he had, like, a wicked scar, which I was into, for some reason. It was kind of dark and mysterious and my relationship with Hector was open, so, I thought, whatever, like, this guy's hot. Nobody dies. Anyway, so, we get to the room, and then suddenly I realize there's another guy in the room who looks identical to him. Like, identical. An identical twin. I know, right? Twins are so creepy." The last line is delightfully ironic, but beyond this, she has sex on a whim and keeps her options open. Clearly, she believes with her whole heart in her materialistic, rather self-centered life.

Nonetheless, there's a sweetness about her as she adds, "I feel like what I do is quite healing. I don't know if you feel that way, you know? ... But that's just my gift, and I just feel like, you know, in spite of everything, as hard as it is losing Hector, you can't crush the human spirit" ("Ruthless in Purpose, and Insidious in Method" 308). She reminds the clones of their own innocence, now long gone. Sarah resolves not to tell her the truth and keep her happily naive. However, she's a pawn in her first appearance and also this one, since Rachel's price for helping the others is Krystal's identity. When Felix sneaks in to steal her wallet, he realizes she's trying to break out of her prison of ignorance and longs to tell her after she protests, "Like, I'm not super-smart, but I'm not super-stupid, either.... I just feel like I'm missing something really big."

The best he can leave her with is a moment of truth: "The only thing that you need to know is that you are one of a kind. You're a survivor, Krystal. And you're not alone" ("Ruthless in Purpose, and Insidious in Method" 308). The chilling creepiness comes at episode end when Rachel drugs her into a coma so she can steal not just her identity but her very life. She abandons the other woman, potentially forever.

Two episodes later, Delphine recognizes her from her nail polish and awakens her. Delphine comforts the distraught clone but seems to lose interest on discovering she's the unimportant pawn of the story. Of course, this kidnapping brings Krystal to a point where she can no longer ignore the secret plots. "Why do weird things keep happening to me?" she asks plaintively. Nonetheless, she isn't inducted into Clone Club.

Season four, Krystal reappears and reveals that she's been tracing all the weird happenstances but has reached the wrong conclusion—that it's a cosmetics conspiracy. She's also been learning self-defense, telling her trainer, "Sometimes it just takes a tragedy to find your own resilience" and "You know, you can be a victim, or you can totally get to the bottom of it, you know?" ("Human Raw Material" 405). Though still lighthearted, she's toughening up. She's also a better investigator than her sisters expect.

She's been labeled a non-threat by Neolution and the Leda clones alike, but within only a few weeks, Krystal uncovered nearly as much information as Sarah and the other clones put together over the course of six months. Krystal prides herself in particular on her ability to dig up and expose Neolution's unethical and illegal activities, though she may not get all of the facts right in terms of how they connect to clones and to herself. Everyone from Felix to Susan dismisses Krystal for her naiveté, but she makes some salient points [Griffin and Nesseth].

She goes to the police in "The Scandal of Altruism" (406), and Art catches her and hides her safely at his place. When Felix comes to help, Art introduces him as a detective from Scotland Yard. However, Krystal suddenly maces Felix, saying after, "I'm so sorry. I'm taking self-defense classes, so it was just like a reflex." It's a silly moment, but one that emphasizes her new fighting girl power. Nineties stories specifically made their heroines campy to undermine their strength and make them less threatening. This trope marks Krystal's every scene. As the farce continues, Felix compounds it with bald-faced lies: "Look, Krystal. You need to know that you figured it out. It's all true. All of it. There is this dirty war being waged on stem-cell technology, trying to control it, that's all being orchestrated by the cosmetic companies."

As the season continues, the creators gleefully enjoy *not* telling Krystal the truth. This gets even sillier at the end of season four when she meets Sarah and denies they look identical: "'K, are you, like, blind? 'Cause this girl looks nothing like me. Like, first of all, my tits are way bigger. And secondly, even if you could drag a comb through that hair, she's like, a 7 on a good day and I've been told I'm a 10." Her oblivious, accidental solving of crimes combines with her ridiculous lack of perception, undermining any strength she reveals. Even when she saves Delphine's life, it's an accident, since her phone goes off unexpectedly. Ironically, it plays "The Warriors" by Amalie Bruun, the same as Krystal works out to in the gym. Over and over, the show emphasizes she shouldn't be taken seriously, though she contributes vital pieces of the Neolution puzzle.

In "Manacled Slim Wrists" (506), Krystal returns for another goofy cameo. She and her roommate Bree have been cohosting a popular beauty vlog that teaches how to use party straws as hair curlers and also exposes the lies of "Big Cosmetics." However, when Bree's hair starts falling out, Krystal seeks out Art, convinced her friend has been poisoned by cosmetics corporations. "Did Krystal just fall ass-backwards into something big again?" marvels Sarah.

As usual, her frivolous lifestyle offers useful insights into what's really happening. Blue Zone Cosmetics, whom she's investigating, has just been bought by DYAD. She's even dating the CEO Len Sipp (played by Tom Cullen, Tatiana's real-life partner). Though Sarah plans to take her place, Krystal insists on interrogating Len in her own fashion—tight pink dress and long, involved kisses as Art and Sarah (on her earpiece) urge her to "keep it in your pants." The girl power heroine is often distracted by her own priorities—shopping or cheerleading over the mission. Thus, her more serious sisters deem her ridiculously unreliable. Enjoying her romance, Krystal keeps the flirtation up until she realizes Len doesn't respect her, just wants her body. Enraged, she kicks him in the groin and, wrestling him to the ground, threatens him with hair-removal cosmetic. He spills, and in an act of superficial revenge, she destroys his manly beard before throwing him out. Each time, Krystal is completely wrong in her facts, yet good-hearted, effective, and even heroic. She outfights Donnie, Felix, and several bad guys. Though her sisters find her laughable, she gets in her licks standing up for the silly yet effective strength of girl power.

Scott and Hell Wizard: Sidekicks

Scott Smith (Josh Vokey) first appears at the University of Minnesota in "Conditions of Existence" (105). Cosima asks him to test some of the clone blood. When he asks after the subject, Cosima hesitates. "Ah, subjects," Cosima corrects, "and if I told you that, I'd have to kill you." They laugh lamely, though of course, the situation is deadlier than Cosima is revealing. He agrees to sequence the "bar code" gene, though such a thing shouldn't exist in humans. Memorably, he asks what he'll get out of helping her. "Um," Cosima drawls, "how 'bout you get to have sex? With yourself?"

Scott stutters around a confused laugh, "Aw-Awesome deal," realizing he's somehow the butt of her joke. In this introduction, he's obviously the ultimate geek, socially awkward since Cosima is far out of his league, intellectually as well as sexually.

In season two, Delphine brings hapless Scott to Canada to work on their team. Cosima refuses, since she sees him as an innocent, she insists, "We can't involve him in this" ("To Hound Nature in Her Wanderings" 206). However, disarming her protective gesture, he pipes up that he's figured out what's going on. While his devotion to gaming casts him as terribly geeky, he's capable and perceptive. Further, Cosima discovers that, since Scott has no agenda, he's soon the only he one she can trust in a workplace of endless lies and maneuvering. It comes to resemble a game—chess or *Battleship*, concentrating on trapping and evading the other players. Of course, this is his domain, which he uses to save the day, sneaking Rachel out of DYAD with an alliance of his gaming pals. Meanwhile, Cosima continues teasing him about his perpetual virginity, especially after she meets his friends.

While the men, from Art to Felix, all cave when family is threatened, Scott gives in the fastest. While not precisely feminized, Scott is definitely not macho—a grad student and uber-geek, he's never seen fighting. In one memorable scene, Rudy preys on Scott by threatening to kill his asthmatic cat Denise—a family member strikingly more vulnerable than Scott himself. In this scene, the bully attacks the Clone Club's weakest link and actually succeeds. Though Scott caves and hands over Duncan's precious book, Cosima sympathizes with his softhearted surrender ("Ruthless in Purpose, and Insidious in Method" 308). Despite his softness, he's optimistic, supportive, and dedicated—exactly what Cosima needs in a lab partner.

In season four, Scott and his pal, known only as Hell Wizard, create a safehouse. It's located under a comic and game shop—their ideal franchise and a universe where they have power. "Secret lab under a comic book shop, what more could a girl want, right?" Cosima smirks ("Transgressive Border Crossing" 402). While visiting, Kira and even Krystal play games with them, and Mika the hacker visits online. Beneath the store are not only bedrooms but a lab, where Cosima and Scott continue their research with purloined DYAD equipment. Before this, the women have been the providers of homes and safety, but now it's the helpful male heroes who take over. It should also be noted that, while the men were employed by DYAD in season three, now they are acting on a volunteer basis, first sinking their own finances in the shop, and then continuing to spend all their hours helping the Ledas.

They continue to manage support in season five, even as Cosima runs off to the island and Rachel takes hostages. Easygoing Scott and Hell Wizard help with capers and accept that S. keeps things on a "need to know basis" with good humor ("Let the Children & the Childbearers Toil" 504). Finally, as Helena is kidnapped in the last two episodes, Scott and Hell Wizard become action heroes. They charge into the old DYAD building—Scott posing as a heart surgeon and Hell Wizard using the power of his security guard job. Beside them Art the cop reprises his own action role. As always, they aren't the story's central characters. Instead, Sarah rescues Helena and the two women kill the main villains, Westmorland and Coady. Nonetheless, it's the men's backup that makes the rescue possible.

In the final episode, Scott's still in the comic shop lab, still supporting Cosima in her endeavors. As there's no mention of massive new funds (though Mika conceivably could have left them her millions) they may still be working for free, generously investing all their assets in distributing the cure. These moments of unanswered questions and total benevolence often appear in less-developed fictional sidekicks—nonetheless, it's clear the women never could have stayed safe and created the cure without them. Hell Wizard and Scott end the episode attending Helena's baby shower where they flip burgers, embraced by their new family. While they may not have found worldly success, they've certainly made devoted friends—another story pattern more common for heroines.

Delphine: Dead Lesbian?

Lesbian representation has had a problematic history on television as so many of their romances end in tragic early death. So many, in fact, that it's become a cliché seen in *Watchmen, The Bell Jar, Goldfinger, Northern Exposure, Brookside, 24, Family Affairs, Smallville, ER, Bad Girls, Hex, Band of Gold, Deadwood, Charmed, Xena, NYPD Blue, Buffy the Vampire Slayer, True Blood, The 100, Dark Angel, Supernatural, Torchwood, Skins, Warehouse 13, Ally McBeal, The Vampire Diaries, Babylon 5, Arrow, Rome, Code Black, The Wire, The Catch, Expanse, Marvel's Jessica Jones, Empire, Orange is the New Black, Battlestar Galactica, Stargate-verse, Blindspot, The Magicians, Girl House, The Gemma Doyle* series, *The Sword of Truth* series, *The Long Earth, Victoria,* and *The Handmaid's Tale*, along with others. Another dead lesbian, or at least bisexual, was Veera's devoted friend Niki Lintula from the *Helsinki* comic, whom Veera met when at age seventeen she was cheating on her boyfriend with a girl.

Caroline Framke, a culture critic at *Vox Magazine*, analyzes the body count and explains, "About 10 percent of the deaths that I counted were gay, bisexual or otherwise queer women, which, when you think about it proportionally, is kind of nuts because not many television shows, unless it's *Orange Is the New Black* or something, have more than one or two maybe gay, bisexual or otherwise women. And the fact that most of them—a lot of them end up dead is troubling" (Martin). The key problem isn't merely that LGBT characters are killed off, but the tendency that they, especially lesbian and bisexual female characters, have to be killed off far more often than straight ones. Framke adds, "*Empire* killed off two queer women when *Empire*, a soap, doesn't even kill off that many people. And it still managed to do that" (Martin).

Even those who have moved on and married a man, like Dax on *Star Trek: Deep Space Nine* or Susan on *Seinfeld*, still are suddenly killed. Further, many have specifically unhappy endings. When they are together happily, at least one half of the couple, often the one who was more aggressive in pursuing a relationship, thus "perverting" the other, is suddenly, dramatically shot. All this suggests society's anger at the women's flouting of society, going back to the shockingly influential novel *The Well of Loneliness* in 1928. Framke concludes, "You have to think about it in a bit of a larger context than even just television. If you go back to lesbian pulp novels, in the '50s, '60s especially, they always ended horribly because the editors would only publish them if gay women in the stories ended up dead or renouncing their lesbianism or basically punished in some way for being happy like this. And that was a mandate. There were morality clauses. This doesn't come from nowhere" (Martin).

All this baggage existed before *Orphan Black,* with some of the deaths admittedly on very feminist shows. Thus, when Delphine and Cosima's relationship crumbles (while Sarah and Alison and Gracie and even Helena end season three with stable heterosexual relationships), fans were incensed when Delphine was suddenly shot in a parking lot.

As DYAD's goons approach her from offscreen, Delphine's only thoughts are for Cosima. Selflessly, Delphine asks, "What will happen to her?" The unseen person says nothing and shoots her in the stomach, leaving her to bleed out against a car. After all the womb trouble of the show, this seems another blow to women's reproduction, symbolically, as Delphine loses her rulership over DYAD and her life. Fawcett says, "From the moment Delphine is told she's not going to live through the end of this day, it takes on this emotional flavor of Dead Man Walking. And Delphine knows it" (Ross, "Finale")

Fawcett adds of Delphine's death, "I know this will be upsetting to many fans but the story in our minds has always been a tragic love story.... Trust me, this was a necessary move to make. And it's necessary in Cosima's story and it's necessary going forward in subsequent seasons—in season 4 and season 5" (Ross, "Finale"). Fans filled the internet with their anger. "I knew we were heading into choppy waters," Manson says. "That relationship was portrayed as natural and not oversexualized and was very important to people in terms of their own lives being represented. But we still had to honor the show. We still had to go, 'OK, we're going to mess up this audience. How do we not lose them? But we knew we wanted that relationship to survive" (Schneider). Manson defended his choice, adding that the character truly was dead: "For all intents and purposes, Evelyne [Brochu's character] is dead. But there's always a crack of hope in an actor's busy schedule. They can reappear somehow. But we had to make a bold story choice, and it was a story choice that was very collaborative with Evelyne" (Framke).

Fan outcry was immense. However, possibly spurred by this, Delphine returns from the dead in season five, more in love with Cosima than ever, and their relationship wins another chance. Thus, the cliché was used then averted, fixing some of the gender issues in television. Delphine and Cosima are almost the only couple to find a happy ending, as Rachel's lover has died and Sarah's and Helena's love interests don't appear in the last season (although both might return). Further, Manson suggests Cosima and Delphine might adopt Charlotte, the little girl Cosima fought through the fifth season to protect. He comments, "It's a nice, little open thing of what could happen to Charlotte. I know that the fandom discussed her being adopted by Cosima and Delphine. I love that story, too. That's a beautiful one to have in your imagination. I second that" (Gelman, "*Orphan Black* Boss"). With this, Cosima and Delphine tour the world, expanding their family each day even as they have the love and precious daughter they've long sought.

False Prince Ferdinand

In "The Weight of This Combination" (301), Delphine enlists the clones to reassure Topside's cleaner Ferdinand (James Frain), who's making a surprise inspection. The man is smooth and slimy but quite trickable. Delphine explains why they've delayed surgery by using the mysteries of women's biology, a frequent ploy to drive off male inquiry. "You cannot remove the ovary of a woman who is ovulating. I know it is inconvenient, but she's contained" ("The Weight of This Combination" 301). Clueless about women, he is fooled. Meanwhile, as he gropes the bound Alison-as-Sarah, he shows his utter contempt for the women. Oily and cruel, Ferdinand languorously pulls on rubber gloves before he suddenly shoves his hand up Alison's shirt. Delphine, Sarah, and Alison can only blink in barely concealed horror as he smirks. After, Sarah interrogates him as Rachel and brings BDSM into the bedroom the way Ferdinand likes. Delphine rescues her before things go very far, and they make him call off his hit on the Ledas.

Ferdinand visits Delphine at DYAD in the third season finale, mildly threatening her. He tells her, "Delphine, there is nowhere I like to be more than under the heel of a woman, but sometimes it … makes me seethe.… I want the original. Once I return her to Topside and I have my own seat at the table, and then you can toil under my heel." Clearly, climbing up the patriarchal ladder is his top priority. To his surprise, Sarah steps out from the shadows to offer Ferdinand one chance for a deal and needles him about her Rachel impersonation. Sarah proposes to use Ferdinand in her own plan, calling him "the lesser of two evils." Clearly, she holds all the cards here. As occurred in the season opener, Ferdinand the great killer is manipulated by the clones and they come out on top. The Ledas lay a trap and Ferdinand plays hero, but only at the women's behest.

When Ferdinand meets Rachel in the *Helsinki* prequel comics, he compliments Leekie on "What you've done here" while staring at her legs in her miniskirt. He's a leering misogynist, and Leekie treats her as a child. In fact, Leekie soon orders Rachel to her room while the men are talking and apologizes to Ferdinand for her outburst. She seduces him later in provocative clothes, taking charge of him and with him, her fate. Still, the pair appear to have a loving relationship. When Ferdinand leaves her, she tells him, "I feel so safe here" while she hugs him. He tells her he always wants her to feel that way, and she responds, "You're the only one that can do that for me, Ferdinand." Already she is too dependent.

"The Stigmata of Progress" (403) has him contact the Clone Club, since he has information and, more importantly to him, a message from Rachel. Now he's on a heroic quest to find his lost love. S. enlists him on the spot, and he charges into where Sarah is being strapped down and tortured. He slays the treacherous orderly (admittedly, with a scalpel, not a sword) and saves the day.

In the next episode, as he glowingly describes his adoration of Rachel, he seems the epitome of courtly love. He's devotedly rescuing her from her own imprisonment, and adds, "What can I say? She pierced this armored heart. Shall we breakfast?" ("From Instinct to Rational Control" 404). With this, he politely makes the others food, while describing how he cooks frittatas to his lady love's taste. All this makes him appear the ideal prince down to his name, Ferdinand Chevalier. Of course, his plan is a bit twisted: "I'd like a family of my own, someday. I've squirreled a little away. Enough to recover by the seaside in style. Just Rachel and I. Bide our time before a slow, steady climb back to power."

Worse, in the same episode, Veera discovers he was responsible for killing all her loved ones—Ferdinand took point during "Operation Helsinki," in which six clones and "32 collateral" were eliminated in under 24 hours. She entraps him, coaxing him to sit on a pressure plate, and then, once he's incapacitated, arriving to taunt him in person. "Bastard son of the 10th Earl of Sussex. A stigma you still can't get over.... You discovered your bloodlust in the British SAS. Learned to kill quickly and quietly. Perfect recruit for a Topside cleaner."

He retorts, "What's stopping me from standing up and killing one more?"

However, she sees through him and answers, "You tell me! Cowardice? Narcissism?" In fact, the brave hero suffers from both, and will not sacrifice himself. Sarah arrives to talk Veera down. Reluctantly, she settles for a different revenge. She orders Ferdinand to type in his password, and she transfers his millions to herself, depriving him of his worldly power and comforts. She leaves him there, and S. must rescue him by disarming the plate, even as she orders him to wait until the women are safe before he tries to stand. Pathetically, he asks for a moment to prepare himself for death and adds, "But when I get out of here, I'm going be a little short of funds..."

Siobhan dismisses his predicament with "You're a clever chap. I'm sure you'll find some way to make yourself useful." He finally stands, alone in the darkened room, bested and left with nothing. His ignominious defeat emphasizes his complete depowering. Clearly, modern women shouldn't trust idealized princes but should rescue themselves.

In "Clutch of Greed" (502), Veera, dying, takes Sarah-as-Rachel's place so her sister can escape. On finding her, Ferdinand smirks in sexist fashion, "You have no idea the volcano that outfit is inspiring in me right now. Turn around slowly." When he discovers who she is, he speaks to her as Veera and Rachel in one, enacting all his revenge fantasies on both: "Oh, pardon me, Rachel? After all those years I invested in you. All that money, which is so fantastic, because you stole it from me, didn't you, Veera? This is like two revenge fantasies in one! I even get to finish Helsinki." Repeating this last over and over, taking his own demasculinization and power loss out on the other woman, he stomps gentle Veera to death. She lies under him, completing one more rape metaphor.

In "Guillotines Decide" (508), he rescues Rachel and works with S. to bring down Neolution.

> FERDINAND: Rachel is rather impressed with our transgressive little alliance, aren't you?
> DEPHINE: It made me sick to work with the man who killed M.K.
> FERDINAND: Sarah doesn't know you two are here, does she?
> S.: No, it's just the four of us. And our interests are very firmly aligned as you now have a nice, big, fat target on your back, too. So Neolution goes down for good—or we all do.

After this, S. shares information with Rachel, and Rachel brings it to Ferdinand like a love offering: "Names, dates, amounts. A full record of worldwide influence—payments."

Ferdinand grins and laughs. "Ohhhh, I bloody love you. With this we could squeeze anything we want out of those Neo pricks."

Rachel offers him a different path with a fortune she's saved up. "It wouldn't last forever, but if we wanted, we could destroy Westmorland and Neolution, go somewhere warm—off the grid."

He condescendingly says that she has a nice plan "But with this, we can build a dynasty. Obscene wealth. Anything we want. Who's your daddy?"

She submits, responding, "You are."

After this, Ferdinand meets with the shadowy board all in grey in their stark warehouse. There, he boasts of his power over them and demands billions. All the power and control are his at last ... until he uploads the files to the screen and they come up empty. "There, uh seems to be some, uh, technical difficulty," he blusters, suddenly realizing Rachel and S. have double crossed him. Desperate, he shoots his way out, deprived of power and love as he had so recently been deprived of all his finances.

He rushes back to confront Rachel: "That was a deathtrap, that meeting. You expected them to kill me." Furious, he insists her plan of running away is ridiculous: "What? We just ride off into the sunset when everything we have ever wanted was at our fingertips? You expected me to take a payoff? That is how we win!" She has learned, but he has not. He pushes her down and strangles her, crying, "I gave everything to be under your heel. I could have squirmed there forever, you heartless little bitch!" When she's unmoved, he screams with rage and frustration, abandoning her. In immature fashion, he goes to take his rage out on someone else.

Ferdinand's death scene is hyper masculine as he ambushes Siobhan and tells her he doesn't want to talk. "I just wanna put holes in you with this .45

bigger than the holes you can put in me with that 9 mil." Having the biggest gun is everything to him.

She sweetly replies, "Won't make much a difference in the throat, love. Why don't we put them down." He gloats about disarming her hidden gun, then shoots her with his own. She collapses on her easy chair, shot in the left ventricle and quickly dying. Nonetheless, she shoots him with another hidden gun, in the throat as she threatened. "Ugh! Quite enough lip out of you," she says, watching him horribly choke and claw at his throat. Once more, he's been mastered by a powerful woman.

Mika: Cyber-Anarchist

Anarcha-feminism fights to bring down the patriarchy as a manifestation of enforced hierarchy. Feminism becomes entwined with the underdog's struggle and an anarchic war against the system. The one devoted to this movement of course is M.K.

She was born Veera Suominen in Helsinki, where she grew up with Asperger's and an uncle who monitored her. Visiting DYAD as a child, she was burned by the same lab fire that apparently killed Rachel's parents (*The Clone Club: Rachel*). From this moment, the corporate clone hated her with a special passion and schemed to destroy her.

At age seventeen (in 2001), Veera discovered the truth of her life and went on the run, only to meet Niki Lintula and more clones like herself, making her first friends despite her terrible shyness. Niki promised she and Veera would "live together like sisters" before Ferdinand, sent by Rachel, suddenly murdered them all (*Helsinki*). Fawcett describes the *Helsinki* comic as "like a teen clone Breakfast Club" that would "end basically in a Red Wedding" (Bernstein 89). The last survivor, Veera made a final vow: "I will remind them that you [Niki] are still alive. That we do not simply fade away like ghosts. Or allow ourselves to be tagged, herded and slaughtered like sheep ... buried away and hidden, we will dig deeper for the truth. And for justice..."

Fawcett adds, "I liked the idea of a scarred teenage slightly Aspergers-y clone who survives Helsinki and changes her name and her identity to stay alive" (Bernstein 89). M.K. is an alias based on her genetic code marker, 3MK29A, suggesting that she "owns" her artificiality. Thus, she too becomes a boundary-breaking cyborg, using hacking to battle DYAD and Brightborn.

The popularization of the internet as Veera grew up and became self-aware in the late nineties became the source of her superpower. Many see its new possibilities for outreach and interaction creating a new type of feminism that includes international, disabled, and other more marginalized women. This is called fourth wave. "Despite the ambiguous assertion of feminism in popular culture, there appear to be as many grassroots feminist strategies purveyed through new social media today as there were being produced by grassroots women's groups and the wider women's movement between the 1970s and the 1990s" (Phillips and Cree). Teaming up with Beth, M.K. produces a grassroots Clone Club that battles the great corporation with data and online skill. This makes her a herald of cutting-edge feminism, one that reaches out to those who have learning disabilities or scars, and one that uses the intersectional power of the web. It's a different kind of rebellion, echoed in the sticker on her laptop for the alternative rock band, Garbage.

> Many of the concerns of the second wave women's movement are echoed in contemporary or fourth wave feminist voices, but there are also different issues and less clear or rigid "feminist" parameters. This is partly to do with the evolution of new cultures around sexuality, work, reproductive technologies, communication technologies and what can be seen as the continually changing market-driven commodification of all that is feminine and targeted at women. It is at this intersection of popular culture and feminism that many apparent contradictions arise for those of us who have grown up with the principles of second wave feminism, where every imposition on women had to be confronted or scrutinized [Phillips and Cree].

In season four, she advises Beth over the phone and appears in a tattered Dolly the sheep mask. Her wavy hair is pushed forward, barely covering her scar. She slouches, trying to hide herself. Lynch adds, "Her nerves manifest themselves through biting her cuticles, and you'll also see some patchiness on her skin and some breakouts around her nose, signifying this anxiety. She has a little more wiry, untamed eyebrows" (Bernstein 89). Maslany explains that she dresses like a child and has a very young expression since she hasn't moved past the time when she lost her best friend at age seventeen (Bernstein 89).

M.K. is linked with the concept of an online avatar because of her barely-visible human presence, in contrast with her activity as a hacker. She even appears multiple times in Kira's online game. Hacking culture is "dealing less directly with the transferal of a singular consciousness from one world to another, and more with the disruption of the social structures of fantasy that mediate and limit the relation of consciousness to both worlds" (Benjamin 191). The power of Avatars comes from one's anonymity and self-re-creation—online, one can be anyone she wishes, while the real self remains hidden and protected. The sheep mask too emphasizes her remaking herself as she chooses. "The construction of any specific image of the subject thus raises a complex interaction of multiple 'selves' within the cultural setting of avatar-mediated environments. Each element of identity is constructed as performed by the subject while it uses that specific body to engage with a specific world" (Benjamin 118).

Described by Donna Jeanne Haraway, author of *Simians, Cyborgs and Women: The Reinvention of Nature*, as "trickster figures that might turn a stacked deck into a potent set of wild cards for refiguring possible worlds" (66), the cyborg shatters limitations. Thus, the female cyborg especially represents "transgressed boundaries, potent fusions, and dangerous possibilities" (Haraway 154). Mika has merged with her computer, soaring across the internet with a newer, better self that rises beyond biological limitations. In this, she echoes the women of the story, constructed people struggling to break out of the roles they were created for. Further, they're fictional creations, set in the story to confront its moral questions. "The Woman Fantastic is a gendered textual and cultural construction. Hence, 'she' is entirely fantastic—less projection, stereotype, or image than symbol, sign, or trope, an always already artificial creation" (Helford et al.)

In a show focusing on the difference between biological bodies, Veera has re-envisioned her own almost as dramatically as Tony has. Of all the clones, she is the one who's a barely-perceptible shadow. Leaving behind the body "necessitates a shift away from a presence *or* absence or the body towards the presence *of* absence of consciousness and its gaze" (Benjamin 115). Further, in real life, she does her best not to exist, wandering the world only under cover of darkness as a night watchman. (The concept in the label emphasizes that she is not gazed at, but instead views others. It's also gender hybridizing.) In fact, her profession of spy makes her another kind of silent watcher, unobserved as she unravels others' dark deeds.

Mika's sheep mask functions like a superhero costume, letting the world see the costumed self that is the outward shape or persona one wishes to become—in many ways more "real" than one's birth self. Just as Neo in *The Matrix* claims his true self in the "virtual" world, Mika's life is not one of hiding in her trailer and playing night watchman, but one of dancing through databases and uncovering secrets. She is Mika now (named by her friend Beth), not Veera, the persecuted damaged teen from Helsinki. Sheep and girl, online millionaire and silent lurker, she transcends all definitions. Haraway celebrates hybridity in just this way—the emerging heroine uses this "incorporative transgression of boundaries: organism *and* machines, human *and* animal" (Thweatt-Bates 81).

Fawcett calls Mika "Very elusive. And quite highly skilled and very smart. And it is interesting as Sarah tries to interact with this character who is almost kind of like a Deep Throat kind of character. What's very cool about it is this is a clone who has been self-aware for some time" (Ross, "Orphan Black Season 4"). Mika in particular is the disabled feminist, working behind the scenes on her computer. Thus, she is a mastermind, one who has been unashamedly monitoring DYAD just as DYAD monitors the clones. This fits well with the feminist tropes: "The cyborg is resolutely committed to partiality, irony, intimacy, and perversity. It is oppositional, utopian, and completely without innocence" (Haraway 151). Fawcett adds:

> She's very paranoid. She's very security conscious. She knows more than Sarah does so she knows how dangerous the whole thing is. She's purposefully avoided contact with the sisters to keep herself safe, and Sarah is now trying to draw her out of the shadows and trying to utilize the information that she has so that Sarah can follow her own mystery and fill in the blanks and protect Alison and protect Cosima from Neolution. But this girl is very unwilling [Ross, "Orphan Black Season 4"].

She tracks her nemesis, Ferdinand, in season four, and stages a methodical execution. She adds, "You killed six of my sisters. Murdered 32 of our friends and loved ones.... I always dreamed of putting a name to your face. Of hurting you like you hurt me" ("From Instinct to Rational Control" 404). Luring him to sit on a pressure plate, she maintains complete control, only emerging once he's caged. When Sarah insists that they need him, Mika unwillingly spares him, though she forces him to transfer his millions to her. Mika operates from terror, not greed. Thus, she considers the money protection, as well as revenge. It's a painful moment for her, putting aside years of planned revenge for the Ledas' needs. She's still unwilling to join Clone Club, only returning when her illness worsens.

As Kira and Sarah run from DYAD, Mika valiantly takes Sarah's place, accepting at last that her sisters matter more to her than herself. At the same time, the Leda illness is killing her, echoing her disability as a source of weakness. She insists, "I'm too tired, Sarah. I've been running my whole life" ("Clutch of Greed" 502). While she battles Ferdinand with all her rage, he, the stronger male, brutally kills her. He takes her body, leaving nothing but her sheep mask and the data she discovered. Writer Jeremy Boxen comments, "Ultimately, we felt the best way to serve M.K. was to motivate the showdown through the unfinished, ugly business still unresolved between her and Ferdinand. Facing down this man is a noble sacrifice she makes for Sarah, but it comes from an incredibly personal place for M.K" ("Jeremy Boxen").

Susan and Coady: Ruling Man's World

> Close-up research on families shows a good many households where wives hold authority in practice. The fact of mothers' authority over young sons has been noted in most discussions of the psychodynamics of masculinity. The intersections of gender relations with class and race relations yield many other situations where rich white heterosexual women, for instance, are employers of working-class men, patrons of homosexual men, or politically dominant over

> black men. To cite such examples and claim that women are therefore not subordinated in general would be crass. The point is, rather, that contradictions between local situations and the global relationships are endemic. They are likely to be a fruitful source of turmoil and change in the structure as a whole.—Carrigan et al. 152

Certainly, Susan rules Ira, complete with an incestuous relationship. Coady too is mother and controller to the Castors. Further, both women insert themselves into the male hierarchies, one corporate and one military. Significantly outcompeted by men, both must demonstrate toughness, even cruelty, to be respected. Their ambition, like their professions of rewriting the rules of nature, emphasizes their goal for dominion over all.

"In addition to hierarchy over women, men create hierarchies and rankings among themselves according to criteria of 'masculinity.' Men at each rank of masculinity compete with each other, with whatever resources they have, for the differential payoffs that patriarchy allows men" (Pleck 62). Women can join these social structures, but they must act like men, showing strength and ruthlessness in return for deference. Like the patriarchs, these women teach the emerging clones valuable lessons about ruling the men's world, even as they both compromise their ethics to succeed. Thus, the young heroines learn by discovering how to defeat them. The Ledas have little idea how to be mothers, though Kira, Charlotte, and Helena's twins provide new responsibilities. Learning from Susan and Coady, each so protective of their clone children, the Ledas can discover a mature woman's ferocity.

Susan Duncan helped create the Leda clones, working for Westmorland and Leekie, the patriarchs. The latter apparently has her killed for loving her daughter Rachel too much, instead choosing to raise her by his soulless corporation. Susan disappears, willingly giving up her child to focus on the science. When she returns to Rachel at the end of season three, she reverts to her cold, analytical side.

> SUSAN: It's my curse. Detachment. I've spent my whole life observing you, but I don't know how ... to be with you.
> RACHEL: Because you abandoned me. Father thought Neolution murdered you, but you are Neolution.
> SUSAN: So are you. I'm sorry, Rachel. I wanted to be your mother, but it was necessary to cut the cord.... Rachel, you are the experiment. One day, you may take over. But be patient. Recover! Everyone needs a purpose in life. Ours is all in service ... of the greater good.
> RACHEL: What is it, Mother? What is our greater good?
> SUSAN: To control human evolution, darling. To create a more perfect human being ["The Stigmata of Progress" 403].

Susan even suggests they let little Charlotte die of the Leda illness to bring them useful information. Clearly, she can muster a great deal of detachment.

Despite this, she's framed as a kinder leader than her competition. In flashback, Susan tells Beth she's different from the others because she watches over them all lovingly. She insists, "Beth, whatever you think you know, you must believe this: I have devoted my life to sustaining yours. Without me, your sisters will wither on the vine, and I cannot bear that. I love you all." ("The Scandal of Altruism" 406). No matter how cruel all the corporate thugs act, Susan insists she's the better option, telling Cosima, "The carriers, the device in Sarah ... these are brutish techniques compared to Leda" ("Human Raw Material" 405). Manson adds, "Susan Duncan is not just evil. She's very rich in her ethics, in her science. She's thought long and hard about what she's doing, and, yes, she may be a eugenicist, but she truly believes in her heart that she's trying to improve the human race and the human lot on the planet" (Bernstein 167).

However, on the island, Cosima realizes Westmorland plans to harvest Kira's eggs and implant them in thirteen hundred women. Appalled, she seeks an ally. "Thirteen hundred? That those are Kira's children. Sarah's grandchildren. Do you even think about it like that? You can stop him, Susan," she protests.

Here, Susan acknowledges that she has no powerful role in the hierarchy but is instead treated with no more respect than a Victorian woman: "I can only steer him. And you can help. Together, we can mitigate the damage."

Cosima, however, is appalled. She frames the debate in terms of ethics, insisting: "She's a little girl! You're a woman, you're a human being. If you don't start there, there's nothing left to mitigate" ("Ease for Idle Millionaires" 505). Despite her hesitation, Susan battles Westmorland, arguing with his plans and finally attempting to murder him with drugs in his IV. However, he turns the tables on her and leaves her to die from her own drug cocktail. She perishes as ineffectively as she lived.

Coady, the crueler mother, raised the Castors at the military compound. The creators explain, "She may seem rather sympathetic to one of the Leda clones but is hiding an agenda that even her superiors don't suspect" (Nguyen, "Here's Everything"). In fact, she's militarized the Castors—whoever they have sex with is rendered infertile. Knowing this, she organizes their sexual encounters. "The Castor clones bring home DNA samples, like trophies, to their mother. Freud would want to see them all, in his office, right away" (Donovan 129). Of course, their weaponization grants her military power and acclaim. She gloats, "It could end wars in a single generation without spilling a drop of blood" ("Certain Agony of the Battlefield" 306). Certainly, her climb through the men's world masculinizes her, as do her dress and attitude. "Machiavellian virtue can be fully embodied by a woman. Only a woman who is willing to abandon her femininity or difference, however, can enjoy political success on this basis" (Jensen 9).

Despite this brutality, she considers herself the Castors' mother, cradling and cuddling them. She tells Helena, "They came to me when they were very young. The irony of it? I never wanted kids. Didn't think it was for me. Next thing I know, I've got more than I can count" ("Transitory Sacrifices of Crisis" 302). Donovan adds, "Not only do these clones adore Dr. Coady (think of how, in the same episode, even the most dangerous Castor clone, Rudy, lovingly calls Dr. Coady 'Mom' and displays affection towards her with a kiss on the cheek), she is the lead scientist in charge of the Castor experiment. She embodies what Freud calls 'the Phallic' mother—domineering, intimidating, and ruthless" (129). Taking her cruelty a step further than Susan's (from neglecting subjects to actively damaging them), Coady injects Sarah with Castor blood, endangering her life. She also experiments on one of the clones, Parsons, and cuts open his head in order to save the others. Helena, the force of love, is horrified and mercy-kills him.

Coady and Susan return around the same time in season five, each brought to the island by the ultimate patriarch, Westmorland. While Susan tries to stop Westmorland from exploiting the children he preys on, Coady assists him in all his brutal schemes. In the penultimate episode, Westmorland insists Coady induce Helena and even perform a Caesarian to get him the twins' cord blood that much faster. He also orders her to execute the last Castor, Mark. This she does, promising him the cure and holding him as she lulls him to sleep with happy memories. Co-producer Alex Levine explains, "The struggle you see is the amoral heartless scientist suffocating her own maternal instincts. Kyra is a terrific actor and she definitely showed depth in that relationship and in that scene" (Wilson). As Levine adds, "I think people forget that Virginia is a ruthless eugenicist. She bought into P.T.'s grand vision and had the cold, evil heart to do certain things that no other party would do. She started this thing with him and she had no moral qualms about using humans as experiments. She always saw the big picture, even with the Castor sterilization plan. And she was very loyal to P.T.; she knows he has the grand vision, that she can't do it without him" (Wilson).

Helena tells her, "He makes you do this. Like he made you kill Gracie. You are his puppy dog. Woof, woof! Coward." Still, Coady is unrepentant. When Helena attempts suicide, Coady saves her, but also prepares to perform a Caesarian and sacrifice Helena for her babies if she doesn't awaken. Helena lures her close and knocks her out, telling her once again, "You are shit mother." With this, she asserts her dominance. In the final episode, even as Helena crouches in labor, she lures Coady close enough to stab her fatally with a screwdriver. As she gives birth, the emerging good mother destroys the bad one.

Ira the Emasculated Assistant

Throughout history, many men worried that empowering women would lead to diminished men following women's orders and doing the housework. The show embodies this question, to some extent, as the strong women choose compliant lovers. It offers many unequal romantic relationships, generally with the women taking charge—Alison and Donnie, Susan and Ira, Rachel and Ferdinand. The men react differently, as Ferdinand chafes, but Donnie and Ira seem to appreciate it. Jesse, too, eagerly goes along with whatever Helena says, reacting with easygoing respect. He's the proverbial nice guy, whom Helena chooses over the aggressive guys at the bar. Vic is a stooge, always getting cheated and beaten up by the cleverer women. Paul and Cal offer stronger, more equal relationships for Sarah, as presumably Siobhan's husband did many years before. However, the relationships crumble (offscreen in Cal's case, and with premature deaths in the cases of the others). The strong, independent women are left alone once more. Felix-Colin, Cosima-Delphine, and Cosima-Shay lack these gender-based dynamics, but the main characters take the stronger roles—keeping secrets from their partners and thus controlling information, though they may not be dictating all aspects of the relationship.

Nowhere is this inequality more obvious than in Ira Blair. His contrast with his military brothers is heightened as much as possible. The anomalous Castor clone was separated from his brothers and placed with an upper middle class foster family by Susan Duncan. When Susan met him again while he was attending Yale, the two became lovers. Their power inequality as she helped create the clones, then chose to isolate him as a small child makes this near-incestuous beyond the question of age.

The relationships with a father-daughter feel (Tomas-Helena, Leekie-Rachel, Henrik-Gracie) are violently ended by the women, but Ira doesn't seem to feel abused. On the contrary, he's devoted to his mother-lover. His actor, Ari Millen, says, "I think Ira is a complete innocent. I don't think he knows or cares or judges what that relationship is. That's just what was. And that's what he knows and that's who he is" (Nguyen) Still, every choice Ira makes is for the good of his mistress Susan, even before his own life. Millen says of Ira, "I see him as almost Susan Duncan's doll. She's molded him in the way that she wants, her ideal of her twisted views" (Bernstein 102).

Felix mocks him with "Scarcely believed it. A Castor who favors slacks" when they meet in "The Mitigation of Competition" (409). Lynch made him look different from the other Castors, noting, "He is very polished, very pristine, perhaps cosmetically altered, perhaps he's had his nose fixed" (Bernstein 102). Rachel, who's attracted to violent Ferdinand, regards androgynous Ira with disdain, saying, "And you're a pale shade of Castor, aren't you? Your brothers may be lackeys, but ... at least they're men."

"As I have never met them, I don't carry the same ... antipathy towards my siblings as you," he replies calmly ("The Stigmata of Progress" 403). Ira, raised as the anti–Castor as Rachel is the anti–Leda, regards them with a certain distance. Of course, Ira shares his brothers' glitching, making him especially dependent on Susan as the only one he thinks can cure him. His true passivity is most apparent in "The Scandal of Altruism" (406). The Ledas offer Susan Leda cells so she can cure them, but they insist they won't help save the weaponized Castors. As Ira protests, Susan agrees to the bargain and dismisses him completely. She will not fight for her lover, but sacrifices him without hesitation to save her pet project. Despairing, Ira returns to their shared hotel room and overdoses on pills. Not a fighter, he simply despairs and prepares to die. The stronger Sarah is the one to come and save him.

At season end, Rachel stabs Susan, who returns in season five. It appears Ira has been tenderly nursing her, even as his glitching grows worse. He does not participate in the battle of wills on the island, instead quietly observing and reporting to Susan. In "Manacled Slim Wrists" (506), he selflessly helps Cosima escape with little Charlotte but returns for Susan, limping and dragging himself as he deteriorates. Though he tells Cosima he's not strong enough to escape, preserving Susan's life still motivates him. He arrives, only to find her dead, killed by Westmorland and Coady. With nothing left, he collapses in her lap and dies, choosing not to live on without his mistress. It's a pathetic end for a pathetic, purposeless character. Without the strong woman in his life, he cannot even exist.

Leekie and Westmorland: The Patriarchy

Leekie is the one to set the lab fire, apparently killing Rachel's parents and leaving her to grow up in the little girl's bedroom lab at DYAD. He has fingers in all their lives, as he recruits his student Donnie to monitor Alison (as shown in the prequel comic), and taunts him with his financial leverage, asking, "Do you really want your life with Alison to start out mired down with debt? She deserves better" (*The Clone Club #3: Alison*). He also assigns Paul to be Beth's monitor two years before the series begins, using blackmail from Paul's past. Control is central, as he's so powerful that he can dictate everyone's lives. Further, he's narcissistic, not only believing himself at the center of the universe but dominating the clones without their consent.

Leekie represents the giant corporation and the concept that the elderly white male can dominate everyone. First and second wave feminism labeled this force the enemy—the ruler who tried to keep women childlike and obedient like Rachel or controlled like all the clones in season one. The burden of maintaining his fragile illusion of absolute power makes him, like all tyrants, insecure; any threat to his authority and supremacy causes him to tighten his grasp. The clones set out to fight their way free.

Leekie enters the story when Cosima and Delphine attend his lecture and he describes remaking human biology. There, his cult following emphasizes his status as patriarch. Cosima is struck by his followers' genetic modifications, Leekie smiles, "Oh, my "freaky-Leekies" as they've been dubbed in the media. It was once asked what my perfect human would look like. I offhandedly suggested silver-gray hair and one white eye" ("Variations Under Domestication" 106). He not only attracts true believers but also larger corporate investors who offer millions to fund his research. Through the series, he's seen defying the natural order with Neolution, shown as a quest to reject the ordinary life cycle and instead tame it to his bidding.

Art director Jody Clement describes Leekie's office "We used Carrara marble tiles for the floor. The glass panels gave beautiful reflections when they were shooting through them. The tones of wood and leather couches really spoke to who Doctor Leekie was" (Bernstein 161). All is outwardly impressive but lacks warmth. When the tyrant isn't viewing others as a threat and pushing them down, he sees them as objects to exploit for his own gain. In "Parts Developed in an Unusual Manner" (107), Leekie invites Cosima to apply to the DYAD Institute. He bribes her, "You could be on the cover of *Scientific American*."

Cosima retorts, "*Scientific American* doesn't put scientists on the cover." In fact, they feature subjects—something Cosima worries she'd become. Nonetheless, she soon accepts his offer, using Neolution's vast resources, but also embracing the man's philosophy. This only lasts an episode, before she discovers Leekie has sent Delphine to her as a plant. Nonetheless, Cosima signs a contract and agrees to serve the great patriarch as Delphine and Rachel do, seeking a cure. He wins her over by bribing her with pure knowledge, the patriarch's gift:

> In "Endless Forms Most Beautiful," Dr. Leekie of the DYAD Institute presents contracts to the various members of Clone Club, doing his best to convince them to sign the agreement. To the others, he brings tantalizing proposals of safety and privacy; he promises that the people of DYAD will get out of their lives. When he approaches Cosima, though, he extends the opposite invitation: "This is your complete, sequenced genome—3.2 billion base pairs. My offer is the freedom to study yourself and your sisters—unfettered research." He knows that it's a chance to dig deeper that will tempt Cosima the most, and it works: even though she was the one who discovered the patent in their DNA and warned that "any freedom they promise is bullshit," she can't resist Leekie's offer and is soon designing her own lab in the heart of DYAD headquarters. Despite all the risks and dangers of the job, it is imperative for Cosima to seize this golden opportunity to get answers [Wolfert and Barkman 27–28].

Through season two, the clones find ways to undermine him. In "Nature Under Constraint and Vexed" (201), at the DYAD party, Sarah-as-Cosima hugs Leekie and steals his passcard to infiltrate DYAD. Meanwhile, Delphine runs interference as Cosima's monitor and lover, dodging his attempts to control them both. Rachel rejects his guidance even more directly in "Ipsa Scientia Potestas Est" (205). He tells her, on seeing Helena has killed her monitor, "There is a kinder, gentler way, Rachel. This is all the result of your heavy-handed tactics."

However, she retorts, "Trust me, Aldous, I've only just begun." In "Knowledge of Causes, and Secret Motion of Things" (207), Rachel discovers Leekie killed her parents. She fires him, taking her place as DYAD's head and telling him, "Go now.... Don't get in your car. Don't go home. You might survive." As she adds, "It's foolish to spare you. But you raised me. Nurture prevails" ("Knowledge of Causes, and Secret Motion of Things" 207). When a strong force stands up to bullies, they wither and blow away. Leekie kisses her on the forehead and, thanking her rather pathetically for his life, leaves.

However, he's soon killed by the weakest character of all, as Donnie too resists the bully. It does not take a great force to destroy Leekie, only a bumbler with a gun. Leekie, fleeing, gets into Donnie's car where Donnie subjects him to his rage and misery:

> DONNIE: You came into my house and probed my wife.
> LEEKIE: Listen to me, you turnip. In 100 years' time, no one will care in any way about Donnie Hendrix except as a footnote in this experiment.
> DONNIE: You ruined my marriage. My wife hates me.
> LEEKIE: I gave you your wife. Put the gun away and go home to bed, huh?
> ("Knowledge of Causes, and Secret Motion of Things" 207].

Even while Leekie dismisses him, Donnie, his powerless inverse in every way, accidentally shoots him. Disposing of the body is a grotesque process, with Alison and Donnie pausing to vomit over and over into the grave. This is not enough; two seasons later, they dig him up (amid more retching) and deliver his head to Cosima. "Who's the science now, bitch," she smirks, emphasizing her total power over what remains of him. Scott joins her, mocking Leekie for refusing to give him a raise.

The end of season four hints at another patriarch behind Neolution—the force that controls the Board, that made Susan create Charlotte and give up Rachel. "John and I knew for a long time that in this feminist show that there was a man at the top," Manson said, amid boos from the audience. "So you think of the most evil, patriarchal figure ... this unlikely oldest man in the world ... and kind of like a Doctor Moreau" (Nguyen, "*Orphan Black* Cast").

P.T. Westmorland was "Born in 1843, allegedly. Educated Eaton and Cambridge. Member of the Royal Geographic Society where he published a number of papers" including the arrogant Imperialist British "The Management of Reproduction in Feebleminded Populations," according to Scott ("Let the Children & the Childbearers Toil" 504). The paper suggests the patriarchy at its worst, denigrating less developed nations. In "The Mitigation of Competition" (409), Cosima reads P.T. Westmorland's book and calls him a "racist blowhard who thinks poverty is genetic"; this may nod to Darwin, who, a product of his time, often described the biology of "savages."

In the next episode, she and Rachel each make their way to the village. There, Rachel meets Westmorland and he offers her all she wishes—an end to her existence as property. Instantly, she becomes his disciple. Indeed, the 170-year-old founder of Neolution (or so he claims) dominates his small village, cultishly named Revival. "The way that the Revival villagers see it, Westmorland is a savior figure; they grant him a cult following, calling him the Founder and viewing themselves as his children" (Griffin and Nesseth). In fact, believers flock from around the world to find cures at his "fountain." When he has something to announce, everyone gathers reverently in the square. His longevity is a disturbing image—suggesting he not only subverts the natural order, but that he's been ruling his hidden empire for almost that long, an entrenched monarch or dictator unwilling to relinquish power.

Cosima, however, skeptically continues investigating. Westmorland is arguably creating a second Eden—a tranquil island untouched by modern troubles, where he hopes to offer eternal life. However, the Cyborg "does not expect its father to save it through a restoration of the garden" and "would not recognize the Garden of Eden; it is not made of mud and cannot dream of returning to dust" (151). Cosima and her sisters reject this newer, better world. The real Cosima explains:

> One of the most difficult and important things we tried to integrate here, using longevity and immortality science, was to throw patriarchy and the proliferation of long-ruling ideologies into stark relief. Prolongevity science and the aspirations to live forever, its hubris and its faults, formed the architecture by which we explored the institutional, systemic, and individually embodied regimes of historical, patriarchal ideological power that has oppressed, subjugated, violated, controlled, and prevented diversity, equality, and solidarity [Griffin and Nesseth].

Like Leekie, Westmorland suggests a classically unchanging way of living, supported by social conventions. He holds a formal dinner party in which he insists Cosima and Delphine wear Victorian dresses, though Cosima defies him in a gentleman's suit and continues to needle him during dinner. They dine surrounded by taxidermied animals, nodding to Cosima and Rachel's roles as his specimens. The whole fish on their plates creepily resemble additional biological samples tamed by man. Meanwhile, Cosima swills wine and hurls comebacks and Westmorland's arrogant speeches, apparently claiming power from her borrowed men's clothes and insisting on subverting the patriarch at every opportunity. Asserting his dominance in return, Westmorland interrupts dinner to banish Delphine back to Europe. When the women are alone, Delphine concludes, "This is what he does, he divides women. Then you just go back in there and act like he's divided us" ("Ease for Idle Millionaires" 505). Loving each other is a blow to the patriarchy, one more thing he can't control.

As it turns out, Westmorland's entire persona is a lie. Cosima follows the teenager Mud out into the woods where she discovers a genetically altered man. Susan tells her that this is Yannis, a boy from a Latvian orphanage who was their first subject. Susan synthesized the healing gene and put it in Leda, but it only appeared in Kira, a generation later. Now Westmorland, seeking more patents and eternal life for himself, wants Rachel to harvest her eggs and put them in 1300 surrogates. Thus, he establishes himself as crueler than any of the previous villains. Minutes later, Westmorland challenges Cosima directly, goading her to shoot Yannis and put him out of his misery. Cosima retorts, "You gave me life. I know you can take that away. You can't take away my humanity" ("Ease for Idle Millionaires" 505). She defies her all-powerful creator and tries to comfort the injured monster. However, Westmorland shoots Yannis himself and locks her up.

As his creation, Cosima appears far beneath him—a clever child who's no threat. In fact, Cosima is the one to destroy Westmorland, with help from her friends. She persuades Mud to help her, even as Susan and Ira join the team and free her. Fleeing the mansion, Cosima runs into the villagers, rioting after the innocent child Aisha has died despite Westmorland's promises. Surrounded, Cosima vows that she's not their enemy and adds, "Westmorland isn't ... isn't 170, okay? Look, look. He's a liar." She shows them an old photo. "Okay? That's him and Susan Duncan in 1967. Look, he's a young man." This is the role of the heroine—tearing down the patriarch's illusion of supremacy and revealing him as frail and pathetic. "Woman always denies the emperor has no clothes and in this way Woman is always fantastic" (Helford et al.). As Cosima concludes, "I'm sorry, but the fountain isn't real. He deceived you. I know that's really hard to hear, 'cause he deceived me too. My family, scientists, governments, military, all over the world. He used you all. He's experimenting on your children. Aisha's dead because of him. Would you please just let me leave?" ("Manacled Slim Wrists" 506). They do, but they also riot and set fire to the camp. All Westmorland has built crumbles.

Manson says of the ending "Even when we pitched it to networks, we pitched a loose sort of ending about getting to the top of the pyramid and finding a way to victory and freedom. We began to refer to it as revealing the person that could embody the entire conspiracy and boil it all down" (Bernstein 19). This was P.T. Westmorland. In "One Fettered Slave" (509), Westmorland's board has shrunken to its last two members, emphasizing his dwindling power. He hides in DYAD's old building as the new one is staked out by reporters and police. As Rachel phrases it, "It's not safe there for him anymore. His subjects have rebelled and abandoned him. Powerful people have been exposed, and they're vengeful." He's down to three followers—Art's duplicitous partner Enger, Coady, and Mark, and he orders Mark's death as a failed experiment. His health too is gone as he staggers and reveals a vulnerably bald head under his wig—the patriarch's illusion of power has shattered.

In his desperation, he has his last followers kidnap Helena and induce labor so he can use the twins' stem cells. "No, I can't wait. Cut them out," he says, pitilessly insisting on saving his own ancient life. Co-producer Alex Levine explains, "P.T. was always supposed to epitomize the misogynistic patriarchy that still pervades the world. But he really lets his flag fly in these last few episodes. I think we always knew he had to say some evil things to represent this accursed, awful world view that is the root of all the horrors of Neolution, we just needed to get him to a desperate enough place where he would let loose" (Wilson).

At last, Sarah faces off with her ultimate creator in the finale. She talks to his disembodied voice as camera swirls, emphasizing his apparent all-encompassing power. Playing cat and mouse in his lab of horrors, she shoots at the grey curtain surrounding her and connects. He tries to smother her, but soon enough, he falls. As he lies pathetically on the ground, she tells him, "I survived you. We survived you. Me and my sisters together. This is evolution." He retorts that as her creator, she'll have to remember him forever, but she yells at him to shut up and then more actively silences him, beating him to death with a fire extinguisher. Once again, Sarah stands up to the bully and he vanishes, leaving the Ledas a final legacy of freedom.

The Next Generation: Kira and the Girls

The next generation—the Ledas' children—reveal quite a spectrum. There's Oscar and Gemma Hendrix—ordinary adopted children with no biological connection to Alison. They also have no significant biological problems and are sent away for much of the turbulence of the five-season struggle, though Gemma's birthday party is destroyed when cops invade and arrest her father. The children have little screentime, functioning more as a prop for Alison's controlling motherhood and later Helena's mama bear routine. Nonetheless, they are loved and protected, growing without much interference from DYAD. Art's daughter Maya joins them—adored, sheltered, and occasionally referenced as a hostage, but basically kept out of the conflict.

At the other end of the spectrum, Kira the miracle child is blessed with healing powers and even a science-fiction level of empathy. Helena's babies show signs of the former and may develop the latter. Having a cousin who's already undergone this will be invaluable for them. Significantly, all three are wanted and raised with love, giving them a better start than their mothers. All grow up in stable homes, with loving though nonstandard nuclear families (Kira is raised by mother, uncle, and grandmother, the boys by mother, aunt, and uncle). Of course, Kira spends the five seasons being kidnapped, hidden in safehouses around the world, and forced, even at her young age, to con Rachel and win her trust before Rachel can harvest her eggs and implant them in surrogates. With all this, she gets quite an adult quest for her years.

Kira's art is central. It helps her express warnings, from her drawing of the fire extinguisher in season two to the animal story she writes in season five. Her drawings are also the first indicator that she recognizes the Clone Club—a message Cal comes to understand. She paints a fantasy castle in their Rabbit Hole hideaway and endears herself to Rachel with a friendship bracelet. The BBC crew remark, "Our amazing fan Miriam, who created the bracelets for Rachel and Kira in Episode 507, was generous enough to make us Purple and Orange's baby bracelets.... We loved the idea that Helena asked Kira to help her identify the babies and create friendship bracelets for them" (BBC Staff, "Episode 10"). With this, she shares her art and love with her little cousins, binding them all together.

Graeme says of Kira's insight, "What gives her that connection with the sisters, that empathetic connection? It's not explainable by science. It's the most human thing about her. To me, that's the most simple and beautiful and elegant thing to want to put on screen, and conceptually people can't wrap their heads around it." (Griffin and Nesseth). Kira's sensitivity lets her warn the adults of threats and also counsel them to love even the lost clones—Helena, Rachel, Mika.

Her other "aunt" is the child Charlotte. Though Marion raises her with love, Charlotte grows up isolated in a lab like Rachel. She wears a leg brace and quickly develops the Leda disease. Seasons three through five see her, like Kira, dragged to safehouses and experimented on in labs. Susan even considers letting her die for the good of science. Charlotte's creation from Rachel's imperfect DNA has led to her difficult life.

> Raised by Dyad and Neolution, Charlotte has spent much of her life in a sterile environment while she is poked and prodded by needles and scientists, her fate in the hands of adults who see her for her biology and not for her autonomy and identity. To top it all off, Charlotte also suffers from the clone disease. For all the other Leda clones plagued by the disease, the symptoms don't manifest until their 20s; Charlotte, however, is roughly eight years old. Charlotte was not cloned from Kendall's original biological material, like the rest of the Leda clones, but from

Rachel's biological material, making Charlotte a clone of a clone [Griffin and Nesseth].

Cloning a clone with current technology tends to result in shortened telomeres, the part of the chromosome that changes with age. Thus, Charlotte's aging cells, copied from the older clone Rachel, likely have caused her to manifest the Leda disease much younger than anyone else.

Many children, born and unborn, are sacrificed during the series. There are all the fetuses that couldn't grow to term, with only Charlotte surviving. The Brightborn babies that are euthanized for being deformed. Abel Johanssen, the Castor baby implanted in Mrs. Johanssen, who dies. All these emphasize the cost of progress and the amorality of the scientist creators.

In "Newer Elements of Our Defense" (304), Gracie loses her baby, even while her Castor brother Abel's bones are dug up. Meanwhile, Helena ends the life of Parsons, a tortured Castor. "We've both been abandoned by our families, left to suffer. I will make it go away. No more pain, little one," she tells him. She hums to him like a child as a hymn plays. Since Gracie returns to her family as they sing "Nearer My God to Thee," all the mothers are presented in an image of salvation. Nonetheless, all three children perish. The Castor and Gracie's baby are even both called "lamb," a Christ symbol of innocence.

The grown child who fares worst is Aisha, one of Westmorland's devotees. This Afghan girl has a pediatric cancer of the kidney, called Wilm's tumor, resulting from misexpression of Lin28a. "While Aisha and her mother believe she is at Revival to be cured, most likely Aisha was brought to the island because of PTW's interest in Lin28a, providing him with a chance to study his 'fountain' gene further before she succumbed to her disease" (Griffin and Nesseth). Westmorland treats Aisha like a lab rat, while Cosima shows her respect, asking polite permission before examining her. Of course, Aisha tragically dies—Westmorland has no cure for her condition. His callousness towards her sacrifice emphasizes how he's using all the children of the island—studying them and receiving transfusions of their plasma. In fact, Aisha's death spurs the islanders to hide their children away and revolt, allowing Cosima to snatch Charlotte and embark on a perilous escape.

The final episode welcomes Helena's babies, but also summons Gemma and Oscar back from their grandmother's and Charlotte and Maya back from their own refuge with Art's ex-wife. All attend Helena's baby shower, expanding from her dream party of season three with Kira in a fairy costume to one of children everywhere—black, white, cloned, adopted—all play happily and bond as friends and cousins. This scene offers hope of a next generation who, like the clones worldwide, can grow up safely without the same struggle as their mothers.

Katja to Camilla: Global Feminism

> Many feminist outreach initiatives—the establishment of a movement press, women's studies courses, the institution of shelters, or reproductive rights campaigns—generated diffuse support.... Generally, European surveys conducted in 1983 found favorable attitudes toward women's liberation movements dominant among women in Belgium, Denmark, Germany, France, Ireland, Italy, Luxembourg, and Greece, and in a high minority among women in the Netherlands and the United Kingdom.—Ergas 530

The lists of perished clones, one wave killed by Ferdinand in Helsinki, and one by Helena in Western Europe, nod to the many feminist movements around the globe, particularly there. It's Katja and the Helsinki girls who arguably begin Clone Club, though they must pass on the torch to their New World sisters.

Global feminism is concerned mainly about how globalization and capitalism affect people across nationalities, races, ethnicities, genders, classes, and sexualities. Since it recognizes the importance of intersectionality, Katja's sudden appearance brings a similar message, alerting Sarah to a larger world of clones who need her. Cosima is correct in reminding her their struggle is "life and death"—not just theirs, but all the women like them. Katja is actually the one to alert them all to their status and Helena's killings. Cosima tells Sarah, "So, six months ago, Katja contacted Beth with this crazy story about her genetic identicals being hunted in Europe" ("Variation Under Nature" 103). Global feminism explores the different ways women are affected and denied agency—in fact, discovering Helena's murders alerts the heroines to a larger world of injustice—they cannot remain complacent if they wish to survive. Once awoken, they discover their lovers are spying on them and their biology is killing them—they must act or be destroyed.

Though little is known about them, several clones make an impression on Sarah in the very early episodes as she leafs through their profiles: Janika Zingler from Austria, Danielle Fournier from France, and Aryanna Giordano of Italy have classic names for their nationalities. Further, Katja, from Katherine, means pure; Aryanna means "holy"; Janika, "God is gracious"; and Danielle, "God is my strength." As such, all are cast as the saintly clones, obedient and dead. Since the European clones are killed by Helena before the story starts, there's a suggestion that Canada and the New World are a place of safety and freedom.

There's another set of clones introduced in the *Helsinki* flashback comic: Along with Finnish Veera Suominen, there's her best friend Niki Lintula as well as Ania Kaminska from Poland, Justyna Buzek from the Czech Republic, Danish Sofia Jensen and Dutch twins Fay and Famke. Ania is killed by Helena at age seventeen—she may be the clone seen in the penultimate episode's flashback. Their country-based names (meaning victory, justice, wisdom, faith, grace, and youth) likewise suggest qualities that DYAD murders or endangers. Only Veera (bravery) survives the purge. German clone Katja Obinger was part of the group, becoming self-aware to pass the information on to Beth years later. One of the great devastations of the survivors' lives is that they finally come forward to expose Neolution, but thanks to the worldwide media frenzy over September 11, no one notices—their nonAmerican birthplaces leave them sidelined. Of course, the Helsinki incident makes the Ledas realize their very lives are on the line. Only through teamwork can they persevere.

The heroines of the show hail from London (Sarah), Cambridge (Rachel), Ireland (Siobhan), Ukraine (Helena), France (Delphine), San Francisco and Minnesota (Cosima), the American South (Adele), Toronto (Beth), and Scarborough (Alison) for a multi-country team-up. Inspired by the Euroclones' early sacrifices, they travel the world to stop Neolution. Season one juxtaposes the big city and suburbia. Season two travels further with the wilderness of Mrs. S's birdwatchers, the splinter Proletheans on their farm, and Cal's summer cottage. These hideaways are contrasted against the gleaming artificial DYAD lab—the institution. Their world is expanding bit by bit.

Season three introduces the jarring Castor base, even farther away—the Rendition Camp resembles the Middle East though it's located in the Mexican desert. Fans and dusty yellow light emphasize the heat and starkness. There's wire gratings, sandbags, fake leaf camouflage ... and of course, prison cells. The heroes, trapped there, struggle to escape back to home and family in the city. Meanwhile, Rachel journeys to Taiwan for eye surgery, while Kira and her family flee to Iceland. Near the series end, Felix and Adele head to Switzerland, researching Neolution's patents. There's also Westmorland's mysterious island—in "The Antisocialism of Sex" (407), Susan calls it "the edge of the known world" (407). It's likely in the northern parts of Canada ... though Canada itself basically goes unmentioned.

Of course, the ongoing joke is how obliquely the central city is identified as Toronto. Many fans have discerned it, not just from the filming location but from the currency, the cars with Ontario license plates, Beth's and Mrs. S's Ontario driving licenses, and references to the suburbs of Scarborough and Parkdale. The DYAD Institute is filmed at Toronto's Bridgepoint Health and Don Jail. The series begins at the GO Station at Union Station, while Alison's hometown is really filmed in Markham, another Toronto suburb. Alison's community theater group rehearses at the Jubilee United Church in Toronto; the birdwatchers' hideout is the Valley Halla Estate near the Toronto Zoo. The exterior and lobby of Brightborn are Le Germain Toronto Maple Leaf Square, its spas are from Festival Tower, and its labs from Maple Hill Memorial Hospital.

At the same time, American pronunciations of words like "lieutenant" are used, and place names are often omitted in favor of vague phrasing like "home." Graeme Manson said the setting is deliberately vague. "It's meant to be Generica. It's part of the price you pay for this kind of co-production" (Ross, "*Orphan Black* Was Not Originally"). By this he means that the Canadian show receives BBC funding and wants to appeal to an American audience. (It was BBC America who asked them to make the lead character British, to better fit BBC's brand.)

Manson adds, "It adds a certain universality to the show that we're looking for. Since we don't mind the audience being off-kilter or off-step, it works for us" (Ross, "Sarah Was Not Originally British"). Fawcett tosses in, "To be honest, we don't want to say we're American and alienate the Canadians, or say we're Canadian and alienate the Americans. The bottom line is we're one big happy family. We're just a little bit further North than you. We like the strong international flavor that we have too. It's something we throw our arms around and embrace wholeheartedly" (Ross, "Sarah Was Not Originally British"). The universal setting ties in with this theme, stressing that women everywhere are facing the same struggles. In "Guillotines Decide" (508), Felix finally calls his home country Canada—probably because at two episodes from series end, keeping the audience isn't a serious concern.

The show ends with a move towards true globalism—Cosima and Delphine travel the world, curing 274 additional clones. "They're never gonna have to go through everything that we did," Cosima notes, happy that she can protect them even while saving them ("To Right the Wrongs of Many" 510). Thus, she and her friends spread their hard-won freedom to the other women, emancipating them from the oppression to which they were born—no more abusive monitors and exploitative corporations. Cosima's also seen putting their needs before her own—hiding her face even as she glances at her Colombian sister Camilla Torres with longing. On first finding her, Cosima remarks on her beauty, revealing her love for all these hidden sisters. Other clones mentioned in the episode are Oxana Petrov and Colista Popoudokis, continuing the concept of names that echo the countries of origin. As Cosima and Delphine seek these women out all over the world, they're emphasizing a true sisterhood with women everywhere, all connected on a fundamental level. This is the essence of global feminism.

Looking to the Future

> Manson compares the ending to finishing a novel: "We're paying off each character relationship—each individual character arc. That's the job that we set out to do." [BBC America president Sarah] Barnett doesn't rule out revisiting the *Orphan Black* world, perhaps via a spinoff, and the producers say they've kicked around movie ideas for the franchise. But for now, BBC America is set to say farewell. "There aren't many networks that can really say a show defined them for a period inside of pop culture," Barnett says.— Schneider

Still, the show left a lasting legacy, in its incredibly feminist themes and moral questions. It welcomed an international viewership, not just with the Canadian setting, but with the characters from across the world all working for a happy ending. With a trans character, lesbians, gay characters, people of color, cult escapees, the disabled, and many nontraditional families, the show celebrates all the sidelined people, helping them defeat the all-powerful establishment. After, Delphine and Cosima tour the world together, saving their sisters across the globe.

Orphan Black (2013–2017) in turn opened the door for other shows celebrating marginalization and international heroes. *FlavorWire* reported, "When the 2014–15 television season began, it was easy to characterize this as some groundbreaking year in which networks were finally coming to their senses about diverse programming" (Viruet). 2014 welcomed ABC's clever sitcoms *Black-ish* and *Cristela*, as well as *Fresh Off the Boat*, the first Asian-American sitcom in twenty years. The CW's telenovela-inspired *Jane the Virgin* joined them, as did the return of other breakout multicultural hits—*Devious Maids* (2013–2016), *Scandal* (2012–), and *How to Get Away with Murder* (2014–). 2015 ushered in Fox's hip-hop drama *Empire* and ABC's impressively multiracial *Quantico*. *FlavorWire* adds, "This season it became painfully clear that there is a severe disconnect between—largely white—TV executives and us minority audiences. The fact that there is surprise about *Empire* or *Blackish*'s success is almost offensive; *of course* these are shows that we wanted and shows that we will watch—we just never had them before" (Viruet). Over at BBC, *Doctor Who* introduced an endearing Black lesbian companion in 2017 along with the all-minority teen spinoff *Class*. Over the years, Netflix broadened its horizons with *Orange Is the New Black* (2013–), *Sense8* (2015–2017), *Luke Cage* (2016–), *Dear White People* (2017–), and many more.

The unusual format, with one actress playing all the leads in this genre-crossing show, also broke down boundaries. Michael Schneider in his essay "Game of Clones" suggests that with its "ambitious storytelling, crafty genre mashups and powerful portrayals of gender identity, female empowerment and acceptance of those who are different" it paved the way for story-bending series like *Mr. Robot*, *The OA, Legion* and *Sense8*. This last follows gay, trans, unjustly imprisoned, persecuted, and otherwise disregarded heroes throughout the world as they struggle for freedom and autonomy, much like the heroines of *Orphan Black*.

Jordan Gavaris adds that *Orphan Black* did more than legitimize sci-fi for mainstream fans but also made television safe for more offbeat shows. "It opened the door to some really interesting programming from cable broadcasters," he says. "Look at shows like *Search Party,* which I love so much. It is the weirdest little show. I don't know if that would exist if we didn't have shows like *Orphan Black* making it okay to be weird" (Schneider). In an ever-expanding television universe of internet-based shows and *YouTube* shorts, creators continue to push boundaries, just like the exceptional creators of *Orphan Black*. This show was something special—a step forward in creativity, hallmarking many more exceptional boundary-breaking programs for the future.

Episodes

Season 1

1. Natural Selection
2. Instinct
3. Variation Under Nature
4. Effects of External Conditions
5. Conditions of Existence
6. Variations Under Domestication
7. Parts Developed in an Unusual Manner
8. Entangled Bank
9. Unconscious Selection
10. Endless Forms Most Beautiful

Season 2

1. Nature Under Constraint and Vexed
2. Governed by Sound Reason and True Religion
3. Mingling Its Own Nature with It
4. Governed as It Were by Chance
5. Ipsa Scientia Potestas Est
6. To Hound Nature in Her Wanderings
7. Knowledge of Causes, and Secret Motion of Things
8. Variable and Full of Perturbation
9. Things Which Have Never Yet Been Done
10. By Means Which Have Never Yet Been Tried

Season 3

1. The Weight of This Combination
2. Transitory Sacrifices of Crisis
3. Formalized, Complex, and Costly
4. Newer Elements of Our Defense
5. Scarred by Many Past Frustrations

6. Certain Agony of the Battlefield
7. Community of Dreadful Fear and Hate
8. Ruthless in Purpose, and Insidious in Method
9. Insolvent Phantom of Tomorrow
10. History Yet to Be Written

Season 4

1. The Collapse of Nature
2. Transgressive Border Crossing
3. The Stigmata of Progress
4. From Instinct to Rational Control
5. Human Raw Material
6. The Scandal of Altruism
7. The Antisocialism of Sex
8. The Redesign of Natural Objects
9. The Mitigation of Competition
10. From Dancing Mice to Psychopaths

Season 5

1. The Few Who Dare
2. Clutch of Greed
3. Beneath Her Heart
4. Let the Children & the Childbearers Toil
5. Ease for Idle Millionaires
6. Manacled Slim Wrists
7. Gag or Throttle
8. Guillotines Decide
9. One Fettered Slave
10. To Right the Wrongs of Many

Works Cited

Primary Sources

BBC Staff, "Episode 2: What You Didn't Know About 'Transgressive Border Crossing.'" *BBC America*, 21 Apr 2016. http://www.bbcamerica.com/shows/orphan-black/blog/2016/04/episode-2-what-you-didnt-know-about-transgressive-border-crossing.

_____. "Episode 10: What You Didn't Know About 'To Right the Wrongs of Many.'" *BBC America*, 21 Aug 2017. http://www.bbcamerica.com/shows/orphan-black/blog/2017/08/episode-10-what-you-didnt-know-about-to-right-the-wrongs-of-many.

"Behind the Scenes: Hair and Makeup." *Orphan Black Season 2* Disk 3. Co-Creator/Dir. John Fawcett. Temple Street Productions Inc., 2014.

"Body Horror: The FX of Season Four." *Orphan Black: Season Four*. Co-Creator/Dir. John Fawcett. BBC, 2016.

Chandoo, Kevin. "Orphan Black." *Art of the Title*. http://www.artofthetitle.com/title/orphan-black.

"Clone Club Insiders." *Orphan Black Season 2* Disk 3. Co-Creator/Dir. John Fawcett. Temple Street Productions Inc., 2014.

"Closer Looks 401: Orphan Flashback." *Orphan Black: Season Four*. Co-Creator/Dir. John Fawcett. BBC, 2016.

"Closer Looks 403: Sibling Rivalry." *Orphan Black: Season Four*. Co-Creator/Dir. John Fawcett. BBC, 2016.

"Closer Looks 406: Losing Kendall." *Orphan Black: Season Four*. Co-Creator/Dir. John Fawcett. BBC, 2016.

"Creating the Castor Clones." *Orphan Black Season 3*, Disc 3. Co-Creator/Dir. John Fawcett. Temple Street Productions Inc., 2015.

Darwin, Charles. *The Origin of Species and the Descent of Man*. 1859. Random House, 1962.

"Dissecting the Scenes." *Orphan Black Season 3* Disk 3. Co-Creator/Dir. John Fawcett. Temple Street Productions Inc., 2015.

"Eisenhower's Farewell Address to the Nation." *Eisenhower Archives*, January 17, 1961 https://www.eisenhower.archives.gov/all_about_ike/speeches/farewell_address.pdf.

Gelman, Vlada. "*Orphan Black* Boss on Burning Qs About Kira's Dad, Charlotte's Future and More." *TV Line*, 13 Aug 2017. http://tvline.com/2017/08/13/orphan-black-series-finale-burning-questions-cal-charlotte-art.

_____. "*Orphan Black* Preview: Can Mrs. S. Be Trusted?" *TV Line*, 10 May 2014. http://tvline.com/2014/05/10/orphan-black-season-2-spoilers-mrs-s-interview.

Herter, Cosima. "Eat Me/Drink Me and the Trouble with Cyborgs." *BBC America*, 14 April 2016. http://www.bbcamerica.com/shows/orphan-black/blog/2016/04/eat-medrink-me-and-the-trouble-with-cyborgs.

_____. "Nature Vs. Nurture, or 'Why Does Cosima Wear Glasses?'" *BBC America*, 6 May 2015. http://www.bbcamerica.com/shows/orphan-black/blog/2015/05/nature-vs-nurture-or-why-does-cosima-wear-glasses.

_____. "Why the Poem 'Protest' Served as Inspiration for *Orphan Black*'s Final Trip Episode Titles." *BBC America*, 10 June 2017.

Houser, Jodi, John Fawcett, and Graeme Manson (w) and Alan Quah, Cat Staggs, Nick Runge, and Szymon Kudranski (a). *Orphan Black: Vol. 1 (The Clone Club)*. IDW Publishing, 2016.

Huxley, Aldous. *Brave New World*. 1932. HarperCollins, 2005.

"Insiders: Felix." *Orphan Black Season 1*, Disk 3. Co-Creator/Dir. John Fawcett. Temple Street Productions Inc., 2013.

"Jeremy Boxen: For M.K., It's Personal." *BBC America*, 17 June 2017. http://www.bbcamerica.com/shows/orphan-black/blog/2017/06/jeremy-boxen-for-m-k-its-personal.

Kavner, Lucas. "Tatiana Maslany Talks *Orphan Black*, Clone Origin Stories, and Sarah and Felix's Incredible Loft." *Vulture*, 17 Apr 2015. http://www.vulture.com/2015/04/tatiana-maslany-orphan-black-clone-origin-stories.html.

Kennedy, Heli, John Fawcett, and Graeme Manson (w) and Jack Lawrence (a). *Orphan Black: Deviations*. IDW Publishing, 2017.

Kennedy, Heli, John Fawcett, and Graeme Manson (w) and Alan Quah, Wayne Nichols and Fico Ossio (a). *Orphan Black: Helsinki*. IDW Publishing, 2016.

Loofbourow, Lili. "The Many Faces of Tatiana Maslany." *New York Times*, 5 April 2015. https://www.nytimes.com/2015/04/05/magazine/the-many-faces-of-tatiana-maslany.html.

"Maria Doyle Kennedy Q&A: 'Find Your Tribe'" *BBC America*, 9 Aug 2017. http://www.bbcamerica.com/shows/orphan-black/blog/2017/08/maria-doyle-kennedy-qa-find-your-tribe.

Meynell, Julian. "Playing Rune Wars with Cosima." *Board Game Geek*, 8 June 2014, https://boardgamegeek.com/thread/1184235/playing-rune-wars-cosima.

Miller, Julie. "Here's How *Orphan Black* Transforms Tatiana Maslany into a Cast of Clones." *Vanity Fair*, 20 Apr 2015. https://www.vanityfair.com/hollywood/2015/04/orphan-black-clones.

Newton, Maud. "Science, Chance, and Emotion with Real Cosima." *Longreads*, 24 June 2015. https://longreads.com/2015/06/24/science-chance-and-emotion-with-real-cosima.

Ng, Philiana. "*Orphan Black* Declassified: Michiel Huisman on Cal's Life-Changing Revelation." *Hollywood Reporter*, 3 May 2014. http://www.hollywoodreporter.com/live-feed/orphan-black-michiel-huisman-cal-700948.

Nguyen, Hanh. "Here's Everything You Need to Know About Orphan Black's New Season." *TV Guide*, 15 Apr 2015. http://www.tvguide.com/news/orphan-black-season-3-premiere-guide.

_____. "Here's the Story Behind That Talking Scorpion on Orphan Black." *TV Guide*, 25 Apr 2015 http://www.tvguide.com/news/orphan-black-talking-scorpion-pupok/

_____. "*Orphan Black* Cast and Crew Share 14 Secrets of the Sestrahood—Paleyfest 2017." *Indie Wire*, 24 Mar 2017. http://www.indiewire.com/2017/03/orphan-black-season-5-secrets-paleyfest-2017-1201796514.

Orphan Black: Season One. Dir. John Fawcett. BBC, 2013.

Orphan Black: Season Two. Dir. John Fawcett. BBC, 2014.

"Orphan Black Season 2 Memorable Moments." *TV Line*. http://tvline.com/gallery/orphan-black-season-2-memorable-moments-clones.

Orphan Black: Season Three. Dir. John Fawcett. BBC, 2015.

Orphan Black: Season Four. Dir. John Fawcett. BBC, 2016.

Orphan Black: Season Five. Dir. John Fawcett. BBC, 2017.
"Q&A with Cosima Herter, Science Consultant." *BBC America,* 30 Mar 2013. http://www.bbcamerica.com/shows/orphan-black/blog/2013/03/qa-with-cosima-herter-science-consultant.
Ross, Dalton. "Attack of the Clones." *EW,* 21 Mar. 2014. EBSCOhost.
_____. "*Orphan Black* Creator Answers Season Premiere Burning Questions." *EW,* 10 June 2017. http://ew.com/tv/2017/06/10/orphan-black-season-5-premiere-tatiana-maslany.
_____. "*Orphan Black* Creator Breaks Down That Crazy, Twerktastic Episode." *EW,* 15 June 2015. http://ew.com/article/2015/05/22/orphan-black-creator-crazy-twerktastic-episode.
_____. "*Orphan Black* Creator on the Show's Latest Bloodbath." *EW,* 13 June 2015. http://ew.com/article/2015/06/13/orphan-black-creator-shows-latest-bloodbath.
_____. "Orphan Black Creators Answer Series Finale Burning Questions." *EW,* 12 Aug 2017. http://ew.com/tv/2017/08/12/orphan-black-series-finale-creators-burning-questions.
_____. "*Orphan Black* Finale: What Happened on the 'Tragic' Season Finale." *EW,* 18 June 2015. http://ew.com/article/2015/06/18/orphan-black-creator-breaks-down-tragic-season-finale.
_____. "*Orphan Black*: Jordan Gavaris Talks Felix and Having the Best Fake Accent on TV." *EW,* 16 Mar 2014. http://ew.com/article/2014/03/16/orphan-black-jordan-gavaris-felix.
_____. "*Orphan Black*: Sarah Was Not Originally British (And More Fun Facts from the Creators)" *EW,* 16 April 2014. http://ew.com/article/2014/04/16/orphan-black-creators-season-2.
_____. "*Orphan Black* Season 4: Tatiana Maslany Stars as the Newest Clone in First-Look Photos." *EW,* 28 Dec 2015. http://ew.com/article/2015/12/28/orphan-black-tatiana-maslany-season-4-new-clone.
_____. "Orphan Black: Tatiana Maslany Breaks Down the Series Finale." *EW,* 12 Aug 2017. http://ew.com/tv/2017/08/12/tatiana-maslany-orphan-black-series-finale.
_____. "*Orphan Black*: The Creators Discuss Introducing Tony the Transclone." *EW,* 7 June 2014. http://ew.com/article/2014/06/07/orphan-black-tony-transclone-creators.
"Send in the Clones." *Orphan Black,* Season 1, Disk 3. Co-Creator/Dir. John Fawcett. Temple Street Productions Inc., 2013.
Towers, Andrea. "Orphan Black Co-Creator on That Cosima/Alison Switch, and Meeting Mommy Hendrix." *EW,* 29 May 2015. http://ew.com/article/2015/05/29/orphan-black-co-creator-cosimaallison-switch-and-meeting-mommy-hendrix.
Wheaton, Wil. "The Clonversation." *Orphan Black Season 2,* Disk 1. Co-Creator/Dir. John Fawcett. Temple Street Productions Inc., 2014.
Wilcox, Ella Wheeler. "Protest." *Poets.Org,* 1914. https://www.poets.org/poetsorg/poem/protest.
Wilson, A.R. "Orphan Black 509: Alex Levine Breaks Down the Series' Penultimate Episode." *TV, Eh?* 5 Aug 2017. https://www.tv-eh.com/2017/08/05/orphan-black-509-alex-levine-breaks-down-the-series-penultimate-episode.
Wordsworth, William. "Lines Written in Early Spring." 1798. *Poetry Foundation,* 2006. https://www.poetryfoundation.org/poems/51001/lines-written-in-early-spring.

Secondary Sources

Annas, George J. "Immortality Through Cloning? Reproduction, Regeneration, and the Posthuman." Read et al., pp. 17–38.
Banschick, Mark. "What Awful Marriages & Cults Have in Common." *Psychology Today,*

28 May 2013. https://www.psychologytoday.com/blog/the-intelligent-divorce/201305/what-awful-marriages-cults-have-in-common.
Barbini, Francesca T., editor. *Gender Identity and Sexuality in Current Fantasy and Science Fiction.* Luna Press Publishing, 2016. Kindle Edition.
Begoña, Aretxaga. "Ruffling a Few Patriarchal Hairs: Women's Experiences of War in Northern Ireland." *Cultural Survival,* March 1995. https://www.culturalsurvival.org/publications/cultural-survival-quarterly/ruffling-few-patriarchal-hairs-womens-experiences-war.
Benjamin, Garfield. *The Cyborg Subject: Reality, Consciousness, Parallac.* Pallgrave McMillan, 2016.
Berkeley, Kathleen C. *The Women's Liberation Movement in America.* Greenwood Press, 1999.
Berns, Fernando Gabriel Pagnoni, and Emiliano Aguilar. "Sisterhood's Back in *Orphan Black*." Greene and Robison-Greene, 141–151.
Bernstein, Abbie. *The DNA of Orphan Black.* Titan Books, 2017.
Breger, Esther. "'Orphan Black' Embodies the Female Gaze Better than Anything Else on Television." *New Republic,* 20 June 2014. https://newrepublic.com/article/118277/orphan-black-season-2-recap-and-finale-review.
Campbell, Alex. "Why Is Dystopian Fiction Still So Popular?" *The Guardian,* 18 Nov. 2014. https://www.theguardian.com/childrens-books-site/2014/nov/18/hunger-games-dystopian-fiction-appeal-to-teenagers-alex-campbell.
Carrigan, Tim, Bob Connell, and John Lee. "Toward a New Sociology of Masculinity." Murphy, pp. 151–164.
Carveth, Rod. "Who Owns Clones?" Greene and Robison-Greene, pp. 34–45.
"Clonaid Says It's Cloned First Boy." *CNN,* 23 Jan 2003. http://www.cnn.com/2003/WORLD/americas/01/23/clonaid.claim/index.html.
Crosby, Janice C. "Feminist Spirituality." Reid, pp. 241–253.
Dalton, A.J. "Gender-Identity and Sexuality in Current Sub-Genres of British Fantasy Literature: Do We Have a Problem?" Barbini.
Davis, Lauren. "*Orphan Black*'s Crazy Bioweapon Actually Exists in Nature." *Io9,* 8 June 2015. http://io9.gizmodo.com/orphan-blacks-crazy-bioweapon-actually-exists-in-nature-1709712202.
Dawkins, Peter. "The Magnificence of Bacon's Great Instauration." http://www.fbrt.org.uk/pages/essays/Magnificence_of_Great_Instauration.pdf.
de Beauvoir, Simone. *The Second Sex.* Bantam Books, 1970.
Dixon, Patrick. "Truth About Clonaid Claims: First Human Clone—Eve—Plus Four More?" *Global Change,* 10 Nov. 2010. http://www.globalchange.com/clonaid.htm.
Doll, Darci. "Re: Production." Greene and Robison-Greene, 153–163.
Donovan, Sarah K. "Not Why but Who." Greene and Robison-Greene, pp. 127–139.
Dvorsky, George. "The Real-Life Science Behind *Orphan Black*." *Io9,* 31 Mar 2015. http://io9.gizmodo.com/the-real-life-science-behind-orphan-black-1694765437.
Ergas, Yasmine. "Feminisms of the 1970s." *A History of Women in the West: Toward a Cultural Identity in the Twentieth Century.* Ed. Françoise Thébaud. Harvard University Press, 1994. 527–563.
Framke, Caroline. "*Orphan Black* Co-Creator Graeme Manson on the Season Finale, a New Threat, and 'Shippers." *The AV Club,* 20 June 2015. http://www.avclub.com/article/orphan-black-co-creator-graeme-manson-season-final-221039.
Frankel, Valerie Estelle. *From Girl to Goddess: The Heroine's Journey Through Myth and Legend.* McFarland, 2010.
Gennis, Sadie. "TV'S Most Important Political Debate Is Happening Right Now on *Orphan Black*." *TV Guide,* 5 Jun 2014. http://www.tvguide.com/news/orphan-black-feminist-reproductive-rights-1082607.

Works Cited

Greene, Richard, and Rachel Robison-Greene, editors. *Orphan Black and Philosophy: Grand Theft DNA*. Open Court, 2016.

Griffin, Casey, and Nina Nesseth. *The Science of Orphan Black: The Official Companion*. ECW Press, 2017. Kindle Edition.

Hamilton, Jill. "Five Things We Know About Societies Run by Women." *Dame Magazine*, 10 May 2013. https://www.damemagazine.com/2013/05/10/five-things-we-know-about-societies-run-women.

Haraway, Donna Jeanne. *Simians, Cyborgs and Women: The Reinvention of Nature*. Free Association, 1991.

Helford, Elyce Rae. "Postfeminism and the Female Action-Adventure Hero." *Future Females, the Next Generation*, edited by Marleen S. Barr, Rowman and Littlefield, 2000, pp. 291–308.

Helford, Elyce Rae, Shiloh Carroll, Sarah Gray, and Michael R. Howard. "Introduction." *The Woman Fantastic in Contemporary American Media Culture*, edited by Elyce Rae Helford, Shiloh Carroll Sarah Gray, and Michael R. Howard. University Press of Mississippi, 2016.

Heuslein, Jeremy. "I Am and Am Not You." Greene and Robison-Greene, 75–84.

Higgins, David M. "Science Fiction, 1960–2005: Novels and Short Fiction." Reid, pp. 73–83.

Hughes, Sarah. "Have You Been Watching ... *Orphan Black*, Season Two?" *The Guardian*, 2 July 2014. https://www.theguardian.com/tv-and-radio/tvandradioblog/2014/jul/02/have-you-been-watching-orphan-black-season-two.

Hughes, William, David Punter, Andrew Smith, editors. *The Encyclopedia of the Gothic, 2 Volume Set*. John Wiley & Sons, 2015.

Jaffe, Sarah. "Why Feminism Needs Punk." *Dissent Magazine*, Spring 2015 https://www.dissentmagazine.org/article/why-feminism-needs-punk-viv-albertine-slits-autobiography.

Jensen, Pamela Grande. "Introduction." *Finding a New Feminism: Rethinking the Woman Question for Liberal Democracy*. Rowman and Littlefield, 1996, pp. 1–22.

Kakoudaki, Despina. "Pinup and Cyborg: Exaggerated Gender and Artificial Intelligence." *Future Females, the Next Generation*, edited by Marleen S. Barr. Rowman and Littlefield, 2000, pp. 165–195.

Kaveney, Roz, editor. *Reading the Vampire Slayer: The Unofficial Critical Companion to Buffy and Angel*. Tauris Parke, 2002.

Keegan, Cael. "Horizontal Inheritance: Orphan Black's Transgender Genealogy." *In Media Res*, 15 April 2015. http://mediacommons.futureofthebook.org/imr/2015/04/15/horizontal-inheritance-orphan-blacks-transgender-genealogy.

Kulkarni, Claudette. *Lesbians and Lesbianisms: A Post-Jungian Perspective*. Routledge, 1997.

Kutulas, Judy. "Liberated Women and New Sensitive Men: Reconstructing Gender in the 1970s Workplace Comedies." *The Sitcom Reader: America Viewed and Skewed*, edited by Mary M. Dalton. SUNY Press, 2005.

Lakin-Smith, Kim. "Doll Parts: Reflections of the Feminine Grotesque in Frances Hardinge's Cuckoo Song and Neil Gaiman's Coraline." Barbini.

Law, Keith. "How 6 High-Strategy Board Games Fit into the *Orphan Black* Universe." *Vulture*, 7 July 2017. http://www.vulture.com/2017/07/orphan-black-board-games-runewars.html.

Lepore, Jill. "The History Lurking Behind *Orphan Black*." *the New Yorker*, 16 Apr, 2015. http://www.newyorker.com/culture/cultural-comment/the-history-lurking-behind-orphan-black.

Maloney, Devon. "That Crazy Musical in *Orphan Black*? Yeah, It Exists in Real Life." *Wired*, 7 May 2014. https://www.wired.com/2014/05/orphan-black-musical.

Martin, Rachel. "TV Characters' Rising Death Toll Reveals Troubling Pattern." *NPR*, 5 June 2016. http://www.npr.org/2016/06/05/480820170/tv-characters-rising-death-toll-reveals-troubling-pattern.

Morgan, Cheryl. "Tipping the Fantastic: How the Transgender Tipping Point Has Influenced Speculative Fiction." Barbini.

Mulvey, Laura. "Visual Pleasure and Narrative Cinema." *Screen* vol. 16, no. 3, Autumn 1975, pp. 6-18. http://www.scribd.com/doc/7758866/laura-mulvey-visual-pleasure-and-narrative-cinema.

Murphy, B.M. *The Suburban Gothic in American Popular Culture*. Palgrave Macmillan, 2009.

Murphy, Peter Francis, editor. *Feminism and Masculinities: Oxford Readings in Feminism*. Oxford University Press, 2004, pp. 151-164.

Paglia, Camille. *Free Women Free Men*. Pantheon Books, 2017.

Phillips, Ruth, and Viviene E. Cree. "What Does the 'Fourth Wave' Mean for Teaching Feminism in Twenty-First Century Social Work?" *Social Work Education*, vol. 33, no. 7, Oct. 2014, pp. 930-943. EBSCOhost, doi:10.1080/02615479.2014.885007.

Playdon, Zoe-Jane. "What You Are, What's to Come: Feminisms, Citizenship, and the Divine." Kaveney, pp. 120-147.

Pleck, Joseph H. "Men's Power with Women, Other Men, and Society: A Men's Movement Analysis." Murphy, pp. 57-68.

Post, Stephen Garrard. "The Judeo-Christian Ethic Opposes Cloning." Rantala and Milgram, pp. 153-158.

Rampton, Martha. "Four Waves of Feminism." *Pacific University Center for Gender Equity*, 25 Oct. 2015. https://www.pacificu.edu/about-us/news-events/four-waves-feminism.

Ransdell, Lisa. "Lesbian Feminism and the Feminist Movement." *Women: A Feminist Perspective*, edited by Jo Freeman. Mayfield Publishing, 1993, pp. 641-653.

Rantala, M.L., and Arthur J. Milgram, editors. *Cloning: For and Against*. Open Court, 1999.

Read, Catherine Y., Robert C. Green, and Michael A. Smyer, editors. *Aging, Biotechnology, and the Future*. Johns Hopkins University Press, 2008.

Reed, Evelyn. *Woman's Evolution from Matriarchal Clan to Patriarchal Family*. Pathfinder Press, 1975.

Reid, Robin Anne, editor. *Women in Science Fiction and* Fantasy. Greenwood, 2009.

Reynaud, Emmanuel. "Holy Virility: The Social Construction of Masculinity." Murphy, pp. 136-148.

Riviére, Joan. "Womanliness as Masquerade." *Formations of Fantasy*, edited by Victor James Donald Burgin and Cora Kaplan. Methuen, 1986, pp. 35-44.

Rosenberg, Buck Clifford. "Masculine Makeovers: Lifestyle Television, Metrosexuals and Real Blokes." *Exposing Lifestyle Television: The Big Reveal*, edited by Gareth Palmer. Aldershot, 2008.

Rowe-Finkbeiner, Kristen. *The F-Word: Feminism in Jeopardy: Women, Politics, and the Future*. Seal Press, 2004.

Sayer, Karen. "It Wasn't Our World Anymore. They Made It Theirs: Reading Space and Place." Kaveney, pp. 98-119.

Schneider, Michael. "Game of Clones." *Variety*, vol. 336, no. 4, 30 May 2017, p. 50. EBSCOhost.

Shannon, Thomas A. "The Transhumanist Movement: A Flawed Response to Aging and Its Natural Consequence." Read et al., pp. 39-57.

Sherman, Suzanne. *100 Years in the Life of an American Girl: True Stories*. SZS Publishing, 2014.

Solinger, Rickie. *Reproductive Politics*. Oxford University Press, 2013.

Spencer, Krishanna. "Priestess Path: Under the Aegis of Athena." *The Beltane Papers,* Autumn 2002, p. 24.
Talbot, Margaret. "A Desire to Duplicate." *The New York Times,* February 04, 2001.
Thweatt-Bates, Jeanine. *Cyborg Selves.* Ashgate, 2012.
Tong, Rosemarie. "A Lonely New World—Or Me, Myself, and I." Read et al., pp. 245–257.
VanderMeer, Ann, and Jeff VanderMeer. "The Rise of Science Fiction from Pulp Mags to Cyberpunk." *Electric Lit,* 22 Dec. 2016. https://electricliterature.com/the-rise-of-science-fiction-from-pulp-mags-to-cyberpunk-e00f6efdcab0.
Viruet, Pilot. "Are This Season's Diverse Shows Ushering in a New Era of Multicultural Television?" *FlavorWire,* 4 Mar 2015. http://flavorwire.com/507088/are-this-seasons-diverse-shows-ushering-in-a-new-era-of-multicultural-television.
Wallis, Claudia, et al. "Onward, Women! the Superwoman Is Weary, the Young Are Complacent, but Feminism Is Not Dead. And, Baby, There's Still a Long Way to Go." *Time,* vol. 134, no. 23, 04 Dec. 1989, p. 80. EBSCOhost.
Wieselman, Jarett. "How Orphan Black Pulled Off That Perfectly Disastrous Musical." *Buzzfeed,* 5 May 2014. https://www.buzzfeed.com/jarettwieselman/orphan-black-musical.
_____. "Meet the Woman (Besides Tatiana Maslany) Who Plays Every Single *Orphan Black* Clone." *Buzzfeed,* 24 April 2014. https://www.buzzfeed.com/jarettwieselman/meet-the-woman-beisdes-tatiana-maslany-who-plays-every-singl.
Wolfert, Johanna, and Adam Barkman. "When Clone Club Looks for Answers." Greene and Robinson-Greene, 25–34.
"The Women and the Gunmen." *Time,* vol. 99, no. 16, 17 Apr. 1972, p. 65. EBSCOhost.
Wright, Carmen. "Leda, Castor, and Their Families." Greene and Robison-Greene, 117–126.

Index

abomination 6, 109, 111
abortion 7, 12, 75, 124
abuse 7, 100, 178, 210
Agricola 18, 42, 43
Aisha 146, 204, 207
Aldous Leekie 7, 10, 13, 14, 18, 20, 21, 35, 53, 54, 59, 68, 70–77, 80, 92, 111, 130, 131, 134, 136, 139, 142, 143, 166, 167, 168, 172, 189, 196, 199, 200–203
Alison Hendrix 1, 2, 7–10, 16, 18–28, 32–38, 51, 54, 58, 61, 62, 68, 71, 72, 74, 82, 87, 91, 98, 99, 102–107, 120, 124–139, 144, 148, 151, 157, 169, 179, 188, 189, 195, 199–202, 205, 209; children 13, 124, 128, 205, 207; mother 7, 32, 133, 137
Angie 93, 126
Arthur Bell 20, 21, 27, 31, 38, 40, 45, 67, 79, 81, 87, 93, 101, 103, 105, 106, 112, 121, 124, 159, 160, 174, 176, 184–186, 201, 205
Asperger's 192
Austen, Jane 132, 147
Aynsley Norris 37, 102, 130, 134

babies *see* Brightborn; designer babies; Helena—babies
baby shower 1, 32, 100, 103, 186, 207
Bacon, Francis 48, 54, 55, 56
Bailey Downs 19, 25, 51, 62, 125, 126, 134
barcode gene 25, 72, 83
Berkeley 12, 84, 89, 102, 125, 141
Beth Childs 5, 6, 8, 9, 17, 20–22, 27, 31, 33, 34, 39, 40, 54, 67, 68, 71, 83, 87, 93, 104, 106, 113, 132, 142, 147–150, 162, 176, 181, 193, 194, 197, 200, 208, 209
Bible 55, 90, 98, 110, 112
Blood Ties 130–131
body horror 22, 77, 82
Brave New World 3, 62, 70
Brightborn 16, 21–23, 33, 35, 44, 50, 59, 65, 66, 77, 78, 79, 85, 86, 89, 123, 139, 157, 181, 182, 192, 207, 210
Britain 12, 95, 97, 105, 209
Brochu, Evelyne 143, 188
Brönte sisters 132
Bruun, Kristian 131, 135, 138, 174, 184
Bubbles 133–134
Buffy the Vampire Slayer 71, 156, 157, 181, 187
"By Means Which Have Never Yet Been Tried" 13, 15, 37, 38, 65, 74, 75, 96, 144

Cal Morrison 31, 35–37, 74, 99, 100, 104, 164, 165, 199, 209
camera 1, 23, 26, 36–41, 48, 133, 167, 205
Camilla Torres 210
Canada 12, 20, 43, 72, 95, 105, 208–210
Caprica 66
Castor 17, 18, 21, 22, 38, 53, 56, 62, 70, 73, 74, 76, 80, 81, 85, 87, 108, 120, 156–163, 170, 180, 196–200, 207
Castors 16–21, 40, 56, 57, 62, 64, 65, 75, 82, 83, 86, 118, 120, 156–163, 180
Charlotte 16, 23, 42, 87, 99, 145, 147, 170, 188, 196, 200, 202, 206, 207
cheekbot *see* maggot
chosen family 17, 99, 151
civil disobedience 12
civil rights 11
Cold River 55, 73, 83, 85
Colin 105, 199
comic books 6, 29, 35, 41, 43, 79, 83, 109, 110, 112, 129, 135, 136, 149, 166–167, 186, 187, 189, 192, 200
"Community of Dreadful Fear and Hate" 7, 19, 32, 37, 42, 103, 137, 138
corporation 11, 15, 25, 31, 35, 51, 52, 62, 66, 72–79, 81, 87, 124, 155, 165, 171, 193, 200
Cosima Niehaus 7–11, 14–45, 50, 53–55,

60–83, 86, 89, 91, 96, 99, 101, 102, 105, 112, 133, 139–148, 159, 162, 166, 169–171, 177, 178, 181, 185, 186, 188, 195, 197, 199–204, 207–211; parents 146
cults 3, 13, 55, 62, 66, 83, 91–92, 111–119, 160, 177–179, 201, 203, 211
cure 7, 14, 15, 20, 23, 27, 53, 55, 68, 74, 77, 79, 80, 81, 82, 145, 147, 159, 162, 169, 179, 181, 186, 198, 200, 201, 207
cyborgs 3, 9, 37, 57–59, 66, 71, 96, 97, 122, 140, 160, 170, 171, 176, 192, 194

D&D 41, 43, 45
damsel 139, 146
dance party 1, 28, 100
Daniel Rosen 20, 163, 165, 167
Darwin, Charles 47, 53, 54, 80, 119, 203
Delphine Cormier 14–18, 24, 27, 28, 30, 32, 35, 37, 38, 70, 72, 74, 75, 76, 80–82, 100, 141–146, 169, 182–184, 187–189, 199, 201, 202, 204, 209, 211
designer babies 50, 59, 67, 70, 77–78, 86, 88
dinner party 200, 100
disabled 41, 192, 211
diversity 29, 58, 96, 123, 203
Doctor Who 67, 212
Dollhouse 66
Dolly 84, 86, 88, 193
domestic 32
dominance 136, 198
Donnie Hendrix 13, 20–25, 30, 32, 35, 37, 38, 54, 71, 77, 87, 91, 99–101, 105, 121, 125, 127–139, 151, 162, 174, 185, 199–202
DYAD 9, 13–15, 20–22, 28, 35, 39, 41–45, 55, 62, 68, 70–77, 79, 81, 88, 89, 96, 99, 100, 122, 123, 130, 134, 142–145, 149, 157, 165, 166, 168–173, 177, 185, 186, 189, 192, 194, 195, 200–202, 205, 209

Eden 54, 166, 203
"Effects of External Conditions" 6, 112, 113, 141
Eisenhower, Dwight 56–57
emasculating 37, 137–138, 155, 167, 170, 192, 199–200
Enger 106, 205
"Entangled Bank" 37, 129, 140–143, 153
Equal Rights Amendment 94, 124
Ethan Duncan 14, 55, 65, 73, 74, 83, 89, 166, 168, 181
eugenics 59, 66, 88, 176
European clones 208
Evie Cho 22, 23, 35, 59, 68, 77–80, 85, 92, 123, 124, 145, 150, 171, 181

eye 15, 16, 18, 24, 26, 36, 37, 38, 51, 59, 71, 75, 77, 92, 94, 121, 149, 153, 158, 159, 160, 169–173, 209

Fawcett, John 5, 19, 20, 29, 33, 40, 41, 43, 45, 56, 76, 77, 82, 97, 102, 111, 127, 132, 133, 137, 148, 162, 164, 168, 173, 174, 176, 192, 194, 195, 210
Felix Dawkins 2, 5, 7, 9, 11, 14, 16, 18–21, 23, 26, 27, 29–31, 35, 37, 38, 39, 44, 45, 51, 61, 67, 71, 81, 87, 93, 97–107, 126, 128, 129, 131, 133, 139, 141–145, 150–154, 157, 160–164, 173, 174, 176, 177, 179, 181–185, 199, 210
The Female Man 67, 68
Ferdinand Chevalier 22, 23, 31, 33, 37, 39, 61, 76, 155, 167, 170, 172, 173, 178, 189, 190, 191, 192, 195, 199, 208
first wave 11
fourth wave 9, 43, 59, 60, 101, 150, 192, 193
Frankenstein 3, 61, 64, 70, 176
"From Dancing Mice to Psychopaths" 44, 79, 80, 170, 171
Frontenac 81

"Gag or Throttle" 25, 134, 147, 172
gallery opening 26–27, 100, 105
Gavaris, Jordan 9, 18, 101, 102, 104, 174, 212
glitching 2, 57, 160, 200
golden ratio 144
gothic 34, 71, 73, 104, 126, 128, 130–134
Grace Johanssen 13, 19, 55, 90, 91, 99, 100, 115–118, 154, 161, 162, 177–179, 188, 198, 199, 207; mother 177–178, 207
grandmother 98, 99, 154, 180, 181, 206
"Guillotines Decide" 26, 61, 81, 101, 105–106, 147, 151, 155, 173, 179, 191, 210
gun 31, 76, 81, 93, 106, 113, 121, 125, 128, 136, 146–148, 153, 155, 163, 166, 180, 192, 202

hacking 50, 192
Haraway, Donna 3, 9, 57–59, 68, 89, 96, 97, 160, 167, 170, 176, 194, 195
Helena 1–3, 6–10, 13, 14, 17–20, 25, 27, 30, 31, 33–35, 38, 39, 45, 47, 51, 54, 55, 58, 61–64, 68–76, 81, 82, 87, 91, 97, 98, 100–103, 106, 108, 109–123, 128, 130, 132, 134, 138, 139, 141, 149, 154, 157, 161, 163, 167, 173, 177–179, 186, 188, 196, 198, 199, 202, 205–209; babies 28, 51, 61, 100, 120–121, 134, 198, 205–207
HellWizard 45, 100, 185–186
Helsinki 39, 76, 83, 187, 189, 191, 192, 208, 209

Index

Henrik Johanssen 12–14, 35, 55, 64, 90–92, 100, 115, 117, 160, 177, 199
Herter, Cosima 3, 5, 6, 11, 24, 29, 52, 54, 57–60, 64, 82, 89–90
hierarchy 75, 79, 99, 107, 156, 157, 165, 168, 192
"HistoryYettoBeWritten" 138, 169
homosexual 11, 58, 195

infertility 14, 74–78, 88, 89, 178, 197
Ira Blair 21–24, 37, 76, 79, 80, 146, 170, 196, 199, 200, 204
Ireland 151, 152, 208, 209
island 23, 24, 26, 35, 53, 62–66, 80, 92, 145, 146, 186, 197, 198, 200, 203, 207, 209
The Island of Doctor Moreau 3, 61, 65, 66, 176, 202

Jason Kellerman 137–138
Jesse 32, 35, 100, 199
Jesus Christ Superstar 91

Katja Obinger 8, 39, 112, 132, 139, 153, 208, 209
Kendall Malone 22, 31, 35, 70, 76, 85, 87, 100, 145, 155, 179–181, 206
Kennedy, Maria Doyle 19, 20, 150–155, 180, 181
Kira Manning 5, 9, 15, 17, 18, 20, 23, 25–29, 31, 35, 39, 42–45, 54, 55, 65, 66, 72, 83, 87, 89, 91, 94, 95, 98–100, 104, 114, 115, 120, 143, 144, 146, 149–155, 160, 161, 164–166, 169, 172, 173, 180, 181, 186, 193, 195–197, 204–207, 209
kiss 21, 137, 145, 176, 185, 198, 202
Krystal Goderitch 18, 23, 27, 28, 33, 38, 44, 45, 67, 75, 88, 99, 103, 106, 159, 169, 181–186

Leakey, Louis 53
Leda and the Swan 115, 171
lesbians 33, 68, 88, 104, 140, 142, 177, 187, 211, 212
London 95, 97, 105, 209
Lost Girl 67
Lynch, Stephen 27, 111–113, 125, 141, 142, 165, 193, 199

macho 137, 138, 148, 162, 186
madwoman 33, 35, 134, 157
Maggie Chen 6, 20, 106, 109–112, 149, 151
maggot 16, 21–23, 40, 44, 59, 76, 170
makeup 2, 27, 46, 111, 113, 125, 156, 166, 175, 180
Manson, Graeme 8, 10, 19, 29, 53, 54, 61, 70, 78, 81, 85, 94, 96–98, 114, 115, 127, 130–132, 143, 144, 163, 170, 173, 180, 181, 188, 197, 202, 204, 210, 211
Marci Coates 133
Marion Bowles 74, 160, 166, 206
Mark Rollins 13, 76, 81, 91, 159, 160, 161, 162, 178, 179, 198, 205
Martin Duko 20, 21, 22, 23, 44, 106, 139, 181
masculinity 30, 56, 93, 107, 136, 162, 174, 195, 196
Maslany, Tatiana 6, 7, 21, 27–29, 33, 36, 41, 48, 95, 97, 99, 103, 110, 113, 121, 129, 131, 139, 141, 142, 144, 149, 156, 167, 169, 173–176, 184, 193
matriarchies 99–100, 157
Millen, Ari 21, 156, 158, 199
Minecraft 44
Minnesota 140, 142, 146, 185
mirrors 7, 39, 56, 70, 123, 136, 142
M.K. 8, 21, 22, 23, 27, 35, 39, 41, 44, 50, 51, 58, 79, 99, 148, 149, 186, 191–195, 206
monitor 20, 71, 72, 87, 127, 129, 130, 136, 142, 165, 174, 182, 200, 202
monster 24, 64, 65, 74, 90, 110, 111, 114–118, 121, 132, 161, 178, 204
Mud 146, 204
murder 6, 18, 21, 22, 78, 96, 100, 106, 110, 111, 112, 115, 117, 118, 123, 124, 130, 131, 134, 177, 178, 192, 196, 197
musical 130–131

Neolution 9, 26, 38, 40, 42, 45, 53–55, 57, 59, 61–65, 67, 70–81, 95, 106, 130, 134, 142, 146, 151, 155, 165, 171, 173, 184, 191, 195, 196, 201–206, 209
new men 135, 138, 161
Niki Lintula 187, 192, 209
nun 38, 108
nurture 6, 10, 26, 34, 83, 105, 109, 151, 156, 157, 173

objectification 36–38
Olivier Duval 18, 20, 37, 71
"One Fettered Slave" 6, 31, 38, 45, 204
The Origin of Species 3, 53, 54
ovary 15, 158, 169, 189

Parsons 118, 160, 198, 207
patent 9, 48, 72, 74, 83, 86, 105, 166, 171, 201, 204
patriarch 13, 24, 33, 35, 61, 62, 72, 96, 108, 116, 126, 147, 172, 198, 201–205
patriarchy 2, 25, 40, 41, 68, 71, 89, 94, 100, 113, 132, 140, 145, 147, 157, 161, 171, 196, 203–205

Index

Paul Dierden 2, 8, 17, 20, 35, 36, 39, 40, 56, 57, 71, 76, 93, 95, 142, 148–150, 153, 160–167, 199, 200
pencil 15, 75, 169
Planned Parenthood 12
post-feminism 2, 125
Pouchy 133, 138
pregnancy 16, 78, 87, 91, 117, 120, 123, 138
privilege 11, 16, 129, 167
Proletheans 6, 9, 31, 40, 55, 90, 92, 111, 113, 115–118, 149, 159, 166, 209
protest 3, 29, 59–61
P.T. Westmorland 24, 25, 31, 33, 35, 43, 45, 46, 49, 59, 61–66, 80–82, 92, 120, 145–147, 162, 171, 172, 186, 191, 196–204, 207
punk 31, 33, 50, 94–96, 113, 157
Pygmalion 71

Rabbit Hole Comics 43, 65
Rachel Duncan 8–10, 14–16, 18, 20–28, 31, 33–39, 42, 43, 45, 46, 50, 54, 59, 61, 62, 65, 66, 68, 71–81, 86, 87, 99, 102, 103, 124, 136, 140, 144–146, 151, 155, 157, 163–173, 177, 183, 185–192, 196–209
radical feminism 125, 141, 150
Raj 93, 101
rape 11, 14, 49, 76, 77, 125, 140, 153, 160, 171, 191
rehab 13, 34, 102, 131, 132, 136
Revival 23, 207
Rossum's Universal Robots 68
Rudy 38, 134, 159–162, 182, 186, 198
Runewars 40–41

S&M 33, 37, 170, 189
Sarah Manning 5–9, 12, 14–40, 43–47, 50, 51, 54, 55, 61, 62, 65, 67, 68, 71–82, 84, 87, 89, 91, 93–108, 112–116, 118, 120–129, 131, 132, 139–191, 194, 195, 197–200, 202, 205, 208–210
Scott Smith 7, 18, 21, 23, 30, 40–45, 100, 101, 147, 185, 186
second wave 12, 94, 101, 140, 144, 147, 150, 162, 168, 193, 200
Seed, Richard 91
self-hatred 5–7
Seth 154, 159, 160, 182
Shay Davydov 32, 41, 144, 145, 199
sheep mask 27, 44, 193
Shelley, Mary 64, 132
silencing 38, 51, 60, 82, 115, 155, 177, 192, 205
Siobhan Sadler 9, 12, 16, 18–27, 31, 33, 35, 39, 67, 72, 74, 79, 81, 83, 87, 94, 95, 98–100, 103–106, 121, 122, 139, 150–155, 157, 160, 173, 179–181, 186, 189–191, 199, 209
slavery 58, 83
soap 133, 137, 179, 187
Sokolowski, Sandy 112, 142, 175
spiritual 17, 112, 114, 117, 119, 164
Steel Magnolias 61–62
Steinem, Gloria 148
sterilization 56, 198
striptease 139
suicide 22, 54, 66, 83, 130, 132, 148, 149, 200
Susan Duncan 21–24, 33, 63, 65, 68, 77, 78, 80, 87, 128, 136, 145, 146, 149, 159, 166, 170, 171, 181, 184, 187, 195–200, 202, 204, 206, 209
syllogisms 157, 159

"Things Which Have Never Yet Been Done" 13–15, 64, 132
third wave 2, 94–96, 101, 123, 147, 148, 149, 150, 181, 182
"To Right the Wrongs of Many" 28, 38, 173, 210
Tomas 9, 20, 35, 90, 109, 110–116, 199
Tony Sawicki 1, 2, 8, 11, 20, 27, 28, 30, 37, 51, 54, 99, 103, 106, 168, 174–176, 194
Topside 70, 76, 167, 189, 190
transgender 2, 8, 30, 83, 104, 174–177
trickster 58, 96, 194
twerking 137
twins 5, 8, 47, 66, 70, 72, 73, 81, 82, 87, 106, 121, 123, 196, 198, 205

underwear 137

Van Lier 79, 81
Veera Suominen 83, 187, 190–192, 194, 209
Vic 2, 31, 67, 93, 107–108
Victorian gown 145, 203
Virginia Coady 24, 33, 38, 46, 57, 65, 76, 81, 82, 106, 120, 121, 159–164, 172, 179, 186, 195–198, 200, 205

Wordsworth, William 63

The X-Files 66

Yannis 24, 146, 204

Zeus 73, 108, 122

www.ingramcontent.com/pod-product-compliance
Lightning Source LLC
Chambersburg PA
CBHW032051300426
44116CB00007B/693